THE MOTHER
OF THE SAVIOUR

THE MOTHER OF THE SAVIOUR

By

Fr. Reginald Garrigou-Lagrange, O.P.

PROFESSOR OF DOGMA AND MYSTICAL THEOLOGY IN THE ANGELICO, ROME

Translated by

Fr. Bernard J. Kelly, C.S.Sp., D.D.

"O God, who art the greatness of the humble, reveal to us Mary's humility, which is proportioned to the elevation of her charity."

—2 Timothy 4:3-4

TAN Books
An Imprint of Saint Benedict Press, LLC
Charlotte, North Carolina

Nihil Obstat: Michael L. Dempsey, S.T.D.
                  Theol. Censor Deputatus

Imprimatur: ✠ John Carol
                  Archbishop of Dublin, Primate of Ireland
                  Dublin, December 8, 1948

Imprimi Potest: Patrick O'Carroll, C.S.Sp.
                  Provincial Superior
                  Dublin, December 2, 1948

Imprimi Potest: Fr. Bernard Marie, O.P.
                  Vicar Provincial of the Free Zone
                  July 8, 1941

First U.S. publication was in 1948, by B. Herder Book Company, St. Louis, Missouri.

Library of Congress Catalog Card No.: 93-61564

ISBN: 978-0-89555-499-4

Cover design by Tony Pro.

Cover Image: *La Vierge au Lys* by William Bouguereau, Art Renewal Center, www.artrenewal.org.

Printed and bound in the United States of America.

TAN Books
An Imprint of Saint Benedict Press, LLC
Charlotte, North Carolina
2012

TO THE BLESSED VIRGIN MARY
MOTHER OF GOD
AND OUR MOTHER
who placed all her greatness in God
and was filled by Him with good things,
in token of profound gratitude
and filial obedience.

❧Translator's Preface❧

A theologian of the eminence of Father Garrigou-Lagrange does not himself need to be introduced to the public. This present work of his would, however, seem to invite a few words of explanation.

It is not a devotional book in the ordinary sense of the term: it is too openly theological for that. On the other hand, it is no mere theological treatise: the author's aim has been to inflame hearts no less than to enlighten minds. The result is a work which demands more intellectual application than many others on Our Lady. But, by way of compensation, it touches the will at a deeper and more spiritual level than would a work of less rich content. The author's insistence—a fully justified one—on the doctrinal side of his subject has, of course, left little room for mere literary ornament. But this lack, if lack it be, will not turn away any reader who is sincerely desirous to know Our Lady better.

As for the translation itself, though care has been taken not to attribute to Father Garrigou-Lagrange anything he did not write, it has not been possible always to translate the original with literal fidelity. Theologians who wish to use the book for strictly scientific purposes would be well advised to compare passages they intend to quote with the original. The translator will be glad to supply it, if necessary, as far as possible.

HOLY GHOST MISSIONARY COLLEGE,
KIMMAGE, *Corpus Christi,* MAY 27TH, 1948.

Author's Preface

This book is intended to be an exposition of the principal theses of Mariology in their bearing on our interior life. While writing it I have noticed more than once how often it has happened that a theologian admitted some prerogative of Our Lady in his earlier years under the influence of piety and admiration of her dignity. A second period then followed when the doctrinal difficulties came home to him more forcefully, and he was much more reserved in his judgement. Finally there was the third period, when, having had time to study the question in its positive and speculative aspects, he returned to his first position, not now because of his sentiment of piety and admiration, but because his more profound understanding of Tradition and theology revealed to him that the measure of the things of God—and in a special way those things of God which affect Mary—is more overflowing than is commonly understood. If the masterpieces of human art contain unsuspected treasures, the same must be said, with even more reason, of God's masterpieces in the orders of nature and grace, especially when they bear an immediate relation to the Hypostatic Order, which is constituted by the mystery of the Incarnation of the Word. I have endeavoured to show how these three periods may be found exemplified in the process of St Thomas' teaching on the Immaculate Conception.

These periods bear a striking analogy to three others in the affective order. It has often been noticed that a soul's first affective stage may be one of sense-perceptible devotion, for example to the Sacred Heart or the Blessed Virgin. This is followed by a stage of aridity. Then comes the final stage of perfect spiritual

ix

devotion, overflowing on the sensibility. May the Good God help the readers of this book who wish to learn of the greatness of the Mother of God and men to understand in what this spiritual progress consists.

The doctrines proposed in this book are not personal ones: it has been my aim to give what is most commonly held by theologians—especially those of the Thomistic school—and to explain the various points in the light of St. Thomas's principles.[1] Lastly, every effort has been made to avoid merely metaphorical expressions. There are sometimes too many of them in books on Our Lady. A bibliography is given with each question treated.

---

1. For the positive part of the book, I have made extensive use of Fr Merkelbach's *Mariologia*. Although I have differed from him in some matters, his book seems to me worthy of the highest praise in its speculative parts as well, both as regards the order of the questions and the accuracy of his theological arguments.

❧Table of Contents❧

PART I

The Divine Maternity
and the Plenitude of Grace

Chapter 1

The Divine Maternity: Its Eminent Dignity

THE two truths which stand out like mountain peaks in the chain of revelation concerning Our Blessed Lady, and around which cluster all other truths we hold about her, are her divine maternity and her fullness of grace, both of which are affirmed in the Gospels and in the Councils of the Church. To grasp their importance it will be well to compare them, asking which of the two comes first, and gives, as it were, the true Pisgah view of all Mariology. In that spirit have theologians enquired which was the greater of Mary's prerogatives, her divine maternity (her motherhood of God) or her fullness of grace.

The Problem Stated

There have been theologians[1] who have declared Mary's fullness of grace her greatest prerogative. The words spoken to Jesus by a certain woman as He passed in the midst of the people, and His answer, have led them to adopt this position: "Blessed is the womb that bore Thee, and the paps that gave thee suck. But He said: Yea rather, blessed are they who hear the word of God and keep it." (*Luke* 11: 27-28). On their view the Saviour's answer implies that the fullness of grace

---

1. Gabriel Biel in IIIum Sent. dist. IV, a. 3, dub III, p. 2, Brescia 1574, p. 67 sq. and some others who have followed him more or less closely. Thus, Vasquez, in IIIam, disp. XXIII, c. II and disp. C, c, II, attributes greater dignity to sanctifying grace than to the divine maternity. For this opinion cf. *Dictionnaire de la Théologie Catholique*, art. *Marie* by E. Dublanchy S.M., col. 2356 sqq.

and of charity which was the principle of Mary's supernatural and meritorious acts was superior to her divine maternity, a privilege in itself of the corporeal order only.

According to many other theologians[2] the reason given just now is not conclusive. Their arguments are many. They say that the woman in question did not speak precisely of the divine maternity: she thought of Jesus less as God than as a prophet whose words were heard eagerly, who was admired and acclaimed, and she was thinking therefore of a natural motherhood according to flesh and blood: "Blessed is the womb that bore thee and the paps that gave thee suck." She did not speak of the divine maternity as of something which included a supernatural and meritorious consent to the mystery of the redemptive Incarnation. That was why Our Blessed Lord answered as He did: "Yea rather, blessed are they who hear the word of God and keep it." For it was precisely by hearing the word of God and believing in it that Mary became Mother of the Saviour. She said her fiat generously and with perfect conformity of will to God's good pleasure and all it involved for her, and she kept the divine words in her heart from the time of the Annunciation onwards. Elisabeth, for her part, expressed this when she said: "Blessed art thou that hast believed, because those things be shall accomplished which were spoken to thee by the Lord" (*Luke* 1:45). What a contrast with Zachary who was struck dumb for not having

---

2. Among the Thomists special mention must be made of Contenson, Gotti, Hugon and Merkelbach.

Father Merkelbach quotes the following in his *Mariologia,* 1939, p. 68, as having all admitted more or less explicitly that her divine maternity is the greatest of Mary's titles: St. Epiphanius, St. Ambrose, St. Sophronius, St. Germanus of Constantinople, St. John Damascene, Andrew of Crete, St. Peter Damien, Eadmer, Peter of Celles, St. Bernard, St. Albert the Great, St. Bonaventure, St. Thomas, Denis the Carthusian, St. Bernardine of Siena, St. Alphonsus, and all Thomists in general as, for example, Gonet, Contenson, Gotti, Hugon. Besides, Leo XIII says in his encyclical *Quamquam pluries* of August 15, 1889: "Certe Matris Dei tam in excelso est dignitas, ut nihil fieri majus queat." Cf. *Marie* in *Dictionnaire de la Th. Cath.,* cols. 2349-2359.

believed the words of the Angel Gabriel: "And behold thou shalt be dumb . . . because thou hast not believed my words." (*Luke* 1:20).

Nothing said so far, therefore, is sufficient to solve the problem: which was the greater, the divine maternity as realized in Mary or her fullness of grace and charity?

We must search deeper for a solution. To make the terms of the problem still more precise, it should be noted that the maternity proper to a creature endowed with reason is not the maternity according to flesh and blood which is found in the animal kingdom, but something which demands by its very nature a free consent given by the light of right reason to an act which is under the control of the will and is subject to the moral laws governing the married state: failing this, the maternity of a rational being is simply vicious. But the maternity of Mary was more than rational. It was divine. Hence her consent needed to be not free only, but supernatural and meritorious: and the intention of divine providence was that in default of this consent the mystery of the redemptive Incarnation would not have taken place—she gave her consent, St. Thomas says, in the name of mankind (IIIa, q. 30, a. 2).

Hence the maternity we are discussing is not one which is merely of flesh and blood, but one which by its nature included a supernatural consent to the mystery of the redemptive Incarnation which was about to be realized, and to all the suffering it involved according to the messianic prophecies—especially those of Isaias—all of which Mary knew so well. There can, in consequence, be no question of any divine maternity for Mary except a worthy one: in the designs of God she was to be a worthy Mother of the Redeemer, united perfectly in will to her Son. Tradition supports this by saying that her conceiving was twofold, in body and in soul: in body, for Jesus is flesh of her flesh, the flame of His human life having been lit in the womb of the

Virgin by the most pure operation of the Holy Ghost: in soul, for Mary's express consent was needed before the Word assumed our nature in her.

To the problem so stated the great majority of theologians answer that tradition teaches that the divine maternity, defined in the Council of Ephesus, is higher than the fullness of grace, and that Mary's most glorious title is that of Mother of God. The reasons for their answer are as follows. We ask the reader's special attention for the first few pages. Once they have been grasped the rest follows quite naturally.

Article 1
The Predestination of Mary

Let us examine first the primary object in the predestination of Mary, and the sense in which it was absolutely gratuitous.

Mary's predestination to the divine maternity preceded her predestination to the fullness of glory and grace.

This proposition may appear a little too profound for a beginning. In reality it is quite easy to understand. Most people admit it, at least implicitly. Besides it throws a flood of light on all that follows.

Pius IX affirmed it in effect in the Bull *Ineffabilis Deus,* by which he defined the dogma of the Immaculate Conception, when he said that God the Father predestined Jesus to natural divine sonship—so superior to adoptive sonship—and Mary to be Mother of God, in one and the same divine decree. The eternal predestination of Jesus included not only the Incarnation itself as object but also all the circumstances of time and place in which it would be realized, and especially the one expressed by the Nicene Creed in the words:

"Et incarnatus est de Spiritu Sancto ex Maria Virgine."[3] By the same eternal decree, therefore, Jesus was predestined to be Son of the Most High and Mary to be Mother of God.[4] It follows that as Christ was predestined to natural divine son-ship before *(in signo priori)* being predestined to the summit of glory and to the fullness of grace (the germ of glory) so also the Blessed Virgin Mary was predestined first to the divine maternity, and in consequence to a very high degree of heavenly glory and to the fullness of grace, in order that she might be fully worthy of her mission as Mother of the Saviour. This second predestination was all the more necessary seeing that, as His Mother, she was called to closest association with Jesus, by perfect conformity of her will with His, in His redemptive work. Such, in substance, is the teaching of Pius IX in the Bull *Ineffabilis Deus.*[5]

---

3. The words "natus ex Maria Virgine" are in the creed used in the West from at least the second century.

4. The words of *Ineffabilis Deus* are: "Ineffabilis Deus ab initio et ante saecula *Unigenito Filio Suo, matrem* ex qua caro factus in beata temporum plenitudine nasceretur, *elegit,* atque ordinavit tantoque *prae creatures universis est prosecutes amore,* ut in illa una sibi *propensissima voluntate complacuerit* . . . Ipsissima verba, quibus divinae scripturae de increata Sapientia loquuntur, ejusque sempiternas origines repraesentant, consuevit (Ecclesia), tum in ecclesiasticis officiis, tum in sacrosancta liturgia adhibere, et ad illius Virginis primordia transferre, quae uno eodemque decreto cum divinae sapientiae Incarnation fuerunt praestituta."

The gratuitous predestination of Christ is the exemplary cause of ours, for He merited for us all the effects of our predestination, as St. Thomas explains (IIIa, q. 24, a. 4). But Mary's predestination to the divine maternity has this altogether peculiar to it, that it is one with Christ's predestination to natural divine sonship, that is to say, with the decree of the Incarnation. This follows clearly from the text of Pius IX.

5. The same doctrine is found very beautifully expressed in the collect of the Votive Mass of the Holy Rosary (Dominican Missal): Omnipotens et misericors Deus, qui ab aeterno Unigenitum tibi coaequalem atque consubstantialem Filium *secundum carnem praedestinasti* in Spiritu sanctificationis D. N. J. C., et sanctissimam Virginem Mariam tibi acceptissimam in *matrem eidem a saeculo praeelegisti."*

In predestining Christ to natural divine sonship, the Father loved, therefore, and selected *(dilexit, elegit et praedestinavit)* Mary from all eternity as His Mother, to whom, in consequence, He willed to give fullness of glory and grace. As Pius IX says in *Ineffabilis Deus:* "Et quidem decebat omnino ut perfectissimae sanctitatis splendoribus semper ornata fulgeret."

St. Thomas says: "Post Christum habuit Maria maximam plenitudinem gratiae, quae ad hoc est electa, ut esset mater Dei" (in *Ep. ad Rom.,* VIII, lect. 5; p. 118 in Marietti edition).

Mary's predestination to the divine maternity involves her predestination to

Thus, just as in Jesus the dignity of Son of God, or Word made flesh, surpasses that of the plenitude of created grace, charity, and glory, which He received in His sacred soul as a result of the hypostatic union of two natures in Him by the Incarnation, so also in Mary the dignity of Mother of God surpasses that of the plenitude of grace and charity, and even that of the plenitude of glory which she received through her unique predestination to the divine maternity.

It is the teaching of St. Thomas and many other theologians when treating of the motive of the Incarnation (for the redemption of mankind) that Mary's predestination to be Mother of the Redeemer depended on the divine foreknowledge and permission of Adam's sin. As St. Thomas explains (IIIa, q. 1, a. 3, ad 3), that sin was permitted in view of a greater good, namely that through the redemptive Incarnation "where sin abounded, grace (might) more abound" (*Rom.* 5:20).[6] Just as God wills the human body for the sake of the human soul, and yet, since He wills that the soul give life to the body, does not create a soul till there is a body ready to receive it, so also God allowed in view of the greater good of the redemptive Incarnation that there should be a sin to be atoned for, and He willed the redemptive Incarnation for the sake of the regeneration of souls: thus in the actually existing order of divine providence there would have been no Incarnation had there been no sin. And in this order every-

glory and grace as an immediate consequence, for that maternity is so intimate a relationship with God as to demand a participation in the divine nature. No one thinks of the Mother of God as without grace (cf. Hugon, *De Virgine Maria Deipara,* 1926, p. 734). The divine maternity implies also both confirmation in grace and *impeccability* for there must be *mutual and perpetual love between Mother and Son:* God owes it to Himself to preserve His Mother from every fault that would separate her from Him (cf. Hugon, *ib.,* p. 736).

6. Pius IX says the same in the Bull *Ineffabilis Deus:* "Ineffabilis Deus. . . cum ab omni aetemitate praeviderit luctuosissimam humani generis ruinam ex Adami transgressione derivandam, atque in mysterio a saeculis abscondito primum suae bonitatis opus decrevit per Verbi incarnationem sacramento occultiore complere, ut quod in primo Adam casuram erat, in secundo felicius erigeretur, ab initio et ante saecula Unigenito Filio suo matrem ex qua . . . nasceretur elegit atque ordinavit . . . et ante saecula Unigenito Filio suo matrem ex qua . . . nasceretur elegit atque ordinavit . . ."

thing is subordinated to Christ and His Holy Mother, so that it is true to say with St. Paul (*1 Cor.* 3:23): "All things are yours . . . And you are Christ's; and Christ is God's."[7] Thus the greatness of Christ and of His Mother are in no way lessened by their dependence on Adam's sin.

Mary was therefore predestined first to the divine maternity. This dignity appears all the greater if we recall that Mary, who was able to merit glory, was not able to merit the Incarnation nor the divine maternity, for the Incarnation and the divine maternity lie outside the sphere of merit of the just, which has as outer limit the beatific vision.[8]

There is also another conclusive reason: the principle or beginning of merit cannot itself be merited. Since original sin, the Incarnation is the principle of all the graces and merits of the just; it cannot therefore be itself merited. Neither, then, could Mary merit her divine maternity *de condigno* nor *de congruo proprie*, for that would have been to merit the Incarnation.[9]

As St. Thomas very accurately indicates, what Mary could merit by the first fullness of grace which she received gratuitously in view of the foreseen merits of her Son, was an increase of charity and that higher degree of purity and holiness which was becoming in

---

7. This point has been explained at length in *Le Sauveur et son amour pour nous,* 1933, pp. 129-136, and in *Angelicum,* 1930 and 1939: "Motivum incarnations fuit motivum misericordiae. . . . Causae ad invicem sunt causae." The sin to be atoned for comes first in the order of material causes. The redemptive Incarnation comes first in the order of final causes, and precedes in the divine intention the actual application of the redemption to souls.

8. Cf. St. Thomas IIIa, q. 2, a. II: "Neque opera cujuscumque hominis potuerant esse meritoria hujus unions (hypostaticae) ex condigno. Primo quidem quia opera meritoria hominis proprie ordinantur ad beatitudinem, quae est virtutis praemium et consistit in plena Dei fruition. *Unio autem incarnationis,* cum sit in esse personali, *transcendit unionem beatae mentis ad Deum,* quae est per actum fruentis, et ideo non potest cadere sub merito."

9. *Ibid.:* "Secundo, quia gratia non potest cadere sub merito, quae est merendi principium. Unde multo minus incarnatio cadit sub merito, quae est principium gratiae, secundum illud *Joannis,* I, 17, 'gratia et veritas per Jesum Christum facta est.'" Mary could merit the Incarnation neither *de condigno* nor *de congruo proprie.* Even the second kind of merit must be excluded for it is based on charity, which the just have through the merits of the Redeemer. In other words, the eminent cause of our merits cannot itself be merited.

the Mother of God.[10] Or, as he says elsewhere: "Mary did not merit the Incarnation (nor the divine maternity) but, granted that the Incarnation had been decreed, she merited *(merito congrui,* not *condigni)* that it should come to pass through her, since it was becoming that the Mother of God should be most pure and perfect."[11] That is to say, she merited the degree of sanctity which it was becoming for the Mother of God to have, a degree which no other virgin had in fact merited, or could merit, since none other had received nor was entitled to receive the initial fullness of grace and charity which was the principle of Mary's merits.

This first reason for the eminent dignity of the Mother of God, based on her gratuitous predestination to that glorious title, is clear beyond question. It contains three truths which are, as it were, stars of first magnitude in the heavens of theology: 1st—that by one and the same decree the Father predestined Jesus for natural divine sonship and Mary for the divine maternity; 2nd—that Mary was predestined for the divine maternity before being predestined to the glory and the grace which the Father prepared for her that she might be the worthy Mother of His Son; 3rd—that though Mary merited Heaven *de condigno* she could not merit[12] the Incarnation, nor the divine maternity, since these lie outside the sphere and purpose of human supernatural merit which does not extend beyond gaining eternal beatitude.

Many theologians have considered the argument just given as conclusive. It implies the arguments we shall expose in the following article, which really are but

---

10. IIIa, q. 2, a. II, ad 3: "Beata Virgo dicitur meruisse portare Dominum omnium, non quia meruit ipsum incamari; sed quia meruit ex gratia sibi data illum puritatis et sanctitatis gradum, ut congrue posset esse mater Dei."

11. *III Sent.,* d. IV, q. 3, a. I, ad 6: "Beata Virgo non meruit incarnationem sed praesupposita incarnation, meruit quod per eam fieret, non merito condigni, sed merito congrui, in quantum decebat quod Mater Dei esset purissima et perfectissima."

12. Not even *merito de congruo proprie,* for that would be based on Mary's charity which for its part depended on Jesus" merits, the source of all human merits. But the Blessed Virgin was able to obtain the advent of the promised Saviour by her prayers, the value of which is termed *meritum de congruo improprie* (which is based not on God's justice but on His infinite mercy).

its developments, much as the history of a predestined soul is the unfolding of what was implied in its predestination.[13]

The Gratuitousness of the Predestination of Mary.

A few additional remarks about the uniqueness of Mary's predestination will make its gratuitousness all the more apparent.

Among men Jesus is the first of the predestined, since His predestination is the model and cause of ours. As St. Thomas shows (IIIa, q. 24, a. 3 and 4), He merited for us all the effects which follow on our predestination. But the man Jesus was predestined, as we have said, to natural divine sonship, even before being predestined to glory and grace. Hence, His first or primary predestination is none other than the decree of the Incarnation. This eternal decree covers not only the Incarnation taken in the abstract—its mere substance— but also all circumstances of time and place in which it was to be put into execution, including the fact that Jesus was to be conceived in the womb of the Virgin Mary "espoused to a man whose name was Joseph, of the house of David." (*Luke* 1:27). Mary's predestination to the divine maternity being thus included in Jesus's

---

13. Cf. *Vie Intérieure de la Très Sainte Vierge,* a collection of writings of M. Olier, Rome, 1866, vol. I, ch. I: Mary's predestination to the august dignity of Mother of the Incarnate Word: in decreeing the Incarnation of His Son, God the Father took The Blessed Virgin as His spouse, pp. 53-60. Consequences: wonderful abundance of light and love poured into the soul of Mary at the moment of her conception, pp. 101 sqq. The glory she gives to God from the time of her conception, pp. 106-115. Ch. III: Mary's presentation and life in the Temple. She enhanced the value of the service offered by the Synagogue by herself adoring Jesus in the Temple under all the figures of the Old Testament; she offered Him under the figure of the immolated victims, pp. 136-143. Mary called on the Messiah in the name of Jews and Gentiles, p. 148, Ch. V: Accomplishment of the mystery of the Incarnation. The Holy Ghost fills Mary with a fullness of His gifts which made her actually worthy of the divine maternity, pp. 203 sqq. The inexpressible love of Mary for the Word incarnate in her, and of the Word for Mary, pp. 250 sqq. At the moment of the Incarnation, the Word espouses the Church in the person of Mary, to whom, on that account, He gives the fullness of IIis gifts, p. 253. Explanation of the *Magnificat,* pp. 294-313. Ch. VIII: The birth of Christ; Mary is spiritually the Mother of all Christians, pp. 327-345. Ch. IX: The presentation of Jesus in the Temple by Mary, pp. 363 sqq. Ch. X: The union between Jesus and Mary, pp. 405-434.

predestination to natural divine sonship, it follows that it precedes her predestination to glory, since Jesus is the first of those so predestined. A striking confirmation of the thesis of the preceding pages![14]

It is no less clear that Mary's predestination, like that of Jesus, was gratuitous. Jesus did not merit His predestination to natural divine sonship for the reason that His merits presuppose His Person, which is that of the Son of God by nature. Being therefore the principle of all His merits, His Divine Sonship could not itself be merited: else it would be cause and effect at the same time and under the same respect.[15]

In the same way Mary's predestination to the divine maternity is gratuitous or independent of her merits, for we have seen that to merit it would involve meriting the Incarnation itself, which is the principle of all the merits of mankind since the Fall. That is the reason for Mary's words in the *Magnificat:* "My soul doth magnify the Lord. . . . Because He hath regarded the humility (the lowly condition) of His handmaid." Her predestination to glory and grace is clearly gratuitous also, since it is a result or morally necessary consequence of her predestination to be Mother of God. This does not however involve a denial that she merited Heaven. On the contrary, we affirm that she was predestined to gain Heaven by her merits.[16] For the

---

14. Suarez is in agreement with the Thomists in this matter: cf. in IIIam, *De Mysteriis Christi,* disp. I, sect. 3, n. 3: "Dicitur B. Virginem, nostro modo intelligendi, *prius* secundum rationem *praedestinatam* esse et electam *ut esset Mater Dei,* quam ad tantam gratiam et gloriam. . . . Ideo enim B. Virgo praedestinata est ad tantam gratiam et gloriam, quia electa est in Matrem Dei . . . ut esset ita disposita sicut Matrem Dei decebat." (cf. also *ib.* disp. X, sect, VIII.)

15. Cf. St. Thomas ilia, q. 2, a. II: "In Christo omnis operatio subsecuta est unionem (cum Verbo); ergo nulla ejus operatio potuit esse meritoria unionis." (Item IIIa, q. 24, a, I and 2.)

16. The divergence of Molinist teaching from that of the disciples of St. Augustine and St. Thomas in this matter of predestination is well known. The two great Doctors mentioned (cf. *St. Thomas,* Ia, q. 23, a. 5) teach that the predestination of the elect cannot depend on their foreseen merits, since their merits are the effect of their predestination, That was the point of St. Paul's question, "What hast thou that thou hast not received (*1 Cor.* 4:7). The ultimate reason why one person is better than another is that God loves him more. No one perseveres in grace rather than to fall into sin except for the reason that

whole question of Mary's predestination cf. *Dict. Théol. Cath.,* article *Marie,* col. 2358.[17]

The sequence or order of the divine plan is therefore clear: 1st—God willed to manifest His goodness; 2nd—He willed Christ and His glory as Redeemer—in which will the permission of original sin for the sake of the greater good is included; 3rd—He willed Our Blessed Lady as Mother of the Redeemer; 4th—In consequence He willed her glory; 5th—He willed the grace and merits by which she would attain to glory; 6th—He willed the glory and grace of all the other elect.

The predestination of Mary appears now in all its sublimity. We can understand why the Church extends to her the application of the words of the Book of Proverbs, 8:22-35: "The Lord possessed me in the beginning of His ways, before He made anything from the beginning. I was set up from eternity, and of old before the earth was made . . . when He prepared the Heavens I was present . . . when He balanced the foundations of the earth, I was with Him forming all things: and was delighted every day, playing before Him at all times; playing in the world, and my delights were to be with the children of men . . . He that shall fmd me shall find life, and shall have salvation from the Lord."

Mary had been promised as the woman who would triumph over the serpent (*Gen.* 3:15), as the Virgin who would bear Emmanuel (*Is.* 7:14); she had been prefigured by the ark of alliance, the house of gold, the tower of ivory. All those testimonies show that she was pre-

---

God gives him the grace to persevere. For that reason we ought daily to pray for the grace of final perseverance, the grace of graces, the grace of the elect.

But even if the Molinists differ from the Thomists in their general theory of predestination, it would appear, as Father Merkelbach notes in his *Mariologia,* p. an, that they should make an exception of Mary. For she, having been predestined *gratuitously* to the dignity of Mother of God, her predestination to glory—which was a consequence of her first predestination—must also have been gratuitous. God could not have allowed His Mother to be lost and therefore must have willed efficaciously to lead her to salvation and to stir up in her the merits which would earn heaven for her.

17. Vasquez was the first to affirm that Mary was predestined to the divine maternity because of her foreseen merits. This opinion has been commonly rejected both in his own and in subsequent times.

destined first of all to be Mother of God. And the precise reason why the fullness of glory and grace was
given her was to make her the worthy Mother of God—
"to make her fit to be mother of Christ, as St. Thomas
expresses it (IIIa, q. 27, a. 5, ad 2), This doctrine appeared
to him so certain that we find him saying in the same
article *(corp. art.)*: "The Blessed Virgin Mary came
nearer than any other person to the humanity of Christ,
since it was from her that He received His human nature.
And that is why Mary received from Christ a plenitude
of grace which surpassed that of all the saints."

Pius IX speaks in the same sense at the beginning
of the Bull *Ineffabilis Deus:* "From the beginning and
before all ages God selected and prepared for His only
Son the Mother from whom, having taken flesh, He
would be born in the blessed fullness of time; He loved
her by herself more than all creatures, and with such
a love as to find His delight in a singular way in her.
That is why, drawing from the treasures of His divinity, He endowed her, more than all the angels and
saints, with such an abundance of heavenly gifts that
she was always completely free from sin, and that, all
beautiful and perfect, she appeared in such a plenitude of innocence and holiness that, except God's, no
greater than hers can be conceived, and that no mind
but the mind of God can measure it."[18]

Article 2

Other Reasons for Asserting
The Pre-eminence of the
Divine Maternity

We have seen that by the decree of the Incarnation
ex Maria Virgine the Blessed Virgin was predestined first
of all to the divine maternity and by way of consequence

---

18. The original Latin text will be found on pp. 7 and 54.

to glory and grace. There are still other reasons, which we shall now bring forward, which show that the divine maternity surpassed the plenitude of grace.

The Value of a Dignity of the Hypostatic Order

Since the value or worth of a relation depends on the term which it regards and which specifies it—as, for example, the dignity of the beatific knowledge and love of the elect depends on their object, which is the divine essence known intuitively—the dignity of the divine maternity is to be measured by considering the term to which it is immediately referred. Now this term is of the hypostatic order, and therefore surpasses the whole order of grace and glory.

By her divine maternity Mary is related really to the Word made flesh. The relation so set up has the uncreated Person of the Incarnate Word as its term, for Mary is the Mother of Jesus, who is God. It is not precisely the humanity of Jesus which is the term of the relation, but rather Jesus Himself in Person: it is He and not His humanity that is Son of Mary.[19] Hence Mary, reaching, as Cajetan says, even to the frontiers of the Divinity,[20] belongs terminally to the hypostatic order, to the order of the personal union of the Humanity of Jesus to the Uncreated Word. This truth follows also from the very definition of the divine maternity as formulated in the Council of Ephesus.[21]

---

19. Cf. St. Thomas IIIa, q. 35, a. 4: "*Concipi et nasci personae attribuitur* secundum naturam illam in qua concipitur et nascitur. Cum igitur in *ipso principio conceptionis fuerit humana natura assumpta a divina persona,* consequens est quod vere possit dici *Deum esse conceptum et natum de virgine.* . . Consequens est quod B. Virgo vere dicatur *Mater Dei.*" To deny that Mary is Mother of God it would be necessary first of all to assert that Jesus had been a mere man before becoming Son of God, or, with Nestorius, to deny that He had a divine personality.

20. Cf. Cajet. in IIa, IIae, q. 103, a. 4, ad 2: "Ad fines Deitatis B. V. Maria propria actione attigit, dum Deum concepit, peperit, genuit et lacte proprio pavit." Of all creatures Mary had the closest "affinity" to God.

21. Cf. Denzinger, Enchiridion, no. 113: "Si quis non confitetur Deum esse veraciter Emmanuel, et propterea *Dei genitricem* sanctam virginem (peperit enim secundum carnem factum Dei Verbum), A.S." *(Item* nos. 218, 290.)

But the order of the hypostatic union surpasses wonderfully that of grace and glory, just as this latter surpasses that of nature—of human nature and of angelic
nature, created or possible. The three orders distinguished by Pascal in his *Pensées,* that of bodies, that of
spirits with their powers sometimes amounting to genius,
and that of supernatural charity, are separated by an
immeasurable distance from each other. The same is
true of the hypostatic order and that of glory and grace,
considering the latter even as found in the greatest
saints. "The earth and its kingdoms, the firmament and
all its stars, are not worth a single thought: all spirits
taken together (and all their natural powers) are not
worth the least movement of charity, for it belongs to
another and an entirely supernatural order." Similarly,
all the acts of charity of the greatest saints, men or
angels, and their heavenly glory, are far below the
personal or hypostatic union of the Humanity of Jesus
to the Word. The divine maternity which is terminated
by the uncreated Person of the Word made flesh surpasses therefore immeasurably, because of its term, the
grace and glory of all the elect, and even the plenitude
of grace and glory received by Mary herself.

St. Thomas says (Ia, q. 25, a. 6, ad 4): "The Humanity of Christ since it is united to God, the beatitude
of the elect since it is the possession of God, the Blessed
Virgin Mary since she is the Mother of God—all these
have a certain infinite dignity from their relation to
God Himself, and under that respect there can be nothing more perfect than them since there can be nothing more perfect than God." St. Bonaventure supports
this when he says: "God could make a greater world,
but He cannot make a more perfect mother than the
Mother of God." *(Speculum,* c. 8).

As Fr. E. Hugon, O.P., says: "The divine maternity
is by its nature higher than adoptive sonship. This latter produces only a spiritual and mystic relationship,
whereas the maternity of the Blessed Virgin estab-

lishes a relationship of nature, a relationship of con-
sanguinity with Jesus Christ and one of affinity with
the entire Trinity. Besides, adoptive sonship does not
impose, as it were, such obligations on God: for the
divine maternity imposed on Jesus those obligations
of justice which ordinary children contract naturally
in regard to their parents, and it confers on Mary that
dominion and power over Him which are the natural
right accompanying the dignity of motherhood."[22]

By way of corollary it may be mentioned that the
divine maternity surpasses all the *gratiae gratis datae*
or *charismata,* such as the gift of prophecy, knowledge
of the secrets of hearts, the gift of miracles or of tongues,
for all these graces are in some way exterior and lower
in dignity than sanctifying grace (cf, Ia IIae, q. 3, a.
5). It should be noted also that the divine maternity
cannot be lost, whereas grace can be lost on earth.

The eminent dignity of the divine maternity has
been set in striking relief by Bossuet in his sermon
on the Conception of the Blessed Virgin (towards the
end of the first point): "God so loved the world, said
Our Saviour, as to give His only begotten Son (*John
3:16*) . . . (But) the ineffable love which He had for
you, O Mary, made Him conceive many other designs
in your regard, He ordained that He should belong to
you in the same quality in which He belonged to Himself: and in order to establish an eternal union with
you He made you the Mother of His only Son and
Himself the Father of yours. O prodigy! O abyss of
charity! what mind does not find itself lost to consider the incomprehensible regard He had for you; you
come so near to Him, through this Son common to you
both, this inviolable bond of your sacred alliance, this
pledge of your mutual love which you have given so
lovingly to each other, the Father giving Him in His

---

22. *Marie, Pleine de Grâce,* 5th edition, 1926, p, 63. This book I consider one of the
best written on the Blessed Virgin.

impassible divinity, and you giving Him in the mortal flesh in which He was obedient."

God the Father communicated to His Son the divine nature. Mary gave Him a human nature, subject to pain and death, in which to redeem us. But Mary's Son is the only-begotten of the Father, and in that consists the whole grandeur of her maternity.

The Reason why so many Graces were Conferred on Mary

The eminent dignity of the divine maternity is revealed in a new light if we consider that it is the reason why the fullness of grace was given to Mary, that it is the measure and end of that fullness, and that it is superior to it.

The reason why Mary was given a fullness of grace from the first instant was that she might be enabled to conceive the Man-God in holiness, by uttering her fiat with the utmost generosity on the day of the Annunciation in spite of the sufferings which she knew had been foretold of the Messiah; it was given her, too, that she might bring forth her child while remaining a virgin, that she might surround Him with the most motherly and most holy devotion; it was given her, finally, that she might unite herself to Him in closest conformity of will, as only a most holy mother can, during His hidden life, His apostolic life, and His suffering life—that she might utter her second *fiat* most heroically at the foot of the Cross, with Him, by Him, and in Him.

As Fr. Hugon has so well put it: "The divine maternity postulates intimate friendship with God. Since a mother is bound both by a law of nature and an express precept to love her son, and he to love her, Mary and Jesus love each other mutually; and since the maternity in question here is supernatural the love must be of the same order. But this means that it is a sanctifying love, since by the fact that God loves a soul He makes it lovable and sanctifies it."[23] There is thus the most complete conformity between the will of Mary and her Son's oblation which was, as it were, the soul of the sacrifice of the Cross.

It is clear that it was for the reason we have given and for none other that Mary was given an initial plenitude of grace followed by a consummated plenitude in glory. The same reason or end was the measure of her grace and glory: therefore it surpassed them. Admittedly it is not possible to deduce from the divine maternity each and every one of the privileges received by Mary,[24] but all derive ultimately from it. If, finally, she was predestined from all eternity to the highest degree of glory after Jesus, the reason is that she was predestined first of all to be His most worthy mother, and to retain that title during eternity after having enjoyed it in time. The saints who contemplate in Heaven the sublime degree of glory, so far surpassing that of the angels, in which Mary is enthroned, know that the reason why she was predestined to it is that she might be and might remain for eternity the most worthy Mother of God: *Mater Creatoris, Mater Salvatoris, Virgo Dei Genetrix.*

Such was the teaching of St. Albert the Great on more than one occasion.[25] The poets have sung it in

---

23. Father E. Hugon, O.P. De B. *Virgine Maria Deipara (Tractatus Theologici),* 1926, p. 735.

24. For example, we cannot deduce from it the privilege of the Assumption, except by taking into consideration the further point that the Mother of God was associated intimately with Jesus's complete victory over Satan, sin and death. At the same time, it is clear that the reason for this intimate association is the divine maternity. This is much the same as to say that the second property of the circle cannot be deduced from the definition alone, but follows from it taken in conjunction with its first property.

25. *Mariale* qq. 140 and 141: "Magis est esse matrem Dei per naturam, quam esse filium (Dei) per adoptionem"—"Quidquid claudit alterum in se plus est eligendum quam illud quod non claudit alterum in se. Sed esse matrem Dei per naturam claudit in se filium Dei adoptivum." Suarez says similarly in Illam P., disp. I, sect. 2, no. 4: "Comparatur haec dignitas Matris Dei ad alias gratias creatas tamquam prima forma ad suas proprietates; et e converso aliae gratiae comparantur ad ipsam sicut dispositiones ad formam. Est ergo haec dignitas matris, excellentior, sicut forma perfectior est proprietatibus et dispositionibus." *(Item* Bossuet, cf. *infra* p. 29.)

their verses. We refer in a note to one of their most recent tributes.[26]

The Motive of the Cult of Hyperdulia

A last consideration, which will be found in the works of many theologians, can be adduced in favor of our thesis.

It is because she is Mother of God rather than because she is full of grace that Mary is entitled to the cult of hyperdulia, a cult superior to that due to the saints highest in grace and glory. In other words, hyperdulia is due to Mary not because she is the greatest of the saints but because of her divine maternity. It would not have been her due had she been raised to her present degree of glory without having been predestined to be Mother of God. This is the express teaching of St. Thomas.[27]

---

26. Paul Claudel has written very beautifully on the subject in his *Corona benignitatis anni Dei,* Hymn to the Sacred Heart, 15th ed., p. 64.

> *Three months after the Angel's message—at the end of June,*
> *The Woman who is bright as the sun and fair as the moon*
> *Feels the Heart of her Infant throb beneath hers.*
>
> *In the womb of the Virgin Immaculate a new world begins,*
> *The Child who is older than time enters time for our sins,*
> *And with human breathing the First Mover stirs.*
>
> *Mary, heavy with child conceived by the Holy Ghost,*
> *Is far from the sight of men with her heavenly Host,*
> *Like the dove of the Canticle in the crannied wall.*
>
> *She moves not, she speaks not a word, she adores—no more;*
> *Her life is within, her God is within to adore,*
> *Her work and her son, her child, her all.*
>
> *The world is at peace, the temple of Janus is shut,*
> *The sceptre of David is gone and the prophets are mute,*
> *Lo! darker than Hades, a dawn without light.*
>
> *For Satan holds sway and the world gives him incense and gold,*
> *But into his kingdom God comes like a thief, and behold*
> *A daughter of Eve puts the serpent to flight.*
>
> *The promised Messiah is come, for whom the world prays,*
> *Men know not the good tidings yet, but, far from their gaze,*
> *The Mother is circled by Cherubim bright.*

27. IIIa, q. 25, a. 5: "Cum Beata Virgo sit pura creatura rationalis, non debetur ei adoratio latriae, sed solum *veneratio duliae, eminentius* tamen quam caeteris

In the Litanies of the Blessed Virgin the first title of glory mentioned is the *Sancta Dei Genetrix*. All the others follow as something which pertains to Mary as Mother of God: *Sancta Virgo Virginum, Mater divinae gratiae, Mater purissima, Mater castissima, Mater inviolata, Mater intemerata, Mater amabalis, Mater admirabilis, Mater boni consilii, etc.*

Consequences of the Principles thus far Outlined

It follows from what has been said thus far that, *simpliciter loquendo,* purely and simply, the divine maternity, even considered in isolation, is superior to the plenitude of grace, consummated no less than initial. The ultimate reason for this assertion is that by its term the divine maternity belongs to a higher order, that of the hypostatic union.[28]

Thus the rational soul which, considered even in isolation, pertains to the order of substance, is superior to its faculties of intellect and will: it is their end, for

---

creaturis, *in quantum ipsa est Mater Dei.* Et ideo dicitur quod debetur ei non qualiscumque dulia, sed *hyperdulia.*"

ad I: *Matri regis* debetur quidam honor consimilis (honori qui debetur regi), ratione cujusdam excellentiae."

ad 2: "Honor matris refertur ad filium."

St. Bonaventure speaks in the same sense in *III Sent.,* d. 9, q. 3, a. 1. The Sacred Congregation of Rites said also (June 1st, 1884): "Reginae et dominae angelorum, *in quantum est mater Dei . . .* debetur . . . non qualiscumque dulia, sed hyperdulia."

28. In this assertion we differ, as do many theologians, from Suarez (in IIIam S. Thomae, t. II, disp. I, sect. 2, no. 6 sq.) and the Salamanticenses *(Cursus Theologicus,* tr. XIII, disp. II, 27; tr. XIX, disp. IV, 117 sq.).

The reasons for our position are those so well exposed by E. Dublanchy in the *Dict. Théol. Cath.,* art. *Marie,* cols. 2357-2365. As we read there, Suarez held that were the divine maternity to exist without grace and adoptive childhood by grace, it would be much inferior to the latter. On the other hand, if the divine maternity be understood as including everything that is associated with it in the present order of providence, it is certainly higher than adoptive childhood. Suarez" distinction has been approved and adopted by Novatus, Vega and the Salamanticenses.

However, as Father Dublanchy says *(ibid.* col. 2357): "The greater number of theologians, basing themselves on the principle that the divine maternity pertains to the hypostatic order and that whatever pertains to that order surpasses all gifts of grace, continued to hold both in the seventeenth and the succeeding centuries that the divine maternity surpassed—in dignity, at least—adoptive childhood by grace, even if it be considered, *per impossibile,* as separated from grace."

they proceed from it as accidents and properties in order that it may have the power of knowing and willing. In a somewhat similar way, the divine maternity, considered in isolation from Mary's other dignities, is the end and reason of her fullness of grace, and is therefore higher than it.

It is now clear why Mary was predestined first to be Mother of God before being predestined to the highest degree of glory after Jesus. The dignity of a relation is to be judged more by its term than by anything else; but the divine maternity is something relative to the Person of the Word made Flesh. In much the same way the mother of a king is nearer to him than the most able of his lawyers.

However, under a certain respect—secundum *quid,* as theologians say—sanctifying grace and the beatific vision are more perfect than the divine maternity. As regards sanctifying grace, it makes its bearer holy in the formal sense of the term, whereas the divine maternity, being only a relation to the Word made flesh, does not sanctify in that way.[29] The beatific vision, for its part, unites the intellects of the elect to the divine essence without the intermediary of the Sacred Humanity.[30]

It is evident that the hypostatic union of the two natures in Christ, considered absolutely, surpasses the beatific vision, even though the latter includes a perfection in the order of knowledge not found in the former. In a similar way, and with all due reservations, the divine maternity, if considered absolutely or *simpliciter,* surpasses the plenitude of grace and glory, even though this latter is more perfect in a secondary

---

29. That is a point of difference between the divine maternity and the uncreated grace of union, which is nothing other than the Person of the Word sanctifying the Sacred Humanity. The grace of union confers an inner, substantial, uncreated sanctity, which is higher than the accidental and created sanctity conferred by the accident of sanctifying grace.

30. These theological arguments for the superiority of the divine maternity over the fullness of grace are ably exposed by Father Merkelbach, O.P., in his *Mariologia,* 1939, pp. 64-70 (against Basquez, Van Noort, and others). Father Hugon, O.P., *Tractatus Theologici, de B. V. Maria Deipara,* 1926, p. 736, may also be consulted.

way, or *secundum quid.* For the divine maternity, being but a real relation to the Incarnate Word, is not enough of itself to sanctify Mary. But it called out for, or demanded, the fullness of grace which was granted her to raise her to the level of her singular mission. She could not have been predestined to be any other kind of mother to the Saviour than a worthy one.[31] Everything follows from that certain truth. All Mariology is dominated by it just as all Christology is dominated by the truth that Jesus is the Son of God.[32]

Since Mary pertains by the term of her maternity to the hypostatic order, it follows that she is higher than the angels; higher also than the priesthood, which participates in that of Christ.[33] Of course, not having the priestly character, Mary could not consecrate as does the priest at the altar. But none the less, her dignity is higher than that of the priest and of the bishop, since it is of the hypostatic order. The Victim offered on the Cross, and whom the priest offers on

---

31. The maternity of a rational creature must be worthy or else irrational; an unworthy mother fails in the duties imposed on her by the natural law. Rational maternity of its very nature far surpasses the maternity of an irrational creature, even though this latter is not without nobility, as for example in the mother-hen who gathers her chicks under her wings and sacrifices herself to protect them from the hawk.

32. cf. *Dict. Théol. Cath.,* art. *Marie* by E. Dublanchy, col. 2365: "The dignity of the divine maternity, since it appertains to the hypostatic order, surpasses all other created dignities, even when considered in its *isolation,* and not excluding the dignity of divine adoption by grace and the Christian priesthood."

Father E, Hugon, O.P., in his book *Marie, pleine de grâce,* fifth edition, 1926, p. 213, remarks very pertinently: "The divine maternity calls for holiness and all its effects. It calls for participation in the divine being and the divine friendship. It implies a special inhabitation of the Blessed Trinity. It confers a sovereign power of impetration. It guarantees impeccability. It confers an inalienable right to the eternal heritage and even to dominion over all things. It belongs to the hypostatic order, which is higher than that of grace and glory. Habitual grace can be lost, but not the divine maternity. Mary's other graces are only a consequence of her maternity. By it, Mary is the eldest daughter *(l'ainée)* in all creation."

33. Mary contributes by her maternity to the realisation of the mystery of the Incarnation by giving the Word His human nature, which is more than to make Him really present in the Blessed Eucharist. Besides, the priest may have the priestly character without grace and without God's friendship; the plenitude of grace is, however, inseparable from Mary, because of her special predestination. It is possible to think of an unworthy priest, but not of an unworthy Mother of God. From Mary's maternity, there follow the privileges of her preservation from original sin, and from every personal sin (even venial) and from every imperfection.

the altar, was given us by Mary. The Principal Offerer of our Masses was given us by her. She was more closely associated with Him at the foot of the Cross than anyone else—more than even the stigmatics and the martyrs. Thus, had Mary received the priestly ordination (but it did not form part of her mission), she would have received something less than what is implied in her title of Mother of God. As St. Albert the Great so well expressed it: "The Blessed Virgin was not called by God to be a minister, but a consort and a helper, in accordance with the words 'Let us make him a help like unto himself'" *(Mariale,* 42 and 165). Mary was chosen to be not the minister of the Saviour but His associate and helper in the work of redemption.

The divine maternity is therefore, as is commonly taught, the foundation, source, and root of all Mary's graces and privileges, both those that preceded it as preparation, and those that accompanied it or followed from it as its consequence. It was by way of preparation for the divine maternity that Mary was the Immaculate Conception, preserved from the stain of original sin by the future merits of her Son. He redeemed her as perfectly as was possible; not by healing her, but by preserving her from the original stain before it touched her soul for even an instant. It was because of her maternity that Mary received the initial fullness of grace which ceased not to increase till it reached its consummated plenitude. And because of the same maternity she was exempt from all personal fault, even venial—and from all imperfection, for she never failed in promptitude to obey the divine inspirations even when they came to her by way of simple counsels.[34] The dignity of Mary surpasses therefore that of all the saints combined.

---

34. Thus we see that an imperfection, which is a *failing in promptitude* to follow a divine counsel, is something different from a venial sin. The shade of difference is not easy to detect in ordinary human lives, but it appears quite clear in the light of the perfect holiness of Mary.

Recall, too, that Mary had a mother's authority over the Word of God made flesh. She contributed therefore to His knowledge: not, of course, to His beatific or infused knowledge, but to the progressive formation of His acquired knowledge, which knowledge lit up the acquired prudence in accordance with which He performed acts proportioned to His age during His infancy and hidden life. In this way the Word made flesh was subject to Mary in most profound sentiments of respect and love. How, then, could we fail to have the same sentiments in regard to the Mother of Our God?

In one of the most beautiful books written about Mary, the *Treatise on True Devotion to the Blessed Virgin,* St. Grignon de Montfort says (ch. 1, a. 1): "God made Man found liberty in being enclosed in her womb; He showed His power by allowing Himself to be carried by her, young maiden though she was; He found glory, and His Father found glory too, in hiding His splendor from all creatures of earth, so as to reveal them to Mary alone; He glorified His majesty and His independence by depending on the Virgin in His conception, His birth, His presentation in the temple, His hidden life of thirty years—and even up to the time of His death, for she was present then, and He offered one only sacrifice in union with her, and was immolated to the eternal Father with her consent as once Isaac was immolated to the divine will by the consent of Abraham. . . . It is she who nourished and supported Him, who brought Him up and then sacrificed Him for us. . . . Finally, Our Lord remains as much the Son of Mary in Heaven as He was on earth."

Such is the first reason for the cult of hyperdulia which we owe her. It explains why the voice of tradition, and especially the Council of Ephesus and Constantinople, insisted, before everything else concerning Mary, on the fact that she was the Mother of God, thereby affirming afresh against Nestorianism that Jesus was God.

To conclude this chapter we should note that many christians find it so evident that Mary's greatest title is that of Mother of God, and that all her other titles follow from and are explained by it, that they do not understand why time should be devoted to proving the point. It is quite clear to them that had we, for our part, been in a position to do so, we should have given our mother every gift at our disposal. That is why St. Thomas is content to state quite simply (IIIa, q. 27, a. 5, corp. et ad 2): "To be the worthy Mother of God, Mary needed to receive fullness of grace." Bossuet repeats this in his sermon on the Compassion of the Blessed Virgin (1st point, end): "Since God disposes things with wonderful aptness, it was necessary that He should imprint on the heart of the Blessed Virgin a love going far beyond nature even to the last reaches of grace, so that she might have for her Son sentiments worthy of a Mother of God and of a Man-God."

⮐Chapter 2⮑

Mary's First Plenitude of Grace

"Hail, full of Grace" (Luke 1:28.)

HAVING seen the nobility of Mary's title, Mother of God, it is now appropriate to examine the meaning and implications of the words spoken to her by the Angel Gabriel on the day of the Annunciation: "Hail, full of grace, the Lord is with thee: Blessed art thou among women." (*Luke* 1:28). As a help to understanding these words spoken in God's name we shall consider: 1st—the different plenitudes of grace; 2nd—the privilege of the Immaculate Conception; 3rd—the sublimity of Mary's first grace,

Article 1
The Different Plenitudes of Grace

According to the usage of Holy Scripture, which becomes more and more explicit in the New Testament, it is grace in the strict sense of the term which is implied in the term "fullness of grace"—that is to say, grace which is really distinct from nature, both human and angelic, grace which is a free gift of God surpassing the natural powers and exigencies of all nature, created or creatable.[1] Habitual or sanctifying grace makes us participate in the very nature, in the inner life of God, according to the words of St. Peter (*2 Peter* 1:4): "By whom he hath given us most great and precious promises: that by these you may be made partakers

---

1. "Full of grace," especially if the original Greek word be considered, means "made agreeable in God's eyes" or "well-beloved of God'. But a soul is made agreeable in God's eyes by habitual grace, or *gratia gratum faciens,* which is itself an effect of the active and uncreated love of God which selects the soul as His adopted child.

of the divine nature." By grace we have become adopted children of God, heirs and co-heirs with Christ (*Rom.* 8:17); by grace we are "born of God." (*John* 1:13). It prepares us to receive eternal life as a heritage and as a reward of the merits of which it is itself the principle. It is even the germ of eternal life, the *semen gloriae* as Tradition terms it, since by it we are disposed in advance for the face to face vision and the beatific love of God.

Habitual grace is received into the very essence of the soul as a supernatural graft which elevates and deifies its vitality. From it there flows into the faculties the infused virtues, theological and moral, and the seven gifts of the Holy Ghost, all of which supernatural organism constitutes a sort of second nature of such a kind as to enable us to perform con-naturally the supernatural and meritorious acts of the infused virtues and the seven gifts. We have, too, by habitual grace the Blessed Trinity dwelling within us as in a temple where They are known and loved, even as it were experimentally. And at times we *do* know Them in this quasi-experimental fashion when by a special grace They make Themselves known to us as the life of our life, for ". . . you have received the spirit of adoption of sons, whereby we cry Abba (Father)." (*Rom.* 8:15). Then does the Holy Ghost inspire us with filial love, and in that sense ". . . the spirit himself giveth testimony to our spirit, that we are the sons of God." (*Rom.* 8:16).

While habitual grace makes us thus children of God, actual or transitory grace first of all disposes us for adoptive childhood, and subsequently makes us act, through the infused virtues and gifts working separately or both together, in a manner becoming God's children. This new life of grace, virtues and gifts, is none other than eternal life begun on earth, since habitual grace and charity will outlive the passage of time.

Grace—call it, if you will, a participation in the divine

nature—was no less gratuitous for the angels than for us. As St. Augustine says *(De Civ. Dei,* XII, c. 9): "God created them, at the same instant forming their nature and endowing them with grace." When creating the angels God conferred grace on them, to which grace their nature, richly endowed though it was, could lay no claim. The angels, and man also, could have been created in a purely natural condition, lacking the divine graft whence issues a new life.

The grace intended in the words "Hail, full of grace" addressed to Our Lady is therefore something higher than nature or the exigencies of nature, created or merely possible. It is a participation in the divine nature or in the inner life of God, which makes the soul to enter into the kingdom of God, a kingdom far surpassing all the kingdoms of nature—mineral, vegetable, animal, human, and even angelic. So elevated is grace that St. Thomas could say: "The good of the grace of one soul is greater than the good of the nature of the whole universe."[2] The least degree of grace in the soul of a newly baptised child is worth more than all created natures, including those that are angelic. Being a participation in the inner life of God, grace is something greater than all miracles and exterior signs of divine revelation or of the sanctity of God's favored servants. And it is of this grace, germ and promise of glory, that the angel spoke when he said to Mary: "Hail, full of grace." Gazing at Mary's soul, he saw that, though he himself was in the possession of the beatific vision, Mary's grace and charity far surpassed his for she possessed them in the degree required to become at that instant the Mother of God.

Mary, of course, had received from the Most High natural gifts of body and soul in wonderful perfection. Judged even from the natural level, the soul of Jesus united in itself all that there is of beauty and nobil-

---

2. Ia IIae, q, 24, a. 3, ad 2.

ity in the souls of the great poets and artists, of men of genius and of men of generosity. In an analogous way the soul of Mary was a divine masterpiece because of the natural perfection of her intelligence and will and sensibility. There is no shadow of doubt that she was more gifted than anyone who has ever struck us as remarkable for penetration and sureness of mind, for strength of will, for equilibrium or harmony of higher and lower faculties. Since she had been preserved from original sin and its baneful effects, concupiscence and darkness of understanding, her body did not weigh down her mind but rather served it. When forming the body of a saint, God has in mind the soul which is to vivify it: when forming Mary's body He had in mind the Body and the infinitely holy Soul of the Word made flesh. As St. Albert the Great loves to recall, the Fathers of the Church say that Mary, viewed even naturally, had the grace of Rebecca, the beauty of Rachel, and the gentle majesty of Esther. They add that her chaste beauty never held the gaze for its own sake alone, but always lifted souls up to God.

The more perfect these gifts of nature in Mary, the more elevated they make her grace appear, for it surpasses them immeasurably.

When speaking of fullness of grace it is well to note that it exists in three different degrees in Our Lord, in Mary, and in the just. St. Thomas explains this a number of times.[3]

There is, first of all, the absolute fullness of grace which is peculiar to Jesus, the Saviour of mankind. Taking into consideration only the ordinary power of God, there can be no greater grace than this. It is the eminent and inexhaustible source of all the grace which all men have received since the Fall, or will receive till the end of time. It is the source also of the beati-

---

3. See particularly his *Comm. in Joannem,* c. 1, lect. x.

tude of the elect, for Jesus has merited all the effects of our predestination.[4]

There is, in the second place, the fullness of superabundance which is Mary's special privilege, and which is so named since it is like a spiritual river which has poured of its abundance upon the souls of men for almost two thousand years.

There is finally the fullness of sufficiency which is common to all the just and which makes them capable of performing those meritorious acts—they normally become more perfect in the course of years—which lead them to eternal life.

These three fullnesses have been well compared to an inexhaustible spring, to the stream or river which flows from it, and to the different canals fed by the river, which irrigate and make fertile the whole region they traverse—that is to say, the whole Church, universal in time and space. The river of grace proceeds from God through the Saviour, as we read "Drop down dew, ye heavens, from above, and let the clouds rain the just: let the earth be opened, and bud forth a saviour." (*Is.* 14:8). And then finally it rises once more to God, the Ocean of peace, in the form of merits, prayers, and sacrifices.

To continue the image: the fullness of the spring has not increased; that of the river, on the contrary, which flows from it has increased. Or, to speak in plain terms, the absolute fullness of Our Saviour knew no increase, for it was sovereignly perfect from the first instant of His conception by reason of the personal union with the Word. For, from the first instant, the *lumen gloriae* and the beatific vision were communicated to Jesus's soul, so that the second Council of Constantinople could say (Denz. 224) that Christ did not grow more perfect by reason of His meritorious acts: "Ex profectu operum non melioratus est." Mary's fullness

---

4. IIIa, q. 24, a. 4.

of grace, however, did not cease to increase up to the time of her death. For that reason theologians usually speak of, 1st—her initial fullness or plenitude; 2nd— the fullness of her second sanctification at the instant of the conception of the Saviour; 3rd—the final fullness (at the instant of her entry into glory), its extent, and its superabundance.[5]

Article 2

The Privilege of the Immaculate Conception

The initial fullness of grace in Mary presents two aspects. One is negative, at least in its formulation: her preservation from original sin. The other is positive: her conception, absolutely pure and holy by reason of the perfection of her initial sanctifying grace in which were rooted the infused virtues and the gifts of the Holy Ghost.

The Dogmatic Definition

The definition of the dogma of the Immaculate Conception, made by Pius IX on December 8th, 1854, reads as follows: "We declare, announce, and define that the doctrine which states that the Blessed Virgin Mary was preserved, in the first instant of her conception, by a singular grace and privilege of God Omnipotent and because of the merits of Jesus Christ the Saviour of the human race, free from all stain of original sin, is revealed by God and must therefore be believed firmly and with constancy by all the faithful" (Denz. 1641).

This definition contains three especially important points: 1st—It affirms that the Blessed Virgin was preserved from all stain of original sin from the first

---

5. Cf. IIIa, q. 27, a. 5, ad 2.

instant of her conception. The conception meant is that known as passive or consummated—that in which her soul was created and united to her body—for it is then only that one can speak of a human person, whereas the definition bears on a privilege granted to the person of Mary. The definition states also that the Immaculate Conception is a special privilege and an altogether singular grace, the work of divine omnipotence.

What are we to understand by original sin from which Mary has been preserved? The Church has not defined its intrinsic nature, but she has taught us something about it by telling us its effects: the divine hatred or malediction, a stain on the soul, a state of non-justice or spiritual death, servitude under the empire of Satan, subjection to the law of concupiscence, subjection to suffering and to bodily death in so far as they are the penalty of the common sin.[6] These effects presuppose the loss of the sanctifying grace which, along with integrity of nature, Adam had received for us and for himself, and which he lost by sin, also for us and for himself.[7]

It follows therefore that Mary was not preserved free from every stain of original sin otherwise than by receiving sanctifying grace into her soul from the first instant of her conception. Thus she was conceived in that state of justice and holiness which is the effect of the divine friendship as opposed to the divine malediction, and in consequence she was withdrawn from the slavery of the devil and subjection to the law of concupiscence. She was withdrawn too from subjection to the law of suffering and death, considered as penalties of the sin

---

6. Cf. Second Council of Orange, Denz. 174, 175. Council of Trent, Denz. 788, 789.
7. Council of Trent, Denz. 789: "Si quis Adae praevaricationem sibi soli et non eius propagini asserit nocuisse, acceptam a Deo *sanctitatem et justitiam* quam perdidit, *sibi soli et non nobis etiam perdidisse;* aut inquinatum ilium per inobedientiae peccatum mortem et poenas corporis tantum in omne genus humanum transfudisse, non autem *peccatum* quod est *mors animae,* A.S." Sin is the death of the soul since it deprives it of sanctifying grace which is the supernatural life of the soul, and the germ of eternal life.

of our nature,[8] even though both Jesus and Mary knew suffering and death in so far as they are consequences of our nature *(in carne passibili)* and endured them for our salvation.

2nd—It is affirmed in the definition, as it was already affirmed in 1661 by Alexander VIII (Denz. 1100) that it was through the merits of Jesus Christ, the Saviour of the human race, that Mary was preserved from original sin. Hence the opinion held by some 13th-century theologians—that Mary was immaculate in the sense of not needing to be redeemed, and that her first grace was independent of the future merits of her Son—may no longer be admitted. According to the Bull *Ineffabilis Deus,* Mary was redeemed by the merits of her Son in a most perfect way, by a redemption which did not free her from a stain already contracted, but which preserved her from contracting one. Even in human affairs we look on one as more a saviour if he wards off a blow than if he merely heals the wound it inflicts.

The idea of a preservative redemption reminds us that Mary, being a child of Adam and proceeding from him by way of natural generation, should have incurred the hereditary taint, and would have incurred it in fact had not God decided from all eternity to grant her the unique privilege of an immaculate conception in dependence on the future merits of her Son.

The liturgy had already made this point in the prayer proper to the Feast of the Immaculate Conception, which was approved by Sixtus IV (1476): "Thou hast preserved her (Mary) from all stain through the foreseen death of this same Son." The Blessed Virgin was preserved from original sin by the future death of her Son, that is to say, by the merits of Christ dying for us on the Cross.

It is therefore clear that Mary's preservation from

---

8. This aspect of the dogmatic definition is very well explained by Fr. X. M. le Bachelet, S.J., in the *Dictionnaire Apologétique, art. Marie,* section *Immaculée Conception,* vol. III, col. 220 sqq.

original sin differs essentially from that of the Saviour. Jesus was not redeemed by the merits of another, not even by His own. He was preserved from original sin and from all sin for two reasons: first because of the personal or hypostatic union of His humanity to the Word in the very instant in which His sacred soul was created, since it could not be that sin should ever be attributed to the Word made flesh; secondly, since His conception was virginal and due to the operation of the Holy Ghost, so that Jesus did not descend from Adam by way of natural generation.[9] These two reasons are peculiar to Jesus alone.

3rd—The definition proposes the doctrine of the Immaculate Conception as revealed, that is, as contained at least implicitly in the deposit of Revelation— in Scripture and Tradition, or in one at least of those two sources.

The Testimony of the Scriptures

The Bull *Ineffabilis Deus* quotes two texts of Scripture, Genesis 3:15, and Luke 1:28, 42.

The privilege of the Immaculate Conception is revealed as it were implicitly or confusedly in the book of Genesis in the words spoken by God to the serpent, and thereby to Satan (*Gen.* 3:15): "I will put enmities between thee and the woman, and thy seed and her seed: she shall crush thy head and thou shalt lie in wait for her heel." The pronoun we translate as "she" in "she shall crush thy head" is masculine in the Hebrew text, and stands for the posterity or seed of the woman; this is true also of the Septuagint and the Syriac versions. The Vulgate however has the feminine pronoun "ipsa," referring the prophecy directly to the woman herself. However there is no essential difference of

---

9. As St. Augustine puts it, *De Genesi ad litteram,* bk. X, chs. 19 and 20: Jesus was in Adam "non secundum seminalem rationem" but only "secundum corpulentem substantiam."

meaning between the two readings since the woman is to be associated with the victory of Him Who will be the great representative of her posterity in their conflict with Satan throughout the ages.

Taken by themselves these words are certainly not sufficient to prove that the Immaculate Conception is revealed. But the Fathers of the Church, in their comparison of Eve and Mary, have seen in them an allusion to it, and it is on that account that the text is cited by Pius IX.

To the naturalist exegete the text means no more than the instinctive revulsion man experiences towards the serpent. But to the Jewish and Christian tradition it means much more. The Christian tradition sees in that promise—it has been termed the *protoevangelium*—the first sketch of the Messiah and His victory over the spirit of evil. For Jesus is pre-eminently the posterity of the woman in conflict with the posterity of the serpent. But if Jesus is termed the posterity of the woman, that is not because of His remote connection with Eve, who was able to pass on to her descendants only a fallen and wounded nature, deprived of the divine life. Rather is it because of His connection with Mary, in whose womb He took a stainless humanity. As Fr. F. X. le Bachelet says, in col. 118 of the article referred to already, "We do not find in Eve the principle of that enmity which God will put between the race of the woman and the race of the serpent; for Eve, like Adam, is herself fallen a victim to the serpent. It is only between Mary, Mother of the Redeemer, that enmity ultimately exists. Hence the person of Mary is included, though in a veiled manner, in the *protoevangelium,* and the Vulgate reading "ipsa" (she) expresses something really implied in the sacred text, since the victory of the Redeemer is morally, but really, the victory of His Mother."

For that reason early Christianity never ceased to contrast Eve who shared in Adam's sin by yielding to the serpent's suggestion with Mary who shared in the redemptive work of Christ by believing the words of the angel on the morning of the Annunciation.[10]

The promise of Genesis speaks of a victory that will be complete: "She shall crush thy head." And since the victory over Satan will be complete, so also the victory over sin which makes the soul slave and the devil master. But as Pius IX teaches in the Bull *Ineffabilis Deus,* the victory over Satan would not be complete if Mary had not been preserved from original sin by the merits of her Son: *"De ipso (serpente) plenissime triumphans, illius caput immaculato pede (Maria) contrivit."*

The Immaculate Conception is contained therefore in the promise of Genesis as the oak is contained in the acorn. A person who had never seen an oak could never guess the value of the acorn, nor its final stage of development. But we who have seen the oak know for what the acorn is destined, and that it does not yield an elm nor a poplar. The same law of evolution obtains in the order of progressive divine revelation.

The Bull *Ineffabilis* quotes also the salutation addressed by the angel to Mary (*Luke* 1:28): "Hail, full of grace . . . blessed are thou among woman," as well as the similar words uttered by St. Elisabeth under divine inspiration (*Luke* 1:42). Pius IX does not state that these words are sufficient by themselves to prove that the Immaculate Conception is revealed; for that, the exegetic tradition of the Fathers must be invoked.

This tradition becomes explicit with St. Ephrem the Syrian (d. 373).[11] Among the Greeks it is found on the morrow of the Council of Ephesus (431), especially in the teaching of two bishop-opponents of Nestorious, St.

---

10. For the interpretation of the prophecy of Genesis cf. Terrien, *La Mère de Dieu et la Mère des Hommes,* vol. III, bk. I, ch. 2, pp. 26-49. The Mary-Eve antithesis is brought out by SS. Justin, Irenaeus, Cyril of Jerusalem, Ephrem, Epiphanius, Ambrose, Jerome, Augustine, John Chrysostom, etc. Cf. *Dict. Apol.* article already quoted, col. 119.

11. Cf, *Dict. Theol.,* art. *Ephrem,* col. 192.

Proclus who was a successor of St. John Chrysostom in the chair of Constantinople (431-446) and Theodore, bishop of Ancyra. Later we find it in the teaching of St. Sophronius, Patriarch of Jerusalem (634-638), Andrew of Crete (d. 740), St. John Damascene (d. towards the middle of the 8th century). These different testimonies will be found at length in the article *Marie* of the *Dict. Apol.*, cols. 223-231.

Understood in the light of this exegetic tradition, the words of the angel to Mary "Hail, full of grace"—that is "Hail, thou art fully pleasing to God and loved by Him"—are not limited temporally in their application in such a way as to exclude even the initial period of Mary's life. On the contrary, the Blessed Virgin would not have received complete fullness of grace had her soul been even for an instant in the condition of spiritual death which follows on original sin, had she been even for an instant deprived of grace, turned away from God, a daughter of wrath, in slavery to the devil. St. Proclus says that she was "formed from stainless clay."[12] Theodore of Ancyra says that "the Son of the Most High came forth from the Most High."[13] St. John Damascene writes that Mary is the holy daughter of Joachim and Anne "who has escaped the burning darts of the evil one,"[14] that she is a new paradise "to which the serpent has no stealthy access,"[15] that she is exempt from the debt of death which is one of the consequences of original sin,[16] and that she must therefore be exempt from the common fall.

If Mary had contracted original sin her fullness of grace would have been diminished in this sense that it would not have extended to the whole of her life. Thus, Our Holy Mother the Church, reading the words of the angelic salutation in the light of Tradition and

---

12. *Orat.* VI: *P. G.*, LXV, 733; cf. 751 sqq., 756.
13. *Hom. VI, in Sanctam Mariam Del genetricem*, 11-12; *P. G.*, LXXVII, 1426 sqq.
14. *Hom. I in Nat.*, 7; *P. G.*, XCVI, 672.
15. *Hom. II in dormit.*, 2, col. 725.
16. *Hom. II in dormit.*, 3, col. 728.

with the assistance of the Holy Ghost, saw revealed implicitly in it the privilege of the Immaculate Conception. The privilege is revealed in the text not as an effect is in a cause which could exist without it, but as a part is in a whole; the part is actually contained in the whole at least by way of implicit statement.

The Testimony of Tradition

Tradition itself affirms the truth of the Immaculate Conception more and more explicitly in the course of time. St. Justin[17], St. Irenaeus,[18] Tertullian,[19] contrast Eve, the cause of death, and Mary, the cause of life and salvation. This antithesis is constantly on the lips of the Fathers[20] and is found also in the most solemn documents of the Church's magisterium, especially in the Bull *Ineffabilis Deus.* It is presented as perfect and without restriction; thus, Mary must always have been greater than Eve, and most particularly at the first moment of her life. The Fathers often say that Mary is stainless, that she has always been blessed by God in honour of her Son, that she is *intemerata, intacta, impolluta, intaminata, illibata,* altogether without spot.

Comparing Mary and Eve, St. Ephrem says: "Both were at first simple and innocent, but thereafter Eve became cause of death and Mary cause of life."[21] Speaking to Our Blessed Lord, he continues: "You Lord and Your Mother are the only two who are perfectly beautiful under every respect. In You there is no fault, and in Your Mother there is no stain. All other children of God are far from such beauty."[22]

---

17. *Dial. cum Tryphone,* 100; *P. G.,* VII, 858 sqq., 1175.
18. *Adv. Haereses,* III, xxii, 3, 4; *P. G.,* VII, 858 sqq., 1175.
19. *De carne Christi,* XVII; *P. L.,* II, 782.
20. For example, SS. Cyril of Jerusalem, Ephrem, Epiphanius, Ambrose, Jerome, Augustine, John Chrysostom, etc.
21. *Op. Syriaca,* Roman edit., t. II, p. 327.
22. Cf. G. Bickell, *Carmina Nisibena,* Leipzig, 1866, pp. 28-29. Bickell concludes from this and similar passages that St. Ephrem is a witness to the dogma of the Immaculate Conception.

In much the same way St. Ambrose says of Mary that she is free from every stain of sin "per gratiam ab omni integra labe peccati."[23] St. Augustine's comment is well known: "The honour of the Lord does not permit that the question of sin be raised in connected with the Blessed Virgin Mary."[24] If however the question be put to the saints "Are you sinless? he affirms that they will answer with the Apostle St. John (*1 John,* 1:8): "If we say that we have no sin, we deceive ourselves, and the truth is not in us." There are two other texts which seem to show that St. Augustine meant his words to be understood in the sense of the Immaculate Conception,[25] Many other texts of the Fathers will be found in the works of Passaglia,[26] Palmieri[27] and Le Bachelet.[28]

It should not be forgotten that the Feast of the Conception of the Blessed Virgin Mary has been celebrated in the Church, especially in the Greek Church, since the 7th and 8th centuries. The same Feast is found in Sicily in the 9th, in Ireland in the 1oth, and almost everywhere in Europe in the 12th century.

The Lateran Council, held in the year 649 (Denz., 256) calls Mary "Immaculate." In 1476 and 1483 Pope Sixtus IV speaks favorably of the privilege in connection with the Feast of the Conception of Mary (Denz., 734 sqq.). The Council of Trent (Denz., 792) declares, when speaking of original sin which infects all men, that it does not intend to include the Blessed and Immaculate Virgin Mary. In 1567 Baius is condemned for having taught the contrary (Denz., 1073). In 1661 Alexander VII affirmed the privilege, saying that almost all Catholics held it, though it had not yet been defined

---

23. In Ps. CXVIII, 22, 30; P. L., II, 782.
24. *De natura et gratia,* XXXVI, 42; P. L., XLIV, 267.
25. *Contra Julianum pelagianum,* V, xv, 57; P. L., XLIV, 815; *Opus imperf contra Julianum,* IV, cxxii; P. L., XLV, 1418.
26. *De immaculatae Deiparae conceptu.*
27. Thesis 88.
28. *Dict. Apol.,* art. *Marie, Immac. Concept,,* col. 210-275.

(Denz., 1100). Finally, on December 8th, 1854, we have the promulgation of the solemn definition (Denz., 1641).

It must be admitted that in the 12th and 13th centuries certain great doctors, as, for example, St. Bernard,[29] St. Anselm,[30] Peter Lombard,[31] Hugh of St. Victor,[32] St. Albert the Great,[33] St. Bonaventure[34] and St. Thomas Aquinas appear to have been disinclined to admit the privilege. But this was because they did not consider the precise instant of Mary's animation, or of the creation of her soul, and also because they did not distinguish, with the help of the idea of preservative redemption, between the debt to contract the hereditary stain and its actual contraction. In other words, they did not always distinguish sufficiently between "debebat contrahere" and "contraxit peccatum." We shall see later that there were three stages in St. Thomas's doctrine and that though he appears to deny the Immaculate Conception in the second, he admits it in the first, and probably in the third also.

Theological Reasons for Admitting the Immaculate Conception

The principal argument *ex convenientia,* or from becomingness, for the Immaculate Conception, is an elaboration of the one which St. Thomas (IIIa, q. 27, a. 1) and others give for Mary's sanctification in her mother's womb before birth. "It is reasonable to believe that she who gave birth to the Only-begotten of the Father, full of grace and truth, received greater privileges of grace than all others. . . . We find however that to some the privilege of sanctification in their mother's womb has been granted, as for example to

---

29. *Epist. ad canonicos Lugdunenses.*
30. *De conceptione virginali.*
31. In *III Sent.,* dist. 3.
32. *Super Missus est.*
33. Item *Super Missus est.*
34. In *III Sent.,* dist. 3, q. 27.

Jeremias . . . and John the Baptist. . . . Hence it is reasonable to believe that the Blessed Virgin was sanctified before birth." In a. 5 of the same question we read also: "The nearer one approaches to the source of all grace the more grace one receives; but Mary came nearest of all to Christ, Who is the principle of grace."[35]

But this argument *ex convenientia* needs to be expanded before it will prove the Immaculate Conception.

It is Scotus's glory (Thomists should consider it a point of honour to admit that their adversary was right in this matter) to have shown the supreme becomingness of this privilege in answer to the following difficulty which St. Thomas and many other theologians put forward: Christ is the universal Redeemer of all men without exception (*Rom.* 3:23; 5:12, 19; *Gal.* 3:22; *2 Cor.* 5:14; *1 Tim.* 2:16); but if Mary did not contract original sin she would not have been redeemed; hence, since she was redeemed, she must have contracted original sin.

Duns Scotus answers this objection[36] by referring to the idea of a redemption which is preservative, not liberative. He shows how reasonable this idea is, and in some places at least does not link it up with his peculiar doctrine concerning the motive of the Incarnation, so that it can be admitted independently of what one thinks about the second matter.

This is his line of argument.

It is becoming that a perfect Redeemer should make use of a sovereign mode of redemption, at least in regard to the person of His Mother who was to be associated more closely with Him than anyone else in the work of salvation. But the sovereign mode of redemption is not that which liberates from a stain already contracted, but that which preserves from all stain,

35. IIIa, q. 27, a. 5.
36. In III *Sent.*, dist. III, q. 1 (Edit. Quaracchi); edit. *Vives,* XIV, 159; and *Reportata,* l. III, dist. III, q. 1, edit. *Vives,* XXIII, 261.

just as he who wards off a blow from another saves him more than if he were simply to heal a wound that has been inflicted. Hence it was most becoming that the perfect Redeemer should, by His merits, preserve His Mother from original sin and all actual sin. This argument can be found in embryo in Eadmer.[37]

The Bull *Ineffabilis* gives this argument, in a somewhat different form, along with others. For example, it states that the honor and dishonor alike of parents affect their children, and that it was not becoming that the perfect Redeemer should have a mother who was conceived in sin. Also, just as the Word proceeds eternally from a most holy Father, it was becoming that He should be born on earth of a mother to whom the splendor of sanctity had never been lacking. Finally, in order that Mary should be able to repair the effects of Eve's fall, overcome the wiles of the devil, and give supernatural life to all, with, by, and in Christ, it was becoming that she herself should never have been in a fallen condition, a slave to sin and the devil.

If it be objected that Christ alone is immaculate, it is easy to answer: Christ alone is immaculate of Himself, and by the double title of His Hypostatic Union and His virginal conception; Mary is immaculate through the merits of her Son.

The consequences of the Immaculate Conception have been developed by the great spiritual writers. Mary has been preserved from the two baneful fruits of original sin, concupiscence and darkness of understanding.

Since the definition of the Immaculate Conception we are obliged to hold that concupiscence has been not only bound, or restrained, in Mary from the time she was in her mother's womb, but even that she was never in any sense its subject. There could be no disordered

---

37. *Tractatus de Conceptione sanctae Mariae; P. L.,* CLIX, 301-318. Eadmer, a disciple of St. Anselm, began in the twelfth century to synthesize the elements of the Greek tradition.

movement of her sensitive nature, no escape of her sensibility from the previous control of reason and will. Her sensibility was always fully subject to her rational powers, and thereby to God's Will, as obtained in the state of original innocence. Thus Mary is virgin of virgins, most pure, "inviolata, intemerata," tower of ivory, most pure mirror of God,

Similarly, Mary was never subject to error or illusion. Her judgment was always enlightened and correct. If she did not understand a thing fully she suspended her judgment upon it, and thus avoided the precipitation which might have been the cause of error. She is, as the Litanies say, the Seat of Wisdom, the Queen of Doctors, the Virgin most prudent, the Mother of good counsel. All theologians realise that nature spoke more eloquently to her of the Creator than to the greatest poets. She had, too, an eminent and wonderfully simple knowledge of what the Scriptures said of the Messiah, the Incarnation, and the Redemption. Thus she was fully exempt from concupiscence and error.

But why did the Immaculate Conception not make Mary immune from pain and death since they too were consequences of original sin?

It should be noted that the pain and death which Jesus and Mary knew were not consequences of original sin as they are for us. For Jesus and Mary they were consequences of but human nature, which, of itself, and like the animal nature in general, is subject to pain and death of the body: it was only because of a special privilege that Adam had been exempt from them in the state of innocence. As for Jesus, He was conceived virginally in passible flesh in order to redeem us by dying, and when the time came He accepted suffering and death, its consummation, freely for love of us. Mary, for her part, accepted suffering and death voluntarily in imitation of Him and to unite herself to Him; she was one with Him in His expiation and in

His work of redemption.

There is one wonderful thing, one delight of contemplatives, which we should not overlook. It is that the privilege of the Immaculate Conception and the fullness of grace did not withdraw Mary from pain, but rather made her all the more sensitive to suffer from contact with sin, the greatest of evils. Precisely because she was so pure, precisely because her heart was consumed by the love of God, Mary suffered pains to which our imperfection makes us insensible. We suffer if our self-love is wounded, or our pride, or our susceptibilities. Mary, however, suffered from sin, and that in the measure of her love of God Whom sin offends, and her love of Her Son Whom sin crucifies; she suffered in the measure of her love of us, whom sin wounds and kills. Thus the Immaculate Conception increased Mary's sufferings and disposed her to bear them heroically. Not one of them did she squander. All passed through her hands in union with those of her Son, thus to be offered up for our salvation.

St. Thomas and the Immaculate Conception

As certain commentators have suggested, three periods may be distinguished in St. Thomas's teaching.

In the first—that of 1253-1254, the beginning of his theological career—he supports the privilege, probably because of the liturgical tradition which favored it, as well as because of his pious admiration for the perfect holiness of the Mother of God. It is in this period that he wrote (I Sent., d. 44, q. I, a. 3, ad 3): "Purity is increased by withdrawing from its opposite: hence there can be a creature than whom no more pure is possible in creation, if it be free from all contagion of sin: and such was the purity of the Blessed Virgin who was immune from original and actual sin." This text states therefore that Mary was so pure as to be exempt from all original and actual sin.

During the second period St. Thomas, seeing better the difficulties in the question—for the theologians of his time held that Mary was immaculate independently of Christ's merits—hesitated, and refused to commit himself. He, of course, held that all men without exception are redeemed by one Saviour. (*Rom.* 3:23; 5:12, 19; *Gal.* 3:22; *2 Cor.* 5:14; *1 Tim.* 2:6). Hence we find him proposing the question thus in IIIa, q. 27, a. 2: Was the Blessed Virgin sanctified in the conception of her body before its animation? for, according to him and many other theologians, the conception of the body was to be distinguished from the animation, or creation of the soul. This latter (called today the consummated passive conception) was thought to be about a month later in time than the initial conception.

The holy doctor mentions certain arguments at the beginning of the article which favor the Immaculate Conception—even taking conception to be that which precedes animation. He then answers them as follows: "There are two reasons why the sanctification of the Blessed Virgin cannot have taken place before her animation: 1st—the sanctification in question is cleansing from original sin . . . but the guilt of sin can be removed only by grace (which has as object the soul itself) . . . 2nd—if the Blessed Virgin had been sanctified before animation she would have have incurred the stain of original sin and would therefore never have stood in need of redemption by Christ. . . . But this may not be admitted, since Christ is Head of all men. (*1 Tim.* 2:6)."

Even had he written after the definition of 1854 St. Thomas could have said that Mary was not sanctified before animation. However, he goes further than that here, for he adds at the end of the article: "Hence it follows that the sanctification of the Blessed Virgin took place after her animation." Nor does he distinguish, as he does in many other contexts, between posteriority in nature and posteriority in time. In the answer to the second objection he even states that the Blessed Virgin "contracted original sin."[38] However, it must be recognised that the whole point of his argument is to show that Mary incurred the debt of original sin since she descended from Adam by way of natural generation. Unfortunately he did not distinguish sufficiently the debt from actually incurring the stain.

Regarding the question of the exact moment at which Mary was sanctified in the womb of her mother, St. Thomas does not make any definite pronouncement. He states that it followed close on animation—*cito post* are his words in Quodl. VI, a. 7. But he believes that nothing more precise can be said: "the time of her sanctification is unknown" (IIIa, q. 27, a. 2, ad 3).

St. Thomas does not consider in the *Summa* if Mary was sanctified in the very instant of animation. St. Bonaventure had put himself that question and had answered it in the negative. It is possible that St. Thomas's silence was inspired by the reserved attitude of the Roman Church which, unlike so many other Churches, did not celebrate the Feast of the Conception (cf. *ibid.*, ad 3). This is the explanation proposed by Fr. N. del Prado, O.P., in *Santo Tomas y la Immaculada,* Vergara, 1909, by Fr. Mandonnet, O.P., *Dict. Théol. Cath.,* art. *Frères Prêcheurs,* col. 899, and by Fr. Hugon, O.P., *Tractatus Dogmatici,* t. II, ed. 5, 1927, p. 749. For these authors the thought of the holy doctor in this second period of his professional career was that expressed long afterwards by Gregory XV in his letters of July 4th, 1622: "Spiritus Sanctus nondum tanti mysterii arcanum Ecclesiae suae patefecit."

The texts we have considered so far do not therefore imply any contradiction of the dogma of the Immaculate Conception. They could even be retained if the idea of preservative redemption were introduced. There

---

38. On the basis of these texts many commentators hold that St. Thomas denied the Immaculate Conception. This is the opinion of Fr. Le Bachelet, *Dict. Théol.,* art. *Immaculée Conception,* cols. 1050-1054.

is however one text which cannot be so easily explained away. In *III Sent.,* dist. III, q. 1, a. 1, ad 2am qm, we read: "Nor (did it happen) even in the instant of infusion of the soul, namely, by grace being then given her so as to preserve her from incurring the original fault. Christ alone among men has the privilege of not needing redemption." Frs. del Prado and Hugon explain this text as follows: The meaning of St. Thomas's words may be that the Blessed Virgin was not preserved from original sin in such a way as not to incur its debt, as that would mean not to stand in need of redemption. However, one could have expected to find in the text itself the explicit distinction between the debt and the fact of incurring the stain.

In the final period of his career, when writing the *Exposito super salutatione angelica*—which is certainly authentic[39]—in 1272 or 1273, St. Thomas expressed himself thus: "For she (the Blessed Virgin) was most pure in the matter of fault *(quantum ad culpam)* and incurred neither original nor mortal nor venial sin." Cf. J. F. Rossi, C.M., *S. Thomae Aquinatis Expositio salutationis angelicae, Introductio et textus.* Divus Thomas (Pl.), 1931, pp. 445-479.[40] In this critical edition of the Commentary on the *Ave Maria,* it is stated, pp. 11-15, that the passage quoted just now is found in sixteen manuscripts out of nineteen consulted by the author, who concludes that it is authentic. He gives photographs of the principal manuscripts in an appendix. Let us hope that the same conscientious work will

---

39. Cf. Mandonnet: *S. Th. Aq. opuscula omnia,* Parisiis 1927, t. I, Introduction, pp. xix-xxii.
40. Off-print, Piacenza, Collegio Alberoni, 1931. Monografie del Collegio Alberoni.
41. The objection was raised in the *Bulletin Thomiste* of July-December 1932 (p. 579) that we read in the same opusculum a little earlier: "Ipsa (Virgo) omne peccatum vitavit magis quam alius sanctus, praeter Christum. Peccatum enim aut est originale, et de isto fuit mundata in utero; aut mortale aut veniale, et de istis libera fuit. Sed Christus excellit Beatam Virginem in hoc quod sine originali conceptus et natus fuit. Beata autem Virgo in *originali concepta* sed non nata." Does this text contradict the other one which occurs a few lines later? It is highly improbable that St. Thomas would contradict himself in the space of a few lines. The difficulty vanishes if one recalls that on St. Thomas's view the *conception of*

be performed on the other opuscula of St. Thomas![41]

In spite of the objection raised by Fr. P. Synave[42] the text appears to be authentic. If it is, then St. Thomas returned towards the end of his life—moved, we may believe, by his love of the Mother of God—to the position he had adopted when he affirmed the Immaculate Conception in his Commentary on the *Sentences*. Nor is the text we are considering the only indication of such a return.[43]

Such an evolution of doctrine is not rare among theologians. At first they propose a thesis which they accept from tradition without seeing all its difficulties. Later reflection leads them to adopt a more reserved attitude. Finally they return to their first position, realising that God is more bounteous in His gifts than we can understand and that we should not set limits to Him without good reason. In the case of St. Thomas, we have seen that the reasons he invoked against the privilege are not conclusive, and that they even support it when considered in the light of the idea of preservative redemption.[44]

---

the body and the beginning of the evolution of the embryo preceded by a month at least the *animation* (or consummated passive conception) before which the person did not exist since there was as yet no rational soul.

42. *Bulletin Thomiste,* loc. cit.

43. In the *Compendium Theologiae,* written at Naples in 1272-1273, and interrupted by his death, St. Thomas wrote (ch. 224): "Nec solum a peccato actuali immunis fuit (B. Maria Virgo) sed *etiam ab originali, speciali privilegio mundata. . . .* Est ergo tenendum quod cum peccato originali concepta fuit, sed ab eo, quodam *speciali modo,* purgata fuit." But he could not have spoken here of a *special* privilege if he meant merely that Mary had been purified in the womb of her mother after animation as were Jeremias and John the Baptist. In other places too St. Thomas declares Mary immune from original sin: *Epis. ad Galat.,* iii, 16, lect. 6, "excipitur purissima et omni laude dignissima;" similarly in *Exposit. in Orat. Domini,* petitio Va, "Plena gratia, in qua nullum peccatum fuit;" in Psalm 18:6, "Quae nullam habuit obscuritatem peccati."

44. Recently, Fr. J. M. Voste, O.P., in his Commentarius in IIIam *P. Summae theol. S. Thomae* (in q. 27, a. 2), 2nd edit., Rome, 1940, has accepted Fr. Rossi's thesis that St. Thomas returned at the end of his career to the position he had adopted at the beginning. This view is at least seriously probable.

Article III

Was Mary Exempt from Every Fault, Even Venial?

The Council of Trent[45] has defined that "after his justification a man cannot avoid, during the whole course of his life, every venial sin, without a special privilege such as the Church recognises was conferred on the Blessed Virgin." The soul in the state of grace can therefore avoid any venial sin considered separately, but cannot avoid all venial sins taken together by keeping itself always free from them. Mary however avoided all sin, even the least grave. St. Augustine affirms that "for the honour of her Son Who came to remit the sins of the world, Mary is never included when there is question of sin."[46] The Fathers and theologians consider, to judge from their manner of speaking, that she is free even from every voluntary imperfection, for, according to them, she never failed in promptness to obey a divine inspiration given by way of counsel. Though a minor lack of generosity is not a venial sin, but simply a lesser good, or an imperfection, not even so slight a shortcoming was found in Mary. She never elicited an imperfect *(remissus)* act of charity, that is to say, one that fell short in intensity of the degree in which she possessed the virtue.

St. Thomas gives the reason for this special privilege when he says: "God prepares and disposes those whom He has chosen for a special purpose in such a way as to make them capable of performing that for which He selected them."[47] In that God differs from men, who sometimes choose incapable or mediocre candidates for important posts. "Thus," continues St. Thomas, "St. Paul says of the Apostles (*2 Cor.* 3:6),

---

45. Sess. VI, Can. 23; Denz. 833.
46. *De natura et gratia,* ch. xxxvi.
47. IIIa, q. 27, a. 4.

"It is God Who has made us fit ministers of the new testament, not in the letter, but in the spirit." But the Blessed Virgin was divinely chosen to be the Mother of God (that is to say, she was predestined from all eternity for the divine maternity). Hence, it cannot be doubted that God fitted her by grace for her mission, according to the words spoken her by the angel (*Luke* 1:30): "Thou hast found grace with God. Thou shalt conceive in thy womb, and shalt bring forth a son; and thou shalt call his name Jesus." But Mary would not have been a worthy Mother of God had she ever sinned, for the honor and dishonor of parents is reflected on the children according to the words of the Book of Proverbs: "The glory of children are their fathers." Besides, Mary had a special affinity to Jesus, from Whom she took flesh, but "What concord hath Christ with Belial?" (*2 Cor.* 6:15). Finally, the Son of God, Who is Divine Wisdom, inhabited Mary in a very special manner, not in her soul only but in her womb also; and it is said (*Wisdom* 1:4): "Wisdom will not enter into a malicious soul, nor dwell in a body subject to sins." Hence it must be said without any reservation that the Blessed Virgin committed no sin, mortal or venial, so that the words of the Canticle of Canticles are fully verified in her regard (*Cant.* 4:7): "Thou art all fair, my love, and there is not a spot in thee.'"

Mary had therefore *impeccantia* (the term is parallel to *inerrantia)* or freedom from sin, and even impeccability. Her title to these endowments is not however the same as her Son's. In her case it was a matter of preservation from every sin through a special privilege.[48] This privilege includes first of all a very high degree of habitual grace and charity, which gives the

---

48. Our Blessed Lord has absolute impeccability under three titles: by reason of His Divine Personality; by reason of the beatific vision which He had in a permanent way since His conception; by reason of the absolute and inalienable fullness of grace and charity, the fervour of which could not diminish. Besides, He always received efficacious grace.

soul a strong inclination to the act of love of God and withdraws it from sin. It includes also confirmation in grace, which when granted to a saint is had normally through an increase of charity, especially that proper to the state of transforming union, and an increase of actual efficacious graces which preserve the soul *de facto* from sin and move it to ever more meritorious acts. Thus Mary enjoyed a special assistance of Divine Providence. This assistance—more effective than even that which belonged to the state of innocence—preserved all her faculties from faults, and kept her soul in a state of the most complete generosity. Just as confirmation in grace is an effect of the predestination of the saints, so this preservative assistance granted to Mary was an effect of her peculiar predestination. Far from diminishing her liberty or free will, the effect of this preservation from sin was to confer on her full liberty in the order of moral goodness, with no inclination to evil (just as her mind never tended to error). Hence her liberty, following the example of that of Jesus, was a faithful and most pure image of God's liberty, which is at once sovereign and incapable of sin.

If human masterpieces of art, in architecture, painting and music, and if the precision instruments produced by human skill all reach such perfection, what must not be the perfection of God's masterpieces? And among these, if the works of the natural order are so perfect—the majesty of the ocean and the high mountains, the structure of the eye and ear, the human mind and the mind of the angels—how perfect must not the works of the supernatural order be, among which so remarkable a place is held by the soul of Mary which was adorned with every choice gift from the first moment of her existence?

NOTE

The distinction between imperfection and venial sin

The problem[49] has been taken from its proper context by the casuists. It is one which concerns interior souls, advanced in the spiritual life, and careful to avoid every more or less venial sin. Those who consider the problem in relation to less advanced souls run the risk of taking for imperfection what is really a venial sin.

At one time the problem was closely associated with another one: is it possible to commit no more than a simple imperfection by resisting a religious vocation? The answer ordinarily given to this question is that though the religious vocation does not oblige under pain of sin, sin is always involved in rejecting it for the reason that religion is a way of life that embraces the whole of life, and the other ways of life, being less safe than it, are never chosen in preference to it except through some inordinate attachment to the things of this world, as is seen in the example of the rich man in the Gospel. Thus, the rejection of a vocation involves an inordinate attachment (which is forbidden by divine precept) and not only a lack of generosity.

To see the problem of an imperfection as distinct from a venial sin in its proper perspective, it must be viewed in its relation to very generous souls, and still more in relation to the impeccability of Christ and the sinlessness of Mary. Here we may ask: Was there any voluntary imperfection in the lives of Jesus and Mary? The question is obviously a most delicate one.

The answer usually given to this problem is that there was never any imperfection, however slightly voluntary, in the lives of Jesus and Mary, for they never failed in their prompt obedience to every divine inspiration given by way of counsel. But if there had been any lack of promptitude, it would have been a

---

49. I have treated it at length in *L'Amour de Dieu et la Croix de Jésus*, t. I, pp. 360-390.

mere lack of generosity, not a moral disorder in the
strict sense of the term, as is an inordinate attachment to the things of this world.

As regards interior souls, it may be said that as
long as they have not taken the vow of always doing
the most perfect thing, they are not bound under pain
of venial sin to act always with the maximum of generosity possible to them at any given instant.[50] It is
becoming, however, that those more advanced should,
without binding themselves by vow, promise the
Blessed Virgin always to do what will appear to them
evidently the most perfect in any given circumstance.

Article 4

The Perfection of
Mary's First Grace

The habitual grace which the Blessed Virgin received
at the instant of the creation of her holy soul was a
fullness or plenitude to which the words of the angel
on the Annunciation day might have been applied: "Hail,
full of grace." This is what Pius IX affirms when he
defines the dogma of the Immaculate Conception. He
even says that, from the first instant, Mary "was loved
by God more than all creatures. *(prae creaturis universis),* that He found most extreme pleasure in her,
and that He loaded her in a wonderful way with His
graces, more than all the angels and saints."[51] Many
texts might be quoted from tradition to the same effect.[52]

---

50. Strictly speaking, a counsel obliges only when one would offend against a precept by not obeying it. (Cf. IIa IIae, q. 124, a. 3, ad 1.)
51. *Ineffabilis Deus . . .* ab initio et ante saecula unigenito filio suo *Matrem,* ex
quo caro factus in beata temporum plenitudine nasceretur *elegit* atque *ordinavit, tantoque prae creaturis universis est prosecutus amore, ut in illa una sibi
propensissima voluntate complacuerit. Quapropter illam longe ante omnes angelicos Spiritus, cunctosque Sanctos caelestium omnium charismatum copia de thesauro Divinitatis deprompta ita mirifice cumulavit* ut ipsa an omni prorsus
peccati labe semper libera ac tota pulchra et perfecta eam *innocentiae et sanctitatis plenitudinem prae se ferret,* qua maior sub Deo nullatenus intelligitur,
et quam praeter Deum nemo assequi cogitando potest.
52. Cf. Terrien, *La Mère de Dieu,* t. II, l. VII, pp. 191-234; De la Broise, S.J., *La
Sainte Vierge,* chs. II and XII; *Dict, Apol.* art, *Marie,* cols. 207 sqq.

St. Thomas explains the reason of this plenitude of grace when he says[53]: "The nearer one approaches to a principle (of truth and life) the more one participates in its effects. That is why St. Denis affirms *(De caelestia hierarchia)* that the angels, who are nearer to God than man is, participate more in His favors. But Christ is the principle of the life of grace; as God He is its principal cause and as Man (having first His humanity is, as it were, an instrument always united to the Divinity: 'Grace and truth came by Jesus Christ' *(John* 1:17). The Blessed Virgin Mary, being nearer to Christ than any other human being, since it is from her that He received His humanity, receives from Him therefore a fullness of grace, surpassing that of all other creatures."

It is true that St. John the Baptist and Jeremias were sanctified, according to the testimony of Sacred Scripture, in their mother's womb, without, however, being preserved from original sin. But Mary received grace from the very first instant in a degree far excelling theirs, and received as well the privilege of being preserved from every fault—even venial—a privilege we find accorded to no other saint.[54]

In his *Expositio super salutatione angelica* St. Thomas describes Mary's plenitude of grace (and his words are applicable to the initial plenitude) in terms of which the following is a summary:

Though the angels do not manifest special respect for men, being their superiors by nature and living in holy intimacy with God, yet the Archangel Gabriel when saluting Mary, showed himself full of veneration for her. He understood that she was far above him through her fullness of grace, her intimacy with God, and her perfect purity.

(a) She had received fullness of grace under three respects. First, so as to avoid every sin, however slight,

---

53. IIIa, q. 27, a. 5.
54. Cf. *Ibid.*, a. 6, ad 1.

and to practice all the virtues in an eminent degree. Secondly, so as to overflow from her soul upon her body and prepare her to receive the Incarnate Son of God. Thirdly, so as to overflow upon all men[55] and to aid them in the practice of all the virtues.

(b) Further, she surpassed the angels in her holy familiarity with the Most High. On that account, Gabriel saluted her saying: "The Lord is with thee." It was as if he said: "You are more intimate with God than I. He is about to become your Son, whereas I am but His servant." In truth, Mary, as Mother of God, is more intimate with the Father, Son and Holy Ghost, than are the angels.

(c) Finally, she surpassed the angels in purity, even though they are pure spirits, for she was both pure in herself and the source of purity to others. Not only was she exempt from original sin[56] and from all mortal and venial sin, but she escaped the curse due to sin, namely, "In sorrow shalt thou bring forth children . . . into dust thou shalt return" (*Gen.* 3:16, 19). She will conceive the Son of God without loss to her virginity, she will bear Him in holy recollection, she will bring Him forth in joy, she will be preserved from the corruption of the tomb and will be associated by her Assumption with the Ascension of the Saviour.

Already she is blessed among women, for she alone, with and through her Son, will lift the curse which descended on the human race, and will bring us blessings by opening the gates of Heaven. That is why she is called the Star of the Sea, guiding Christians to the harbour of eternity.

Elisabeth will say to her: "Blessed is the fruit of thy womb." Whereas the sinner looks for that which he cannot find in the object of his sinful desires, the just finds everything in what he desires holily. From this

---

55. Theologians commonly hold that Mary merited for us with a merit of becomingness *(de congruo)* all that Christ merited in strict justice *(de condigno)*.
56. This is the text we have quoted on p. 48.

point of view, the fruit of the womb of Mary will be thrice blessed.

(a) Eve desired the forbidden fruit, so as to have the knowledge of good and evil, and thereby to become independent and free from the yoke of obedience. She was deceived by the lying promise "You will be as God," for far from becoming like God, she was turned away from Him. Mary, on the contrary, found all things in the blessed fruit of her womb. In Him she found God, and she will lead us to find God in Him.

(b) By yielding to the temptation, Eve sought joy and found sadness. Mary, on the contrary, found joy and salvation for herself and us in her Divine Son.

(c) Finally, the fruit sought by Eve had beauty only for the senses, whereas the fruit of Mary's womb is the splendor, the eternal and spiritual glory of the Father. Mary is blessed herself, and still more blessed in her Son, Who has brought all men blessing and salvation.

The preceding is a synopsis of what St. Thomas has to say of Mary's fullness of grace in his commentary on the *Hail Mary*. He has in mind most of all the fullness of the Annunciation day. But what he says is applicable also to her initial fullness, just as what is said of the stream is applicable also to its source.

Mary's Initial Grace compared with that of the Saints

It has been asked if Mary's initial grace was greater than the final grace of the greatest of angels and men, or even than the final grace of all angels and men taken together. The question is usually understood not of the final and consummated grace of Heaven, but of the grace which is final in the sense that it immediately preceded entry into glory.[57]

---

57. Theologians commonly teach that the consummated grace of Mary in Heaven is higher than that of angels and saints combined; also that the final grace of Mary at the moment of death, and even her grace at the moment of the Incarnation,

As for the first part of the question, theologians commonly hold that Mary's initial grace was greater than the final grace of the highest of angels and men. This is the teaching, for example, of St. John Damascene,[58] Suarez,[59] Justin of Miechow, O.P.,[60] Contenson,[61] St. Alphonsus,[62] Fathers Terrien,[63] Godts, Hugon, Merkelbach, etc. Today, all textbooks of Mariology are unanimous in considering this teaching certain. It can even be found expressed by Pius IX in the Bull *Ineffabilis Deus* in the passage we have quoted already. The principal argument in favor of this teaching is arrived at from a consideration of the divine maternity, which is the reason for all the privileges conferred on Mary. There are two ways of outlining it: from the point of view of the end to which Mary's initial grace was ordained, and from the point of view of the divine love which was its cause.

Mary's initial grace was given her as a worthy preparation for the divine motherhood—to prepare her to be a worthy Mother of the Saviour, said St. Thomas (IIIa, q. 27, a. 5, ad 2). But even the consummated grace of the other saints is not a worthy preparation for the divine maternity, for it pertains to the hypostatic order. Hence the first grace of Mary surpasses the consummated grace of the other saints. Pious authors express this truth by taking in an accommodated sense the words of Psalm 86: "The foundations thereof are in the holy mountains." They say that the summit of the perfection of the other saints is not as yet the beginning of the perfection of Mary.

The same conclusion is reached by considering the

---

grace of all the saints at the term of their earthly lives. The question under discussion here is whether or not the same may be said of Mary's initial fullness of grace. We know, of course, that the degree of glory of the saints in Heaven corresponds to the degree of grace and charity which they had before entry there.

58. *Orat. de Nativitate Virginis* P. G., XCVI, 648 sqq.
59. *De mysteriis vitae Christi,* disp. IV, sect, I.
60. *Collat. super litanias B. Mariae Virginis,* col. 134.
61. *Theol. mentis et cordis,* l. X, diss. VI, c. I.
62. *Glorie di Maria,* IIe P., disc. 2.
63. *La Mère de Dieu,* t. I.

uncreated love of God for the Blessed Virgin. Since grace is the effect of the active love of God which makes us pleasing in His eyes as adoptive children, the more a person is loved by God the more grace he receives. But Mary, since she was to be the Mother of God, was more loved by Him in the first instant of her being than any angel or saint. Hence she received from the first instant a greater gift of grace than any of them, however favored.

Was Mary's First Grace higher than the Final Grace of all the Angels and Saints taken together?

A number of theologians, both ancient and modern, have answered this question in the negative.[64] However, the affirmative answer, which is given by Ch. Véga, Contenson, St. Alphonsus, Godts, Monsabré, Billot, Sinibaldi, Hugon, L. Janssens, Merkelbach and others, is at least probable.

For it there is, first of all, the argument from authority. Pius IX favors it in his Bull *Ineffabilis Deus,* when he says: "Deus ab initio . . . unigenito filio suo Matrem . . . elegit atque ordinavit, tantoque prae creaturis universis est prosecutus amore, ut in illa una sibi propensissima voluntate complacuerit. Quapropter illam longe ante omnes angelicos Spiritus, cunctosque Sanctos coelestium omnium charismatum copia de thesauro Divinitatis deprompta ita mirifice cumulavit, ut . . . eam innocentiae et sanctitatis plenitudinem prae se ferret, et qua major sub Deo nullatenus intelligitur, et quam praeter Deum nemo assequi cogitando potest." (This text is translated on page 14.) Taken in their

---

64. Théophile Raynaud, Terrien, and Lépicier, admit it only in regard to Mary's fmal grace. Others, like Valentia, admit it for the grace of her second sanctification at the time of the Incarnation. However, most theologians join St. Alphonsus in admitting it for her initial grace. Among these three opinions, the first two are certain; the third, as Fr. Merkelbach shows in his *Mariologia,* 1939, pp. 178-181, is at least very probable.

obvious sense all these expressions, especially the
"cunctos sanctos," mean that Mary's grace surpassed
that of all the saints together from the first instant
mentioned in the text. If Pius IX wished to say that
Mary's grace surpassed that of each angel and saint
individually, he would have said "longe ante quemli-
bet sanctum et angelicum" rather than "longe ante
omnes angelicos Spiritus cunctosque sanctos." Nor
would he have said that God loved Mary above all
creatures, "prae creaturis universis," and that He took
greater delight in her alone, "ut in illa una sibi propensissima voluntate complacuerit." It cannot be con-
tended that in all this there is no question of the first
instant of Mary's existence since Pius IX goes on to
say, immediately after the passage just quoted, "Decebat omnino ut beatissima Virgo Maria perfectissimae
sanctitatis splendoribus *semper* ornata fulgeret."

A little further on in the same Bull, we are told that,
according to the Fathers, Mary is higher by grace than
the Cherubim, the Seraphim, and the whole Heavenly
Host *(omni exercitu angelorum)—that* is to say, all
united. Though it is universally admitted that these
words refer to Mary in Heaven, it must yet be recalled
that one's degree of heavenly glory is proportionate to
the preceding grace or charity at the hour of death.
And in the case of Mary, this latter was proportionate
to her dignity as Mother of God, a dignity for which
she had been prepared from the very first instant of
existence.

To the argument from the authority of the Bull *Ineffabilis,* two theological reasons can be added. They are
based on the divine maternity, considered as the end
towards which Mary's first grace was ordained and on
the uncreated love which was its cause. As a help to
grasping them, it is necessary to remark that even though
grace is a quality and not a quantified thing, there are
many to whom it is not at once evident that if Mary's
first grace surpassed that of the highest of the saints,

it must also surpass that of all angels and saints united. They say, for example, that though the eagle's vision is more acute than that of the most keen-sighted man, it does not follow that an eagle sees more than all men taken together. Of course, in this example an element of quantity—that is, of extension and distance—enters in, which is not found in the case of Mary's grace, so that it is really irrelevant. But, at the same time, it may be well to clarify the question still more.

1st—Since Mary's first grace prepared her to be the worthy Mother of God, it must have been proportionate, at least remotely, to the divine maternity. But the final consummated grace of all the saints together is not proportionate to the divine maternity, since it belongs to an inferior order. Hence the final consummated grace of all the saints united is less than the first grace received by Mary.

This argument—even though not admitted by all theologians—seems to be quite conclusive. The objection has been raised that Mary's first grace was not a proximate preparation for the divine maternity and hence was not necessarily of a different order from the grace of all the saints. To this it may be answered that, though not a proximate preparation, Mary's first grace was a worthy and proportionate preparation, according to the teaching of St. Thomas (IIIa, q. 27, a. 5, ad 2): "The first perfection of grace (was) as it were dispositive, making the Blessed Virgin worthy to become the Mother of Christ." But the consummated grace of all the saints united is not proportionate to the divine maternity, which is of the hypostatic order. The argument therefore retains its force.

2nd—The person who is more loved by God than all creatures united receives grace surpassing theirs, for grace is the effect of uncreated love and is proportionate to it. As St. Thomas says (Ia, q. 20, a. 4): "God loves one more than another by the fact that He wills him a higher good, for the divine will is the cause of the good that is in creatures." But God has loved Mary from all eternity more than all creatures united, as being she whom He was to prepare from the first instant of her conception to be the worthy Mother of the Saviour. In the words of Bossuet: "He always loved Mary as His Mother, and considered her as such from the moment she was conceived."[65]

This does not, of course, exclude the possibility that Mary advanced in holiness, or grew in grace. For grace, being a participation in the divine nature, can always increase though still remaining finite; Mary's final fullness of grace is limited, while yet being so full as to overflow on all souls.

To these two arguments, taken from the divine maternity, another may be added, which will become increasingly evident as we speak of Mary's universal mediation. It is that Mary could obtain by her merits and prayers—even on earth, and from the time when she could first merit and pray—more than all the saints together, for they obtain nothing except through her universal mediation. Mary is, as it were, the aqueduct which brings us grace; in the mystical body she is, as it were, the neck which joins the members with the Head. In short, from the time she could merit and pray, Mary could obtain more without the saints than they could without her. But merit corresponds in degree to charity and sanctifying grace. Hence Mary received from the beginning of her life a degree of grace superior to that which the saints and angels united had attained to before their entry into Heaven.

There are other indirect confirmations, or more or

---

65. Cf. E. Dublanchy, *Dict. Théol. Cath.,* art. *Marie,* col. 2367: "The teaching of Pius IX in the Bull *Ineffabilis Deus* resumes the argument upon which theological tradition has always relied: God's love of special predilection for Mary more than all other creatures, a love such that He made her alone the object of His greatest satisfaction, and gave her that which was dearest to Him, His own Son. And since it is the teaching of St. Thomas (Ia, q. 20, a. 3) that the good which God produces in creatures is proportioned to the love He has for them, it may be concluded with certainty that Mary, loved by God more than all creatures, has been the recipient of divine favors greater than those given to all creatures, taken even collectively.

less close analogies. For example, a precious stone—a diamond—is worth more than a number of other stones united; a saint like the Curé of Ars could do more by his prayers and merits than all his parishioners together; a founder of an order like St. Benedict surpasses all his first companions by the grace he has received, for without him they could not have made the foundation whereas, had they failed him, he could have enlisted others to take their place; the intellect of an archangel surpasses that of all inferior angels united; the intellectual worth of St. Thomas is greater than that of all his contemporaries; the power of a king is greater, not only than that of his prime minister, but also that of his ministers combined.

Early theologians did not examine the question of the degree of Mary's first grace, but that is probably because its solution appeared evident to them. They taught, for example, at the end of the treatises on grace and charity that whereas a ten-franc piece is worth no more than ten one-franc pieces, the charity signified by the ten talents of the parable is worth more than ten charities of one talent.[66] That is why the devil tries to keep souls called to high sanctity by their priestly and religious vocation at the level of mediocrity. He wishes to prevent the growth of their charity, knowing that one man of great charity will do much more than many whose charity is at a lower, lukewarm level.[67] Thus Mary, in virtue of the first grace which disposed her for the divine maternity, was worth more in God's eyes than all the apostles, martyrs, confessors, and virgins united, more than all men and all angels created from the beginning.

---

66. Cf. Salamanticenses, *De caritate,* disp. V, dub. III, par. 7, nos. 76, 80, 85, 93, 117.
67. Attention must be drawn to the nature of the order of pure immaterial quality to which sanctifying grace belongs. The reason why the vision of the eagle is not better than that of all men united, even though it is better than that of the most keen-sighted man, is that quantity or distance in space intervenes; all men, situated at different places on the globe, can obviously see more than one eagle, even if perched on the highest mountain. But quantity does not enter at all into the order of pure quality.

The thought of the marvellous instruments which human skill can produce is a reminder of what the Divine Artist can do in this soul of His special choice, in her of whom it is said "Elegit eam Deus et prae-elegit eam," in her who the liturgy tells us was raised above all the angelic choirs. The first grace she received was already a worthy preparation for her divine maternity and her exceptional glory which is inferior only to that of Our Lord Jesus Christ. Nor should we forget that she suffered proportionately as He did, for she was called to be a victim with Him so as to be victorious with and by Him.

These reasons permit us to get some glimpse of the dignity and elevation of Mary's first grace.

One more point before concluding. The classics in the literature of every country mean much more to us when we take them up in mature age, than they did when we first read them at the age of fifteen or twenty years; and the same is true of the works of the great theologians, of St. Augustine and St. Thomas. Must there not, then, be beauties hidden as yet from our eyes in God's masterpieces, in those composed immediately by Himself, and especially in that masterpiece of nature and grace, the soul of Mary, God's Mother? This thought alone is enough to make one begin by affirming the richness of her initial grace. Perhaps the next thing will be, to wonder if the affirmation has not been too hasty, if a probability has not been made into a certainty. But last of all, there will come a return to the first position; not now because it is beautiful, but because careful study has shown that it is true; not because it has a merely theoretical becomingness but because its becomingness acted as a motive in determining the choice that God actually made of it.

Article 5

The Consequence of Mary's Plenitude of Grace

From the instant of her conception, Mary's initial plenitude of grace included the infused virtues and the seven gifts of the Holy Ghost, which are the different parts or functions of the spiritual organism. Even from before St. Thomas's time, habitual grace was called "the grace of the virtues and the gifts" because of its connection with them; for the infused virtues, theological and moral, flow from grace (in a degree proportioned to its perfection) as its properties, just as the faculties flow from the substance of the soul.[68] The gifts flow from it also (in a similar proportionate degree) as infused permanent dispositions which make the soul docile to the inspirations of the Holy Ghost, somewhat as the sails of a boat make it docile to a favorable wind.[69]

Furthermore, the infused virtues and the gifts are linked up with charity which makes their acts meritorious,[70] and they keep pace with it in their growth as do the five fingers of the hand with one another.[71] It may well happen that the gifts of wisdom, understanding and knowledge, which are both speculative and practical, will manifest themselves in one saint more in their practical and in another more in their speculative roles. But normally all seven exist in every soul in the state of grace in a degree proportionate to its charity—the charity itself being proportionate to the sanctifying grace of the soul.

From these principles, which are commonly accepted in treatises on the virtues in general and the gifts, it is usually deduced that Mary had the infused theological and moral virtues and the gifts from the first instant

---

68. Cf. Ia, IIae, qq. 62, 63 (a. 3), 110, aa. 3 and 4; IIIa, q. 7, a. 2.
69. Ia IIae, q. 66, a. 2.
70. *Ibid.*, a. 5 and q. 65.
71. Ia IIae, q. 66, a. 2.

of her conception, and that they flowed from and were proportionate to her initial fullness of grace. Mary—destined even then to be Mother of God and men—could not have been less perfect than Eve was at her creation. Even if she did not receive in her body the privileges of impassibility and immortality, she must have had in her soul all that pertained spiritually to the state of original justice—all, and more, even, since her initial fullness of grace surpassed the grace of all the saints together. Her virtues in their initial state must, therefore, have surpassed the heroic virtues of the greatest saints.[72] Her faith, lit up by the gifts of wisdom, understanding and knowledge, was unshakably firm and most penetrating. Her hope was unconquerable, proof against presumption and despair alike. Her charity was most ardent. In fine, her initial holiness, which surpassed that of God's greatest servants, was born with her, and did not cease to grow all through life.

The only difficulty in this matter is that of the exercise of the infused virtues, already so perfect, and the gifts. Their exercise demands the use of reason and of free will. We must, therefore, ask if Mary had the use of her rational faculties from the first instant.

All theologians admit that the holy soul of Christ had the use of intellect and will from the beginning.[73] They admit too that He had the beatific vision, or the immediate vision of the divine Essence,[74] a doctrine which the Holy Office declared on June 6th, 1918, to be certain. Jesus is the Head in the order of grace, and therefore He enjoyed from the first instant, as a consequence of the personal union of His humanity to the Word, the glory He was to give to the elect. He had also infused knowledge similar to that of the angels, but in a much more perfect degree than it has been found in some of the saints—in those, for example, who

---

72. Cf. H. B. Merkelbach, *Mariologia,* 1939, pp. 184-194.
73. Cf. IIIa, q. 34, aa. 2 and 3.
74. *Ibid.,* a. 4 and q. 9, a. 2.

had the gift of understanding and speaking languages they had never learned.[75] Theologians teach that these two knowledges—the beatific and the infused—were perfect in Jesus from the beginning. It was only the knowledge which He acquired by experience and reflection which developed. Jesus, the sovereign priest, judge, and king of the universe, offered Himself for us, says St. Paul,[76] from the moment of His entry into the world and knew everything in the past, present and future, that could be submitted to His judgement.[77]

Though there is little serious difference of opinion among theologians regarding Jesus" knowledge, the problem of Mary's knowledge is much disputed. It would appear that there is no reason to assert that she had the beatific vision here on earth, especially from the first instant of her conception.[78] But many theologians hold that she had *per se* infused knowledge from the beginning, at least from time to time—though some contend that she had it in a permanent way. On this view she would have had the use of her intellect and of her free will in her mother's womb—on certain occasions at least—and would, in consequence, have had the use of the infused virtues and the gifts which she possessed in so high a degree. One can hardly deny this view except by asserting that Mary's intellect, will and infused virtues remained as it were asleep, as they

75. IIIa, q. 9, a. 3.
76. *Heb.* 10:5-9: "Wherefore when he cometh into the world he saith . . . Behold I come . . . Sacrifice and oblation (of the Old Law) thou wouldst not . . . Behold I come to do thy will."
77. In Jesus' infused knowledge we distinguish the knowledge which is infused *per se* from that which is infused *per accidens*. Knowledge is infused *per se* if it deals with an object about which, from the very nature of the object, knowledge cannot be acquired; such infused knowledge can be used without the help of imagery even in the womb. Knowledge is infused *per accidens* when the object with which it deals is of such a kind that it could be known by acquired knowledge; this knowledge is used with the help of imagery. An example of knowledge which is infused *per accidens* is knowledge of a language; for such knowledge can be acquired in the ordinary way by study.
78. Ch. Véga is the only theologian who has held that Mary had the beatific vision, excluding faith and merit of eternal life, from the first instant. It cannot be established with certainty that she had it in a passing way before death. Cf. Merkelbach, *Mariologia*, pp. 197 sqq. This latter opinion is at most very probable. It is suggested by the fact that St. Paul enjoyed the privilege for some few instants.

do in other children, and did not wake up till she attained the ordinary age of the use of reason.

For our part, we may say, first of all, that it is at least very probable, according to the teaching of the majority of theologians, that Mary had the use of her free will through her infused knowledge from the first instant of her conception, at least in a passing manner. Such is the teaching of St. Vincent Ferrer,[79] St. Bernardine of Sienna,[80] St. Francis de Sales,[81] St. Alphonsus,[82] Suarez,[83] Vega,[84] Contenson,[85] Justin de Miéchow,[86] and most modern theologians.[87] Fr. Terrien goes so far as to say that he found only two opponents of the doctrine: Gerson and Muratori.[88]

The following are the reasons that can be adduced in favor of the privilege:

1st—It is not becoming to hold that Mary, Queen of patriarchs, prophets, apostles, and all the saints, lacked a privilege granted to St. John the Baptist.[89] We read of him in *Luke* 1:41 and 44, while he was still in the womb: "When Elisabeth heard the salutation of Mary, the infant leaped in her womb," and Elisabeth herself said: "For as soon as the voice of thy salutation sounded in my ears, the infant in my womb leaped for joy." St. Irenaeus, St. Ambrose, St. Leo the Great, and St. Gregory the Great have noted that the joy of St. John the Baptist before his birth was not merely of the sense

---

79. *Manuscript. Tolos.,* 346.
80. *Sermon IV de B.M.V.,* a. I, c. II, t. IV, p. 86.
81. *Sermon* 38 *for the Feast of the Purification.*
82. *Glorie de Maria,* IIe P., II discors., 2 punt.
83. *De mysteriis vitae Christi,* disp. IV, sect. 7 and 8.
84. *Theologia Mariana,* no. 956.
85. Lib. X, diss. 6, cap. 1.
86. *Collat.* 93 *super litan. B. V.*
87. Cf. *Tractatus dogmatici* by Fr. Hugon, O.P., t. II, p. 756; *Mariologia* by Fr. Merkelbach, O.P., pp. 197 sqq.; *La Mère de Dieu* by Fr. Terrien, S.J., t. II, p. 27; cf. also the article *Marie* in the *Dict. Apol.* where Fr. d'Ales quotes Fr. de la Broise to the same effect.
88. Cf. Terrien, *ibid.*
89. St. Thomas (IIIa, q. 27, a. 6) cites Jeremias and John the Baptist as having been sanctified before birth. However, the sacred text does not state that Jeremias had the use of reason and of free will in the womb, whereas of St. John the Baptist we read (*Luke* 1:44): "The infant in my womb leaped for joy."

order, but was elicited by the coming of the Saviour, Whose precursor he was.[90] Thus Catejan notes that this joy, being a spiritual order, presupposes the use of reason and will, and at the time there could be no question of acquired but only of infused knowledge (Comment. in IIIa P., q. 27, a. 6). The church too sings in her liturgy, in the hymn for Vespers of St. John the Baptist "Senseras Regem thalamo manentem . . . Suae regenerationis cognovit auctorem: You have recognised your kind and the author of your regeneration." If, therefore, St. John the Baptist had the use of reason and will before birth, because of his vocation as precursor of Christ, the same privilege can hardly be denied to Christ's mother.

2nd—Since Mary received grace and the infused virtues and the gifts in the first instant in a degree higher than that of the final grace of the saints, she must have been sanctified in the way proper to adults, that is, by disposing her through actual grace for habitual grace, and by using this latter as a principle of merit from the moment she received it; in other words, she offered herself to God as her Son did on His entry into the world. "Then I said: Behold I come to do thy will, O God" (*Heb.* 10:9). Mary did not, of course, know then that she would be one day the Mother of God, but none the less she would accept all that the Lord asked and would yet ask of her.

3rd—Mary's initial fullness of grace, virtues, and gifts which surpassed already the final fullness of all the saints, could not have remained inactive at the beginning of her life. Such inactivity would appear opposed to the sweet and generous dispositions of Divine Prov-

---

90. St. Irenaeus, *Adv. Haer.* III, 16; *P. G.,* VIII, 923: "John who was still in his mother's womb, recognizing the Saviour Who was in Mary's womb, saluted Him;" St. Ambrose, in *Luke* I, II, c. xxxiv; *P. L.,* LIV, 232: "He who thus leaped for joy had the use of reason;" St. Leo, *Sermo XXXI* in *Nativ. Domini, c.* iv; *P. L.,* LIV, 232: "The precursor of Christ received the prophetic spirit in the womb of his mother, and before his birth manifested his joy in the presence of the Mother of God"; St. Gregory, *Moral.,* l. III, c. 4; *P. L.,* LXXV, 603: "He was filled with the prophetic spirit in the womb of his mother."

idence in favor of the Mother of the Saviour. But unless she had the use of her free will through infused knowledge, the virtues and gifts which she possessed in so high a degree would have remained inactive for a considerable part of her life (that is, the beginning).

Almost all present-day theologians admit that it is at least very probable that, in her mother's womb, Mary had the use of her free will through infused knowledge—transitorily, at any rate. They admit too that she had the use of this infused knowledge on certain occasions, such as the Incarnation, the Passion, the Resurrection, the Ascension; also that she had the use of it for the purpose of acquiring a more perfect knowledge of the divine perfections and of the mystery of the Blessed Trinity. There is all the more reason for admitting that Mary had this privilege when we recall that infused knowledge was given to the apostles on the first Pentecost when they received the gift of tongues, and that the great St. Teresa, after arriving at the Seventh Mansion, had frequent intellectual visions of the Trinity such as can only be explained by infused ideas. Even those theologians who are most conservative in their views do not hesitate to admit this much of Mary.[91] It is in fact the least that may be attributed to the Mother of God who enjoyed the visit of the Archangel Gabriel, who was on terms of saintly familiarity with the Incarnate Word, who was constantly enlightened by Him during the hidden life, who must have received special revelations during and after the Passion, and who received on the day of Pentecost the light of the Holy Ghost in more abundant measure than the apostles themselves.

---

91. Cf. H.-B. Merkelbach, O.P., *Mariologia,* 1939, p. 200: "Cognitionem infusam transeuntem Mariae fuisse communicatam conveniens erat in quibusdam specialibus adjunctis, v.g. in primo instanti conceptionis et sanctificationis, aut dum huiusmodi cognitio hic et nunc opportuna aut decens videbatur ad pleniorem intelligentiam cuiusdam mysterii, aut ad interpretationem cuiusdam loci Scripturae; et si prophetis videatur aliquando concessa, aut etiam sanctis, quo altius in contemplando assurgerent, sicut testantur auctores mystici, non est tale privilegium B. Virgini denegandum."

Was Mary's Use of Reason and Free Will in her Mother's Womb only Transitory and Interrupted?

According to St. Francis de Sales,[92] St. Alphonsus,[93] and theologians of the standing of Sauve,[94] Terrien[95] and Hugon,[96] Mary's use of her privilege was uninterrupted. Fr. Merkelbach and other theologians assert that there is no convincing argument in proof of that thesis.[97] It is our opinion that though it cannot be demonstrated with certainty that Mary enjoyed the uninterrupted use of reason and free will in her mother's womb, it is seriously probable and difficult to disprove that she had it. For if it be conceded that she had it in the first instant, it follows that she would become less perfect when deprived of it. But it does not appear becoming that so holy a creature should fall in any way without guilt on her part, all the more so since her dignity demanded that she should progress continuously and that her merit should be unbroken.[98]

It has been objected that St. Thomas regards the privilege as peculiar to Christ.[99] Certain it is that Christ's permanent exercise of reason and will belongs to Him alone as a strict right and consequence of the beatific vision. Mary cannot lay any such claim to the privilege. But it appears altogether becoming that the future Mother of God should have been granted it as a special and most appropriate favor. Besides, St. Thomas's words may be explained by the fact that the Immaculate Conception had not been defined in his time and, in consequence, prominence had not been

---

92. *Loc. cit.*
93. *Loc cit.*
94. *Jésus Intime,* t. III, p. 262.
95. *La Mère de Dieu,* t. II, ch. I.
96. *Tractatus Dogmatici,* 1927, t. II, p. 759; also *Marie Pleine de Grâce,* 5th edit., 1926, pp. 24-32.
97. *Mariologia,* pp. 199, 201.
98. This is the argument of Fr. Hugon, *loc. cit.*
99. IIIa, q. 27, a. 3: ". . . non habuit usum liberi arbitrii in ventre matris existens: hoc enim est speciale privilegium Christi. . . .

given to the motives we have adduced for admitting the privilege in Mary's case.[100] Today, however, after the Bull *Ineffabilis,* we realise that Mary was favored from the first instant more than all the saints united. Besides, as we have said, almost all theologians admit that she had the privilege at least transitorily from the first instant. If so, it is hard to see why it should ever have been withdrawn, interrupting her merit and progress, and leaving the initial plenitude, as it were, unproductive and sterile—all of which is opposed to the sweet and strong way in which Providence cared for Mary.

Such was the initial fullness of grace which accompanied the Immaculate Conception, and such were its first consequences. More and more can we see the implications of the angelic salutation: "Hail, full of grace."

---

100. Cf. Hugon, *locis citatis.*

❧ Chapter 3 ❧

Mary's Plenitude of Grace at and after the Incarnation

IN this chapter we shall speak of Mary's spiritual
progress up to the Annunciation, of the increase
of grace at that instant, of her perpetual virginity, of her growth in charity on certain important occasions which followed—notably on Calvary; finally we
shall speak of Mary's wisdom, of her principal virtues
and charismatic gifts.

Article 1
Mary's Spiritual Progress
Up to the Annunciation

The method which we have adopted in this book is
first to treat principles, bringing out their force and
their sublimity, and then to apply them to the Mother
of God. Hence we begin this article by recalling that
spiritual progress is, most of all, progress in charity,
the virtue which inspires, animates, and renders meritorious the other virtues. All the other infused virtues
are connected with charity, and grow to the rhythm of
its growth, just as the five fingers of a child's hands
grow proportionately.[1]

In the sections that follow we shall see why and how
charity developed in Mary, and examine the stages of
its growth.

---

1. Ia IIae, q. 65 and q. 66, a. 2.

The Rapidity of the Growth of Charity in Mary

Why is it that charity grew in Mary up to the time of her death? First of all, because such growth is in accordance both with the nature of the charity which is tending to eternity and with the divine precept: "Thou shalt love the Lord thy God with thy whole heart, and with thy whole soul, and with all thy strength"—a precept which is so worded as to denote progress. This divine precept, which takes precedence over all other precepts and counsels, obliges all christians to tend towards the perfection of charity and the other virtues in the manner appropriate to their condition of life—some in the married state, others in the priestly or the religious state. Not all are obliged to the practice of the three evangelical counsels. But all are obliged to strive to acquire their spirit, which is one of detachment from self and the things of this world in view of closer union with God.

Of Our Blessed Lord alone can it be said that He never grew in grace or charity, for He alone received the complete fullness of them both at His conception in consequence of the hypostatic union. Thus, the Second Council of Constantinople declares that Jesus did not develop spiritually through progress in good works,[2] even though He followed the normal sequence in performing the acts of virtue peculiar to each period of life. Mary, however, was continually growing in grace all through her life. What was still more, her growth was an accelerated one, in accordance with the principle formulated by St. Thomas *à propos* the text: ". . . comforting one another, and so much the more as you see the day approaching." (*Heb.* 10:25). In his commentary *in loc,* he writes: "It may be asked why we should thus always progress in faith and love. The reason is that a natural (or connatural) movement always

---

2. Cf. Denz., 224: "Si quis defendit . . . Christum . . . ex profectu operum melioratum . . . A.S."

becomes more rapid the nearer it approaches its term (the end which attracts it). With violent or unnatural movement, it is quite different." [Today we remark that the downward movement of a falling body is uniformly accelerated while the upward movement of one thrown into the air is uniformly slowed down.] "But," continues St. Thomas, "grace perfects the soul and makes it tend to the good in a natural way (like a second nature); it follows then, that those who are in the state of grace should grow more in charity according as they come nearer to their final end (and are more strongly attracted by it). That is why it is said in the Epistle to the Hebrews: 'Not forsaking our assembly . . . but comforting one another, and so much the more as you see the day approaching'—that is to say, the end of your journey approaching. We read elsewhere: 'The night is passed, and the day is at hand.' (*Rom.* 13:12). 'But the path of the just, as a shining light, goeth forwards and increaseth even to perfect day.'" (*Prov.* 4:18).[3]

St. Thomas wrote this at a time when the law of universal gravitation was not yet known, and the rate of acceleration of falling bodies had not been calculated accurately. Nevertheless, his genius enabled him to find in the little that had been observed a symbol of the accelerated progress of the saints who gravitate towards the Sun of justice and the Source of all good. His point is, therefore, that the intensity of the life of the saints increases, that they move more promptly and generously towards God, the nearer they come to Him. That is the law of universal attraction in the spiritual life. Just as bodies attract one another in proportion to their mass and in inverse proportion to the square of their distances, so souls are attracted to God in proportion to their holiness and their nearness to

---

3. Cf. also St. Thomas in l. i *de Coelo,* ch. viii, lect. 17, end: "Terra (vel corpus grave) *velocius* movetur quanto magis descendit." Ia IIae, q. 35, a. 6: "Omnis motus, naturalis *intensior est* in fine, cum appropinquat ad terminum suae naturae convenientem, quam in principio . . . quasi natura magis tendat in id quod est sibi conveniens, quam fugiat id quod est sibi repugnans."

Him. The trajectory of the spiritual motion of the saints is towards a zenith from which it does not descend. There is no twilight for them. Age weakens only their bodily powers. Their progress in love is even more rapid in their last years. They advance, not with a regular, but with an ever hastening step, in spite of the weight of years, and their "youth shall be renewed like the eagle's." (*Ps.* 102:5).

Mary's progress was the most continuous of all. It encountered no obstacle, was not halted nor delayed by attachment to self or to the things of this world. It was the most rapid of all, because the rate at which it commenced was determined by Mary's fullness of grace and therefore surpassed that of all the saints. Thus there was in Mary (especially if, as is probable, her infused knowledge gave her the use of reason and will during her hours of sleep) a wonderful increase in the love of God of which the accelerated motion of bodies under the force of gravitation is but a distant image.

Modern physical science tells us that the velocity of a falling body increases uniformly. This is an image of the growth of charity in a soul which allows nothing to hold it back, and which moves faster towards God according as increasing nearness to Him increases His attraction. Such a soul usually makes each sacramental or spiritual communion more fervently, and in consequence more fruitfully, than the preceding one. The movement of a stone thrown in the air, which grows uniformly slower and finally falls back, is a symbol of the lukewarm soul, especially if through a growing attachment to venial sin its communions become less fervent.

The principles outlined in this article show what must have been Mary's spiritual progress from the time of her Immaculate Conception, especially if she had, as is probable, the uninterrupted use of reason and will in her mother's womb and afterwards.[4] Besides,

----

4. We have quoted the authorities who support this view on p. 71. The following are

since it appears that Mary's initial fullness of grace surpassed that of all the saints, her subsequent progress cannot but exceed our powers of description.[5] Nothing held her back, neither the consequences of original sin, nor any venial sin, neither negligence, nor distraction, nor imperfection. She was like a soul which, having taken the vow always to do the most perfect thing, proved completely faithful to it.

Saint Anne must have been struck by the unique holiness of her child. But she could not have suspected the Immaculate Conception nor the future divine maternity. Her child was much more loved by God than she thought. In a somewhat similar way, each soul in the state of grace is more loved by God than it thinks. To know fully how much it is loved, it would need to understand grace, and the glory of which grace is the germ, just as to know the full value of the acorn it is necessary to have seen a fully developed oak tree. The greatest things often lie concealed in the most insignificant, as in a mustard seed, or in the tiny trickle which is the beginning of a mighty river.

Mary's Progress by Merit and Prayer

If Mary's charity grew uninterruptedly in accordance

---

the words of St. Francis de Sales: "How much more probable is it that the mother of the true Solomon had the use of reason in her sleep:" *Treatise on the Love of God*, L. III, c. 8, à propos the words of the Canticle of Canticles: "I sleep and my heart watcheth."

5. It is necessary to explain what is meant by the expression "to exceed our powers of description". It is not a denial of the certain fact that Mary's grace remained limited. To attribute to her what is peculiar to her Divine Son would be unpardonable exaggeration. We know that her progress in grace could not go beyond certain limits. In other words, we know on the negative side what she could not do; but we do not know on the positive side all she could do, nor the degree of holiness to which she could attain, nor what was her point of departure. This is like our knowledge of the forces of nature: we do not know all they can do, but we do know certain things they cannot do—such as to cause the restoration to life of a dead man.

In a similar way, we do not know positively all that the angels are capable of by their natural powers, especially the highest angels; but we know for certain that the least degree of grace is higher than the nature of the highest angel. To know fully the value of the least degree of grace, germ of glory, it would be necessary to have enjoyed the beatific vision momentarily. Much less then can we understand the grace of Mary.

with the great law of love, we may ask what were the sources of its growth. They were merit, prayer, and a certain spiritual communion with God who was present in Mary's soul from the first moment of her existence.

It must be recalled first of all that it is not precisely in extension that charity grows, for even the least degree of charity extends to God and to all men without exception—though it is true that we can and do extend the field of our active goodwill. Charity grows most of all in intensity. It takes ever deeper root in the will, or, to lay metaphor aside, it makes the will determined to avoid both evil and that which is less good and to tend generously to God. The growth of charity is not quantitative—as is that of a heap which grows by having more added to it—but qualitative, as is the growth of knowledge which, even if no fresh conclusions are drawn, can become more penetrating, more profound, more unified, more certain. Charity grows by tending to love God above all things, more perfectly, more purely, and more firmly, and our neighbour as ourselves, so that all may be united in glorifying God in time and in eternity. This growth brings the formal object and motive of charity into fuller relief than it usually is at the beginning of a spiritual life. At first, we love God more for what He has given and for what we hope He will yet give, and less for His own sake. But gradually we come to realise that the Giver is greater and more lovable than the gift, and that He deserves to be loved for the sake of His own Infinite Goodness.

In our case, a number of different influences contribute to the growth of charity—merit, prayer, the sacraments. We shall now consider the first of these in relation to Mary.

A meritorious act, proceeding from charity or from a virtue inspired by it, establishes a right to a supernatural reward, and first of all to the reward of an increase of habitual grace and charity itself. The increase of grace and charity is not caused directly by the meritorious act, for grace and charity are not acquired but rather infused habits. God alone can produce them, for they participate in the depths of His life; He alone can increase them. That is why St. Paul says: "I have planted (by preaching and baptism), Apollo watered, but God gave the increase" (*1 Cor.* 3:6); and again: "He will . . . increase the growth of the fruits of your justice." (*2 Cor.* 9:10).

But though our acts do not directly increase charity, they contribute in two ways to its growth: morally, by meriting it; physically, by disposing for it. Meritorious acts confer on the soul the right to receive from God an increase of charity so as to love Him more purely and more firmly. Besides, they dispose the soul for this increase by opening out in some way, or by unfolding, its higher faculties, enabling the divine life to enter them, to elevate them, and to purify them.

It often happens that our meritorious acts remain imperfect—remiss, as theologians put it—that is to say, below the level or degree in which the virtue of charity exists in us. Oftentimes, though we have a charity of three talents, we act as if we had one of but two, It is as when an intelligent man is careless and does not apply himself seriously to what he is doing. Remiss acts are meritorious. But St. Thomas and the older generation of theologians teach that they do not obtain for the soul at once the increase of charity which they merit, precisely because they do not dispose it to receive it.[6] A person who, having three talents of charity, acts as if he had only two, is obviously not preparing or disposing himself to have his charity increased to four talents. He will receive the increase he merits only when he disposes himself for it by a more generous or more intense act of charity or of one of the virtues which it controls.

These few principles throw a flood of light on what has been said about Mary's progress by way of merit.

---

6. Cf. IIa IIae, q. 24, a. 6, ad I.

She never performed a remiss or imperfect meritorious act, for that would have been a moral imperfection, a lack of generosity in God's service such as theologians declare she was never guilty of. Hence her meritorious acts were rewarded at once by the increase of charity which they merited.

But there is something more. Theologians tell us that God is more glorified by a single act of charity of ten talents, than by ten acts of one talent. Similarly, one devout soul gives more glory to God than many who are lukewarm. In the spiritual order especially, quality means more than quantity. Hence, Mary's merits grew continuously in perfection. Her most pure heart dilated, and her capacity for the divine increased, as is described in *Psalms* 118:32: "I have run the way of thy commandments, when thou didst enlarge my heart." Whereas we often forget that we are journeying towards eternity and treat this world as if it were to last for ever, Mary never withdrew her eyes from the goal of her life, God Himself, and never wasted a moment of the time He gave her. Each instant of her life on earth entered into the single instant of eternity through her accumulating ever richer merits. She saw the present not along the horizontal line of time which ends in a future on earth, but along the vertical line which ends in an eternity that never passes.

Another thing to be noted is that, according to the teaching of St. Thomas, no deliberate act really performed in the course of a lifetime is ever indifferent. For an act which is indifferent in itself, such as to take a walk or to teach mathematics, becomes good or bad in performance because of the end to which it is directed, and a reasonable being is obliged always to act for a reasonable or good end, and not simply for self-gratification or for some other disordered purpose.[7] From this it follows that every deliberate act

---

7. Cf. Ia IIae, q. 18, a. 9.

of a person in the state of grace which is not a sin is morally good; in consequence, it is virtually ordained to God, the final end of the just, and is meritorious. "Every act of those who have charity is either meritorious or de-meritorious" (De Malo, a. 5, ad 17). This is an additional reason for saying that all Mary's deliberate acts were good and meritorious. And we may add that none of the acts she performed during her waking hours were indeliberate or machine-like, but all were under the control of her intellect and her grace-directed will.

When we meditate on the outstanding occasions in Mary's life, it is especially in the light of the preceding principles that we should do so. And since, just now, we are concerned with those which preceded the Incarnation, let us turn to her Presentation in the Temple, when she was as yet a child, or to her participation in the great feasts of Israel, or to her reading of the Messianic prophecies—those particularly of Isaias—which increased so wonderfully her faith, her hope, her love of God, and her longing for the advent of the Messiah. How much she must have penetrated the depth of meaning in Isaias' words: "For a child is born to us, and a son is given to us, and the government is upon his shoulder; and his name shall be called, Wonderful, Counsellor, God the Mighty, the Father of the world to come, the Prince of peace." (*Is.* 9:6). Though she was still so young, Mary's vivid faith must have grasped better than even Isaias did the meaning of the words "God the Mighty." She understood already that the plenitude of the divine power would be in that Child, that the Messiah would be an eternal and immortal King, always the Father of His people.[8]

---

8. No one can affirm as certain beyond question that Mary did not understand the *God the Mighty* of the prophecy of Isaias as attributing divinity to the Messiah. The Church, enlightened by the New Testament, understands the term in that sense in the Masses of Christmas. Who then will assert that Mary did not understand as much before the Incarnation? *The Messiah is the Anointed of the Lord.* In the light of New Testament teaching, we today realize that the anointing is

The life of grace increases not by merit only but by prayer as well, which has its own peculiar efficacy (of impetration). For that reason, we pray every day to grow in the grace of God, saying: "Our Father, who art in Heaven, hallowed be Thy Name; Thy Kingdom come (more and more in us); Thy Will be done (may Your precepts be better observed by us)." Similarly, the Church makes us pray on the 13th Sunday after Pentecost: "Grant us, O Lord, an increase of faith, hope and charity."

After justification, one can therefore grow in grace both by the way of merit—which is based on the divine justice, and gives a right to a reward—and by the way of prayer—which relies on the divine mercy. Prayer is efficacious in the degree in which it is humble, confident, persevering, and desirous of an increase of virtue rather than of temporal favors: "Seek ye first the kingdom of God and His justice, and all these things shall be given to you." And it can happen that the soul in the state of grace will receive at once, in answer to fervent prayer, more than it merits. In other words, a person may, on occasion, receive an increase of grace through the impetratory power of a prayer which exceeds that due to prayer's meritorious value.[9]

Mary's prayer was most efficacious from her very childhood, not only because of its meritorious value, but also because of its wonderful impetratory value, proportionate to her humility, her confidence, and her perseverance in a continually growing generosity. Through it she grew continuously in the pure and strong love of God. She obtained also all the actual efficacious graces which cannot be merited strictly, such as

---

constituted first of all by the *grace of union,* which is the *Word Himself, who* communicates substantial and uncreated holiness to the Sacred Humanity. (Cf. IIIa, q. 6, a. 6; q. 22, a. 2, ad 3.)

9. This explains how the just can obtain by prayer graces which cannot be merited, as, for example, the grace of *final perseverance,* or actual *efficacious grace* which at the same time preserves from mortal sin and conserves and augments the state of grace. The same can be said of the *special inspiration* which is the principle, through the gifts of understanding and wisdom, of infused contemplation.

those which incline to new meritorious acts, or the special inspiration which is the principle of infused contemplation. This must certainly have happened when she repeated in her prayer the words of the Book of Wisdom 7:7: "Wherefore I wished, and understanding was given me: and I called upon God, and the spirit of wisdom came upon me: and I preferred her before kingdoms and thrones, and esteemed riches nothing in comparison with her . . . for all gold in comparison of her, is as a little sand, and silver in respect of her shall be counted as clay." In this way, the Lord came to her to nourish her with Himself, and each day gave Himself more fully to her by prompting her to give herself more fully to Him.

More appropriately than anyone else except Jesus, she said with the psalmist: "One thing I have asked of the Lord, this will I seek after: that I may dwell in the house of the Lord all the days of my life; that I may see the delight of the Lord. . . (*Ps.* 26:4). Day after day brought her a fuller understanding of the infinite goodness of God to those who seek Him and to those who find Him. Even before the institution of the Blessed Eucharist, Mary enjoyed, therefore, that spiritual communion which consists in the simple and intimate prayer of the soul in the unitive stage when it enjoys God present within it as in a spiritual temple: "O taste and see that the Lord is sweet." (*Ps.* 33:9).

The psalmist expresses his thirst for God in burning words: "As the hart panteth after the fountains of waters; so my soul panteth after thee, O God. My soul hath thirsted after the strong living God." (*Ps.* 41:2). What must have been Mary's thirst for God from the moment of the Immaculate Conception up to the day of the Incarnation!

St. Thomas tells us that Mary's progress in charity was not such that she merited the Incarnation, for the Incarnation is the principle of all merit since the sin of Adam, and could not itself be merited by one who was redeemed. Nevertheless, her progress merited for her gradually (as a result of the first grace which came from the future merits of her Son) that eminent degree of charity, humility, and purity which made her, on the Annunciation day, the *worthy* mother of the Saviour.[10]

Neither did she merit the divine maternity; that would have been equivalently to merit the Incarnation. She did, however, merit the degree of charity which was the proximate disposition for being made Mother of God. This proximate disposition must have been an unimaginable summit of holiness, since even the remote disposition—Mary's first fullness of grace—surpassed the united holinesses of all the saints.

Finally, we may add that Mary's years in the temple accelerated her growth in the grace of the virtues and the gifts in a way with which the growth of the most generous of souls is quite unworthy to be compared.

It is, of course, possible to exaggerate Mary's growth in grace and to attribute to her a perfection which belongs only to her Son. But even if we are careful to confine ourselves to what were really her prerogatives, we are utterly incapable of forming a worthy idea of the elevation of her beginning and her progress in the spiritual life. The most we can do is to attain to some small measure of understanding of so sublime a mystery.

NOTE

When in our lives do the less fervent or remiss acts of charity obtain the increase of charity due to them?

According to St. Thomas,* every act of charity of the "wayfarer" is meritorious, meriting an increase of this virtue and disposing the soul, at least in a

---

10. Cf. IIIa, q. 2, a, II, ad 3: "Beata Virgo dicitur meruisse portare Dominum omnium, *non quia meruit ipsum incarnari,* sed quia *meruit* ex gratia sibi data *ilium puritatis et sanctitatis gradum,* ut *congrue* posset esse Mater Dei."
* IIa IIae, q. 24, a. 6.

remote manner, to receive it; but only fervent acts dispose one proximately, *i.e.* acts at least equal in intensity to the degree of the infused virtue from which they proceed. Therefore only fervent acts obtain immediately the increase of charity that they merit.

When do the less fervent acts obtain it?

One might think that it is as soon as a fervent meritorious act is made. However, there is a difficulty, for whereas this act certainly obtains the increase due to it and to which it disposes one proximately, it is not certain that it obtains at the same time the increase due to the less fervent meritorious acts which have preceded it and which has not yet been given.

One way by which these arrears can be obtained is by fervent acts of charity which are themselves meritorious, and which also dispose one to receive already in the present life not only what they merit themselves but even more than they merit.

This is the case with the fervent act of charity by which one prepares oneself for a good communion, which confers "ex opere operato" an increase of charity corresponding to the actual fervent disposition *and* to the "arrears". This must be quite frequent with good priests and good christians, especially at the more fervent communions which they make on certain feast-days or on the First Friday of the month. More so must this take place when, with good dispositions, one receives Holy Communion as Viaticum, or with Extreme Unction, which, effacing the remains of sin *(reliquiae peccati),* produces an increase of charity in proportion to the fervour with which it is received; it can therefore produce also the "arrears" merited but not yet obtained.

One's "arrears" may be obtained also by a fervent prayer for an increase of charity; for this prayer is at once meritorious, inasmuch as inspired by charity, and impetratory; and on this latter score it obtains more than it merits and can dispose one proximately to receive the "arrears" already merited but not obtained.

Finally, it remains probable that the soul which may not have obtained its "arrears" during this life by any of the means we have mentioned, can dispose itself proximately to receive them by its fervent acts in Purgatory, acts which, however, are no longer meritorious. It is certain that these souls in Purgatory, as their purification advances, make more and more fervent acts (non-meritorious), which attain at least to the degree of intensity of the infused virtue from which they proceed. These acts do not merit an increase of this virtue, but it is probable that they dispose one actually to receive the "arrears" already merited "in via" and not yet obtained. Thus a soul which entered Purgatory with a charity of five talents, could leave it with a charity of seven, the degree of glory corresponding always to the degree of merit.

And if this is true, it would appear to be true especially with regard to the final act by which the soul disposes itself *(in genere causae materialis)* to receive the light of glory, an act which is produced *(in genere causae efficientis et formalis)* under the influence of this light at the exact moment of its infusion, just as the last act which immediately disposes one for justification proceeds from charity at the exact moment of its infusion. Thus the "arrears" would be obtained at least at the last moment, on one's entry into glory.*

Article 2

Mary's Wonderful Increase in Grace at the Annunciation

As St. Thomas explains,[11] it was becoming that the mystery of the Incarnation should be announced to the Blessed Virgin so as to instruct her in its meaning and

---

* These different explanations, which are quite probable, have been proposed by several commentators on St. Thomas in IIa, IIae, q. 24, a. 6, We have exposed them more at length elsewhere: L'Amour de Dieu et la Croix de Jésus, t. I, pp. 415-422, and Les Trois Ages de la Vie Intérieure, t. 1, p. 180 sqq.

11. IIIa, q. 30, aa. 1, 2, 3, 4.

that she might give her consent to it. Thereby she conceived the Word spiritually, as the Fathers say, before conceiving Him physically. And St. Thomas adds that her supernatural and meritorious consent was given in the name of the whole human race which stood in need of the promised Redeemer.

It was becoming also that the Annunciation should have been made by an angel, coming as ambassador of the Most High. A rebellious angel had caused the Fall; a holy angel, the highest of the archangels, announces the Redemption.[12] Becoming, as well, that Mary should have been enlightened before St. Joseph about the mystery, for by her predestination she was greater than he. Becoming, in the last place, that the Annunciation should have taken the form of a corporeal vision accompanied by an intellectual illumination, for the corporeal vision is, in itself, more certain and reliable than the imaginative one, and the grace of the intellectual illumination revealed with certainty the meaning of the words spoken.[13] Joy and confidence succeeded reverential fear and astonishment as the angel spoke: "Fear not, Mary, for thou hast found grace with God. Behold thou shalt conceive in thy womb, and shalt bring forth a son; and thou shalt call his name Jesus. He shall be great, and shall be called the Son of the Most High. . . . The Holy Ghost shall come uponthee and the power of the Most High shall overshadow thee. And therefore also the Holy which shall be born of thee shall be called the Son of God." And the angel adds, both as sign and as explanation of what is to come to pass: "And behold thy cousin Elisabeth, she also hath conceived a son in her old age, and this is the sixth month with her that is called barren. Because no word shall be impossible with God."

And Mary consented, saying, "Behold the handmaid

---

12. IIIa, q. 30, a. 3.
13. Ib., a. 4.

of the Lord; be it done to me according to thy word."

Bossuet tells us in his *Elevations on the Mysteries,*
12th Week, 6th Elevation, that Mary manifested principally three virtues in her consent: virginity, by her
noble resolution to renounce the joys of the senses for
ever; perfect humility in regard to God who so favored
her; and faith, by conceiving the Son of God in her
soul before she conceived Him in her body—which is
why Elisabeth saluted her: "And blessed art thou that
hast believed, because these things shall be accomplished that were spoken to thee by the Lord." She
manifested also confidence in God and courage, for she
was not ignorant of the messianic prophecies—those
especially of Isaias—which foretold the great sufferings of the Messiah in which she was called to share.

Many interior souls are struck most by Mary's total
self-forgetfullness at the Annunciation, and see in it
the highest humility. She thought only of God's will,
of all that the Incarnation would do for His glory and
for our salvation. And God, Who is the greatness of
little ones, regarded her humility, and made her faith,
her confidence, and her generosity all they were called
to be by her participation in our redemption. There
are men who think that their greatness consists in
their genius and their gifts of nature. Mary, the greatest of creatures, turned her gaze from herself, and
sought her greatness in God. *Deus humilium celsitudo,*
God, who art the greatness of the humble, reveal to
us the greatness of Mary, the loftiness of her charity.[14]

St. Thomas tells us[15] that Mary's fullness of grace
increased notably at the Incarnation, through the pres-

---

14. *Deus humilium celsitudo* is the opening of the Collect of the Mass of St. Francis of Paula, April 2nd, and of the Blessed Martin Porres, November 5th, in the
Dominican Missal. St. Albert the Great has some magnificent pages in his *Mariale* about the humility of Mary whom he regarded as his mother and his inspiration.
15. IIIa, q. 27, a. 5, ad 2: "In Beata Virgine fuit triplex perfectio gratiae. Prima quidem quasi dispositiva, per quam reddebatur idonea ad hoc quod esset mater
Christi, et haec fuit prima perfectio sanctificationis. Secunda autem perfectio gratiae fuit in Beata Virgine ex praesentia Filii Dei in eius utero incarnati. Tertia
autem est perfectio finis, quam habet in gloria."

ence of the Word of God made flesh. If she had not been already confirmed in grace, she would have been so from that moment.

The Reason for Mary's Increase in Grace and Charity at the Incarnation

Three reasons have been given for Mary's increase in the divine life at the Incarnation: the finality, or purpose, of her grace; the cause of her grace; the mutual love of Jesus and His Mother.

In the first place, an increase in grace and charity was most becoming as a proximate and immediate preparation for the dignity of the divine motherhood. It is a general principle that the proximate preparation (ultimate disposition) for any perfection is proportionate to it. But the divine maternity is superior by its term—which is of the hypostatic order—to every other dignity of nature or of grace. Hence, Mary must have received as proximate preparation for it a special increase of her fullness of grace. This special increase made her proximately worthy to be the Mother of God and to take her unique place in regard to the Word made flesh.

In the second place, the Son of God owed it to Himself to enrich Mary with a still greater grace when He became present in her by the Incarnation. For by His Divinity He is principal cause of grace, and by His Humanity He is its meritorious and instrumental cause. But Mary was, of all creatures, the one who entered into closest contact with Him in His Humanity since He took flesh in her womb. Hence, it was appropriate that she should have received a notable increase of grace at the Incarnation. Receiving the Word into her womb, she must have experienced all— and more than all—the benefits of a fervent sacramental communion. Jesus gives Himself to us in the Blessed Eucharist under the appearances of bread; He gave Himself to Mary in His true form, and by an immediate contact which produced, *ex opere operato,* an increase in her participation in the divine life more bounteous than even that produced by the greatest of the sacraments.

There is one remarkable point of dissimilarity between Jesus' gift of Himself to Mary and His gift of Himself to us in Holy Communion. He gives Himself to us that we may live by Him. But, though He nourished Mary's soul and gave Himself to her by the Incarnation, in His human nature, He lived by her and received from her the nourishment which His sacred Body required.

In the third and last place, the mutual love of Jesus and Mary demanded an increase of Mary's fullness of grace. As we have said, grace is an effect of God's active love for His creature. But if the Word made Flesh loves all the men for whom He is prepared to shed His blood, if He loves in a special way the elect and among them in a still more special way the apostles and the saints, His love for Mary, who was to be the most closely associated with Him in His work for souls, is the greatest of all. But Jesus is God. Hence His love for her produces grace in her soul—such an abundance of grace as to be capable of overflowing on souls. He is man too, and as man has merited all the effects of our predestination.[16] Hence, in His love for her, He communicated to her the effects of her special predestination, most particularly that increase of charity which brought her nearer to the final fullness that was to be hers in glory. We must remember too that Mary was never in the slightest degree unresponsive to Jesus' love for her; on the contrary, her maternal love for Jesus answered most fully to Jesus' love for her. On that account it was possible for Him to give Himself to her much more fully than to any of the great saints. To

16. IIIa, q. 24, a. 4.

form some idea of Mary's maternal love for Jesus, we have only to think of the heroic love and of the immense sacrifices of which mothers are capable for their children in their hour of trial and suffering. Think too of how loving Mary's pure virgin heart was; and of how she loved her Son as her God; and of how her love was supernatural as well as natural, growing continuously in intensity. Such thoughts will enable you to glimpse Mary's love in a distant way.

Speaking of the time when the Body of the Saviour was formed in Mary's virginal womb, Fr Hugon says:[17] "She must have made uninterrupted progress in grace during those nine months—ex *opere operato,* as it were—through her permanent contact with the Author of holiness. If her plenitude of grace is incomprehensible at the time of the Incarnation, what must it have been at the Nativity. . . . Each time she fed him at her virginal breast, she was nourished with grace. . . . When she held Him in her arms and gave Him the kisses of a virgin-mother, she received from Him the kiss of the divinity, which made her still purer and holier." These words are but an echo of the liturgy.[18] Even when physical contact with Jesus in her womb had ceased, Mary's charity and motherly love continued to grow, and this up to the hour of her death. In her case, grace perfected nature in a degree which will remain for ever beyond the powers of the human tongue to express.

---

17. *Marie, pleine de grâce,* 5th edit., 1926, p. 46.
18. Cf. Vespers Hymn for the Feast of the Holy Family:

O Lux beata caelitum   Maria dives gratia
Et summa spes mortalium   O sola quae casto potes
Jesu, o cui domestica   Fovere Jesum pectore,
Arrisit orto caritas: Cum lacte donans oscula.

Article 3
The Visitation and the "Magnificat"

1. The Visitation

After the Annunciation the Blessed Virgin went to visit her cousin, St. Elisabeth. As soon as Elisabeth heard Mary's salutation, the child she bore leaped in her womb for joy, and she was filled with the Holy Ghost. And she cried out: "Blessed art thou among women, and blessed is the fruit of thy womb. For behold, as soon as the voice of thy salutation sounded in my ears, the infant in my womb leaped for joy. And blessed art thou that hast believed, because those things shall be accomplished that were spoken to thee by the Lord." In the light of divine revelation Elisabeth understands that the Fruit of Mary's womb is beginning to bless men through His mother. She knows that it is the Lord Himself who comes to her. The Son of God comes, through His mother, to His precursor; and the precursor, through his mother, recognized the Son of God.

St. Luke gives the canticle of the *Magnificat* in the verses which follow. The context, the authority of the great majority of the best manuscripts, and the unanimous voice of the oldest and most learned Fathers (Irenaeus, Origen, Tertullian, St. Ambrose, St. Jerome, St. Augustine, etc.) all point to Mary as its author.

What strikes one most of all in the *Magnificat* is its simplicity and its dignity. In substance it is a song of thanksgiving, which recalls that God is the greatness of the humble, that He lifts them up even while He casts down the pride of the mighty. Bossuet sums up well what the Fathers say about the *Magnificat* in his *Elevations on the Mysteries,* 14th week, 5th Elevation. We shall follow him in the next few pages.[19]

---

19. St. Francis de Sales' two sermons on the *Visitation* should also be studied. In one place he asks if by "the humility of his handmaid" Mary referred to her lowly

2. God has done great things in Mary

"My soul doth glorify the Lord." Mary leaves self, as it were, to glorify God alone and to find in Him all her joy. She is in perfect peace, for no one can take from her Him of whom she sings.

"My spirit hath rejoiced in God my Saviour." What Mary cannot find in herself she finds in God, who is the Supreme Treasure. She rejoices "because He hath rewarded the humility of His handmaid." She does not think herself capable of attracting His gaze, for she is nothing. But He, in His goodness, has turned towards her, and now she has a sure ground for confidence—the Divine mercy. No longer does she fear to recognise all she has received freely from Him: rather is that a debt of gratitude to be paid. "For behold from henceforth all generations shall call me blessed"—a prophecy which is still fulfilled after two thousand years with each "Hail Mary" that men say.

And now she sees that her joy will be the joy of all men of good will: "He that is mighty hath done great things to me; and holy is His name. And His mercy is from generation unto generation, to them that fear Him." He who is mighty has performed in her the greatest work of His might—the redemptive Incarnation: He has given a Saviour to the world through her, while yet leaving her virginity intact.

The Most High is holy, is Holiness. This is all the more evident to us who believe that the Son of God, who is also the Son of Mary, has bestowed mercy, grace and holiness on men of so many different times and nations who feared God with that childlike fear which is the beginning of wisdom, and accepted the yoke of His commandments by grace.

---

condition as a creature or also to her humility. With some of the Fathers—though against many authorities—he answers that it is more probable that she spoke of her humility; for she knew from the angel's words that she was full of grace, and had, in consequence, the virtue of humility in a high degree. But to God she gave the glory due to her virtue.

3. God raises up the humble and through them triumphs over the pride of the mighty

To explain these wonderful effects Mary appeals to the Divine Power: "He hath showed might in His arm; He hath scattered the proud in the conceit of their heart. He hath put down the mighty from their seat, and hath exalted the humble." God did all she mentions when He sent His only Son to confound the proud by the preaching of His gospel, and to make use of the weakness of the apostles, confessors and virgins, to bring the strength of a proud paganism to naught. His sublime mysteries He has hidden from the wise and revealed to little ones. (*Matt.* 11:25). Mary is herself an example of what God does by the little ones. He raised her above all because she looked on herself as the least of all. The Son of God chose for His dwelling not the rich palaces of kings but the poverty of Bethlehem, and He manifested His power by the very weakness in which He came to exalt the little ones.

"He hath filled the hungry with good things; and the rich He hath sent empty away." Jesus in His turn will say: "Blessed are ye that hunger now, for you shall be filled. . . . Woe to you that are filled, for you shall hunger." (*Luke* 6:21, 25). In Bossuet's words, it is when the soul sees the glory of the world in ruins and God alone great that it finds peace.

The *Magnificat* concludes as it began, with thanksgiving: "He hath received Israel His servant, being mindful of His mercy: As He spoke to our fathers, to Abraham and to his seed for ever." We should make our own the words of St. Ambrose: "Let Mary's soul be in us to glorify the Lord; let her spirit be in us that we may rejoice in God our Saviour."[20] May His Kingdom come in us through the accomplishment of His will.

---

20. *In Lucam,* 1. II, n. 26.

Article 4
Mary's Perpetual Virginity

The Church teaches three truths concerning Mary's virginity: that she was a virgin in conceiving Our Saviour, that she was a virgin in giving Him birth, and that she remained a virgin her whole life through. The first two truths were defended against the Cerinthians and the Ebionites towards the end of the 1st century; against Celsus, who was refuted by Origen; in the 16th century against the Socinians, whom Paul IV and Clement VIII condemned; and recently against the rationalists—Strauss, Renan, and the Pseudo-Herzog in particular.[21] The second truth was attacked by Jovinian, who was condemned in 390. The third truth was denied by Helvidius and defended by St. Jerome.[22]

The Virginal Conception

Mary's virginity in the conception of her Son was foretold by Isaias (*Is.* 7:14): "A virgin shall conceive, and bear a son." The virginal conception is clearly the literal sense of this text; otherwise, as St. Justin pointed out to Tryphon,[23] there would be no question of a *sign,* as Isaias had promised. Gabriel also gave testimony to the virginal conception at the Annunciation: "The Holy Ghost shall come upon thee, and the power of the Most High shall overshadow thee." The message given by the angel to St. Joseph is to the same effect: "Joseph, son of David, fear not to take unto thee Mary, thy wife, for that which is conceived in her is of the Holy Ghost" (*Matt.* 1:20). And St. Luke says of Jesus: ". . . being (as it was supposed) the son of Joseph." (*Luke* 3:23).

Tradition confirms that the conception of Christ was

---

21. Cf. Denzinger, nos. 20, 91, 113, 143 sqq., 201, 214, 255 sqq., 282, 290, 344, 429, 462, 708, 735, 993, 1314, 1462.
22. *De perpetua virginitate B. Mariae adversus Helvidium*, P. L., XXII, 183-205.
23. *Dial. cum Tryphone,* LXXXIV; *P. G.,* VI, 673.

virginal, as can be learned from the testimonies of St. Ignatius the Martyr, Aristides, St. Justin, Tertullian, St. Irenaeus. All the creeds teach that the Son of God made flesh "was conceived by the Virgin Mary, by the operation of the Holy Ghost."[24] It was defined by the Lateran Council under Pope Martin I in 649[25] and it was reaffirmed by Paul IV against the Socinians.[26]

The arguments which show the appropriateness of the virginal conception are exposed by St. Thomas[27]: 1—It is appropriate that He who is the natural Son of God should have no father on earth, but only in Heaven; 2—The Word, conceived eternally in the most complete purity, should be conceived virginally when being made flesh; 3—That the human nature of the Saviour be exempt from original sin it was appropriate that it should not be formed by the ordinary process of human generation, but virginally; 4—By being born of a virgin Christ showed that His members should be born by the Spirit of His virginal and spiritual spouse, the Church.

The Virginal Birth

St. Ambrose bears witness to the virginal birth when commenting on the text of Isaias: "A virgin shall conceive, and bear a son;" she will be a virgin, he says, in giving birth as well as in conceiving.[28] The same had been said earlier by St. Ignatius the Martyr,[29] Aristides,[30] Clement of Alexandria.[31] It was defined by the Lateran Council.[32]

St. Thomas gives the following arguments to show

---

24. Denz., 6 sqq.
25. Denz., 256.
26. Denz., 993.27.
27. IIIa, q. 28, a. 1.
28. Epist. XLII ad Siricium Papam, *P. L.*, XVI, 1124: "Non enim concepturam tantum modo virginem, sed et parituram (Isaias) dixit."
29. *Ad Ephes.*, xv, 1.
30. *Ex vita Barlaam et Josaphat, P. G.*, XCVI, 1121.
31. *Strom.*, VII, xvi; *P. G.*, IX, 529.
32. Denz., 256; item 993.

the appropriateness of the virginal birth: 1—The Word, who is conceived and who proceeds eternally from the Father without any corruption of His substance, should, if He becomes flesh, be born of a virgin mother without detriment to her virginity; 2—He who came to remove all corruption should not by His birth destroy the virginity of her who bore Him; 3—He who commands us to honor our parents should not Himself diminish by His birth the glory of His holy mother.

The Perpetual Virginity of Mary after the Saviour's Birth

The Lateran Council affirmed this point of doctrine in 649, as did Paul IV later against the Socinians.[33]

Among the Greek Fathers two deserve special mention as having explicitly taught it: Origen[34] and St. Gregory the Wonderworker.[35] The expression *semper virgo*—"always a virgin"—is common in the 4th century, especially in the works of St. Athanasius and Didymus the Blind.[36] It was also used by the 2nd Council of Constantinople.[37] The Latin Fathers are represented by Saints Ambrose,[38] Augustine,[39] and Jerome.[40] St. Ephrem voices the mind of the Syriac Church.[41]

St. Thomas's arguments to show the appropriateness of the perpetual virginity are as follows (IIIa, q. 28, a. 3): 1—Helvidius's error is opposed to the dignity of Christ Himself, for just as He is the only Son in eternity of the Father so also He ought to be the only Son in time of the Virgin; 2—It is opposed also to the

33. Denz., 256; 993.
34. *In Matt.*, t. X, xvii; *P. G.*, XIII, 876 B; *Homil. VII in Luc.*; *P.G.*, XIII, 1818.
35. *Serm. in Nativit. Christi; P. G.*, X, 391.
36. St. Athanas., Orat. II contra *Arianos*, LXX; *P. G.* XXVI, 296; Didymus, *De Trinitate*, I. xxvii; *P. G.*, XXXIX, 404.
37. Denz., 214, 218.
38. *Epist. XLII* ad Siricium Papam; *P. L.*, XVI, 1124.
39. *Serm. III in Natali Domini*, n. 1; *P. L.*, XXXVIII, 995.
40. *De perpetua virginitate B. Mariae adversus Helvidium.*
41. *S. Ephrem Syri opera*, ed. Rom., 1743, t. II, p. 267.

dignity of the Holy Ghost who sanctified once and for ever the virginal womb of Mary; 3—It is opposed to the dignity and holiness of the Mother of God as it would imply that she was dissatisfied with having borne such a Son; 4—Finally, St. Joseph would have been guilty of the greatest presumption had he violated the virginity of her whom he knew, by the angel, to have conceived of the Holy Ghost.[42]

St. Thomas explains also (IIIa, q. 28, a. 4) the commonly accepted teaching that the Blessed Virgin had taken a vow of perpetual virginity. Her words to the angel prove the point: "How shall this be done, because I know not man?" Tradition is summed up in the phrase of St. Augustine's: "Virgo es, sancta es, votum vovisti."[43]

Article 5

The Principal Mysteries which Contributed to Mary's Increase in Grace after the Incarnation

These mysteries are those especially which the Rosary proposes for our consideration.

The Nativity

Mary grew in humility, poverty and love of God by giving birth to her Son in a stable. His cradle was but a manger. But, by contrast, there were the angels there to sing "Glory to God in the highest; and on earth peace to men of good will." Those words were sweet to the ears of the shepherds and of St. Joseph, and still more sweet to the ears of Mary. They were the beginning of a *Gloria* which the Church does not cease to

---

42. Those mentioned in the New Testament as brothers of the Lord were merely relatives, as tradition has always taught. The Hebrew word corresponding to "brother" signified near relative, and was used to cover *cousins, nephews,* etc. Cf. *Gen.* 13:8; 14:6. Cf. A. Durand, *Frères du Seigneur* in *Dict. Apol.*
43. *Sermo CCCX in Natali Joannis Bapt.; P. L.,* XXXVIII, 1319.

sing at Mass while this world endures, and the liturgy of eternity has not yet replaced that of time.

It is said of Mary that she kept all these words, pondering them in her heart. Though her joy at the birth of her Son was intense, she treasured it up in silence. St. Elisabeth alone received her confidences. God's greatest actions defy human expression. What could Mary say to equal what she had experienced?

The Presentation in the Temple

Mary said her *Fiat* in peace and holy joy on the day of the Annunciation. There was sorrow too in her heart at the thought of the sufferings which Isaias had foretold would befall her Son. Still more light is thrown for her on the mystery of the Redemption when the holy old man Simeon speaks of the Child Jesus as the "Salvation, which thou hast prepared before the face of all peoples: A light to the revelation of the Gentiles." Mary remains silent in wonder and thanksgiving. Simeon continues: "This child is set for the fall, and for the resurrection of many in Israel, and for a sign which shall be contradicted." Jesus, come for the salvation of all, will be the occasion of the fall of many, He will be a stumbling block (*Is.* 8:14) for many of the Jews, who, refusing to recognise Him as the Messiah, will fall into infidelity and thence to eternal ruin. (*Rom.* 9:32; *1 Cor.* 1:3). Jesus Himself will say later: "Blessed is he that shall not be scandalised in me." (*Matt.* 11:6).

Turning then to Mary herself, Simeon addressed to her the prophetic words: "And thy own soul a sword shall pierce, that out of many hearts thoughts may be revealed." Mary will have a share in the Saviour's trials. His sufferings will be hers. Her very heart will be pierced by a sword of sorrow.

Had the Son of Man not come thus on earth we should never have known the full malice of pride's revolt against truth. The hidden thoughts of hypocrisy and false zeal were revealed when the Pharisees cried out for the crucifixion of Him Who is Holiness.

Jesus' fullness of grace had two apparently contradictory effects: the most perfect peace of soul; the will to offer Himself as a redemptive victim. Mary's grace produced two similarly contrasting effects: the pure joys of the days of the Annunciation and the Nativity; the desire to be united most generously to the sufferings of her Son for our salvation. Thus, presenting Him in the temple, she already offers Him for us. Joy and sorrow are wedded in the heart of the Mother of God who is already the Mother of all who will believe in her Son.

The Flight into Egypt

St. Matthew tells us how, after the Magi had come to adore, an angel appeared to Joseph in his sleep saying: "Arise, and take the Child and his mother, and fly into Egypt; and be there until I shall tell thee. For it will come to pass that Herod will seek the Child to destroy him." True to the angel's prophecy, Herod ordered the massacre of all the children of two years and under, in and around Bethlehem.

It is Jesus whom this king fears. He fears where there is no reason to fear, and despises God's anger which he should hold in dread. Mary and Joseph are called to share in Jesus' sufferings. "Before, they had lived in peace and earned their bread without anxiety by the labour of their hands. But as soon as Jesus is given to them their tranquil calm is broken . . . they must share in His Cross."[44] The Holy Innocents share also in the Cross. Their massacre shows us that they were predestined from all eternity for the glory of martyrdom.

When Herod has died, an angel appears again to

---

44. Bossuet, *Elevations,* 19th Week, 3rd Elevation.

Joseph to tell him that the time has come to go to Nazareth in Galilee.

The Hidden Life of Nazareth

Mary grew continuously in grace and charity as she carried the Infant in her arms, fed Him, embraced Him and was caressed by Him, heard His first words, guided His first steps.

"Jesus advanced in wisdom and age and grace with God and men." Arrived at the age of twelve years, He accompanied Mary and Joseph to Jerusalem for the Pasch. When the day of departure came, He remained in the city unknown to His parents. It was only after three days that they found Him in the midst of the doctors. And He said to them: "How is it that you sought me: did you not know that I must be about my Father's business?" But Mary and Joseph "understood not the word that he spoke to them."

Mary accepted in faith what she could not as yet understand. The depth and the extent of the Mystery of the Redemption will be revealed to her only gradually. She is glad to have found Jesus again. But in her joy sounds many an overtone of sadnesses yet to come.

Bossuet has some remarkable reflections on the hidden life, which lasted up to the time of Jesus' public ministry.[45]

"There are some who feel ashamed for Jesus' sake that He should have endured the wearisomeness of so long a retirement. They experience much the same feelings in regard to Mary, and try to enliven her period at Nazareth by attributing continual miracles to her. Rather let us pay heed to the words of the gospel: "Mary kept all these words in her heart." Was not that a task worthy of her? And if the mysteries of His

---

45. *Elevations,* 20th Week, 9th and 10th Elevations.

infancy were so rich a subject for her meditation, what of the mysteries that succeeded them? Mary meditated on Jesus . . . she remained in perpetual contemplation, her heart melting, as it were, in love and longing. What then shall we say to those who invented so many pretty fables about Our Lady? What, if not that humble and perfect contemplation did not seem enough in their eyes? But if it was enough for thirty years of Mary's—and of Jesus'—life, it was enough for the other years too. The silence of the Scriptures about Mary is more eloquent than all discourses. Learn, O man, in the midst of your restless activity, to be satisfied to think of Jesus, to listen to Him within, to hear again His words. . . . Of what are you complaining, human pride, when you say you count for little in this world? Did Jesus count for much there? Or Mary? They were the wonder of the world, the sight that ravished God and angels. And what did they do? What name did they bear? Men wish to bear an honored name, to take part in brilliant movements. They do not know Jesus and Mary. . . . You say you have nothing to do. The salvation of souls is in your hands—in part, at least! Do you not know enemies whom you could help to reconcile, quarrels you could mend? Are there not souls in misery you could save from blasphemy and despair? And even if you have nothing of all that, have you not the work of your own salvation, which is for every soul the true work of God?"

Reflecting on the hidden life of Nazareth and on Mary's spiritual progress in its silence, and reflecting by way of contrast on what the world terms progress, we are forced to conclude: men never talked more of progress than since they began to neglect its most important form, spiritual progress. And what has been the result? That the baser forms of progress, sought for their own sake, have brought pleasure, idleness and unemployment in their train, and prepared the way for a moral decline towards materialism, atheism—and even barbarism, as the recent world wars prove. In Mary, on the contrary, we find the ever more perfect realization of the gospel words: "Thou shalt love the Lord thy God, with thy whole heart, and with thy whole soul, and with all thy strength, and with all thy mind." The further she advances the more she loves God with all her heart, for the more she sees the opposition to Jesus growing in the course of His ministry up to the consummation of the mystery of the Redemption.

The Cause of Mary's Dolors on Calvary and the intensity of her Love of God and of her Son and of Souls

What was the profound cause of Mary's sorrows on Calvary? Every christian soul for whom practice has made the Stations of the Cross familiar will answer: the cause of Mary's sorrows, as of those of Jesus, was sin. Happy the souls for whom that answer is a vital truth, who experience true sorrow at the thought of their own sins—a sorrow that only grace can produce in them.

We understand but little of the sorrows of Mary, for little grieves us except what wounds our bodies, our self-love, our vanity, or our pride. We suffer too from men's ingratitude, from the afflictions of our family or our native land. But sin grieves us but little. We have but little sorrow for our faults considered as offenses against God. In theory, we admit that sin is the greatest of evils since it affects the soul itself and its faculties, and since it is the cause of the disorders which we deplore in society; it is only too evidently the cause of the enmity between classes and nations. But in spite of that we do not experience any great sorrow for the faults whereby we contribute more or less ourselves to the general disorder. Our superficiality and our inconstancy prevent us from seeing what an evil sin is; precisely because it strikes so deep it cannot be known by those who look only at the surface. In its manner of ravaging souls and society, sin is like one of those diseases which affect vital but hidden organs, and which the sufferer is ignorant of even while they near a crisis.

To experience salutary grief, grief for sin, it is necessary truly to love God whom sin offends and sinners whom it destroys. The saints suffered from sin in the degree in which they loved God and souls. St. Catherine of Siena recognized souls in the state of mortal sin by the insupportable odor which they exhaled. But to know just how far grief for sin can go, one must turn to the heart of Mary. Her grief sprang from an unequalled love for God, for Jesus crucified, and for souls—a love which surpassed that of the greatest saints, and even of all the saints united, a love which had never ceased to grow, a love which had never been restrained by the slightest fault or imperfection. If such was Mary's love, what must her grief have been! Unlike us who are so superficial, she saw with piercing clarity what it was that caused the loss of so many souls" the concupiscence of the flesh, the concupiscence of the eyes, the pride of life. All sins combined to add to her grief; all revolts against God, all outbursts of sacrilegious rage, such as that which reached its paroxysm in the cry "Crucify Him" and in utter hatred of Him who is the Light Divine and the Author of Salvation.

Mary's grief was deep as was her love, both natural and supernatural, of her Son. She loved Him with a virginal love, most pure and tender; loved Him as her only Son, miraculously conceived, and as her God.

To understand Mary's dolours, one would need to have received, as did the stigmatics, the impression of the wounds of the Saviour; one would need to have relived with the mystics His physical and moral sufferings, and to have shared with Him the hours of His Passion and Death. We shall try once more to speak of this matter when considering Mary as Mediatrix and Co-Redemptrix, and the reparation which she offered with, and by, and in her Son.

Mary's love in her dolours was meritorious for us and for her also. By her sufferings she grew in charity as well as in faith, and hope, and religion; she grew in fact in all the virtues—those of humility, and meekness, and supernatural courage suggesting themselves especially to the mind. Her virtue in suffering was heroic in the highest degree. Thereby she became Queen of Martyrs.

On the hill of Calvary, grace and charity overflowed from the Heart of Jesus to the heart of His mother. He it was who sustained her, just as it was she who sustained St. John. Jesus offered up her martyrdom as well as His own, and she offered herself with her Son, who was more dear to her than her own life. If the least of the acts of Nazareth increased Mary's charity, what must have been the effect of her participation in the Cross of Jesus!

Pentecost

The glorious resurrection of Our Saviour and His different apparitions all marked new stages in Mary's spiritual growth. She saw in them the realization of so many of Jesus' prophecies. She saw in them too His victory over death, a sign of Good Friday's victory over Satan.

The mystery of the Ascension raised Mary's thoughts still higher heavenwards. The evening of that day, when she withdrew to the Supper-room with the Apostles (*Acts* 1:14) she must have felt, as they too did, how empty the world was without Jesus. The difficulty of converting the pagan world loomed up in all its magnitude. The presence of Our Lady helped the Apostles to face it. In union with Jesus she merited, *de congruo,* the graces they were about to receive in this room where the Blessed Eucharist had been instituted, where they had been ordained priests, and where the Master had appeared to them after His Resurrection.

The day of Pentecost comes. The Holy Ghost descends on Mary and on the Apostles in the form of tongues of fire, to give the final enlightenment concerning the mysteries of man's salvation, and to impart the strength needed for the immense and arduous task that awaited its accomplishment. On that day, the Apostles were confirmed in grace. St. Peter went forth to manifest by his preaching that he had received fullness of knowledge of the mystery of Jesus Christ, Saviour and Author of newness of life. One and all, from being fearful the apostles became courageous, rejoicing to suffer for the name of Jesus. How marvellous must not Mary's progress have been—she who was to be on earth, as it were, the heart of the infant Church!

Now that Jesus has ascended to Heaven no one will participate as she in His love for His Father and for souls. By her prayer, her contemplation, her ceaseless generosity, she will, in some way, sustain the souls of the Twelve, following them as a mother in the labours and difficulties of their apostolate, right up to the crown of martyrdom. They are her sons. The Church will later call her Queen of Apostles.

Even now she cares for them and makes their work fruitful by a continual oblation of herself in union with the sacrifice of Jesus perpetuated on the altar.

Mary, Model of Devotion to the Eucharist

It is most becoming to insist here a little on what Holy Mass and Holy Communion, received from the hands of St. John, must have meant for Our Blessed Lady.

Why had Mary been committed to St. John on Calvary rather than to the holy women who were also at the foot of the Cross? The reason was that St. John was a priest and had a treasure which they could not give her, the treasure of the Eucharist.

Why among the Apostles was John chosen rather than Peter? One reason is that John alone remained at the Cross, drawn and held there by a strong sweet grace. Another is that he is, as St. Augustine remarks, the model of the contemplative life, of the interior and hidden life which had always been that of Mary and which would be hers till death. Mary's life will be cast in a very different mould from that of Peter, for she will have no share in ruling the Church. Her vocation will be to contemplate and to love Our Saviour in His sacramental presence, and to obtain by her unceasing prayer the spread of the faith and the salvation of souls. She will be thus in a very real sense the heart of the infant Church, for none other will enter as she into the depths and the strength of the love of Jesus.[46]

Let us consider her in this hidden life, especially at the hour when John celebrated Holy Mass in her presence. Mary has not the priestly character; she cannot perform the priestly functions. But she has received, in the words of M. Olier, "the plenitude of the priestly spirit", which is the spirit of Christ the Redeemer. Thus she is able to penetrate deeper than St. John himself into the meaning of the mysteries he celebrates. Besides, her dignity of Mother of God is greater than that of ordained priest; she has given us both the Priest and the Victim of the sacrifice of the Cross and she has offered herself with Him.

Holy Mass was for her, in a degree we can only suspect, the memorial and the continuation of the sacrifice of the Cross. A sword of sorrow had pierced her

---

46. St. Thomas says, IIIa, q. 8, a. 1, ad 3, speaking of the Mystical Body of Christ: "The head has evident superiority over the members, whereas the heart exercises a hidden influence. That is why the Holy Ghost who vivifies and unifies the Church invisibly is compared to the heart, and Christ, in His visible nature, is compared to the head." From another point of view, we say that the Holy Ghost is like the soul of the Church, since the invisible soul is whole in the whole body and whole in each of its parts, though exercising its higher functions in the head. Mary's influence has been well compared to that of the heart, since it remains hidden, and since it is principally of the affective order—the influence of a mother.

heart on Calvary, the strength and tenderness of her love for Jesus making her suffer a true martyrdom. She suffered so much that the memory of Calvary could never grow dim, and each Holy Mass was a fresh renewal of all she lived through there. Mary found the same Victim on the altar when John said Mass. She found the same Jesus, really present; not present in image only, but in the substance of His Body with His Soul and Divinity. True, there was no immolation in blood, but there was a sacramental immolation, realised through the separate consecration of the bread and the wine: Jesus' blood is shed sacramentally on the altar. How expressive is that figure of His death for her who cannot forget, for her who bears always in the depths of her soul the image of her Son, outraged and wounded, for her who hears yet the insults and the blasphemies offered Him. St. John's Mass, with Mary present at it, was the most striking memorial of the Cross as it is perpetuated in its substance on our altars.

Mary Found in the Sacrifice of the Mass the Point of Contact of the Cults of Heaven and Earth

It is the same Victim who is offered at Holy Mass and who, in Heaven, offers His glorious wounds to the Heavenly Father. The Body of Christ never ceases to be in Heaven, it is true. It does not come down from Heaven, in the strict sense of the terms, on to the altar. But, without being multiplied. It is made really present by the transubstantiation of the substance of the bread and the wine into Itself.

There is the same principal priest, or offerer, in Heaven and on earth also, "always living to make intercession for us." (*Heb.* 7:25). The celebrant of the Mass is but a minister who speaks in Jesus' name. When he says "This is my body" it is Jesus who speaks by him.

It is Jesus who, as God, gives to the words their power of transubstantiation. It is Jesus as Man who, by an act of His holy soul, transmits the divine power and who continues to offer Himself thus for us as principal priest. If the human minister ever happens to be slightly distracted, the principal Offerer is not distracted, and Jesus as Man, continuing to offer Himself sacramentally for us, sees all that we miss—sees all the spiritual influence exercised by each Mass on the faithful present and absent, and on the souls in Purgatory.

Jesus continues to offer Himself in each Mass, the actual offering being made through the hands of His minister. The soul of the sacrifice of our altars is the interior oblation which is always a living reality in His Sacred Heart; through that oblation He applies to us continually the merits and satisfaction of Calvary. The saints have sometimes seen Jesus in the priest's place at the moment of consecration. Mary knew the full truth better than any of the saints. Better than any of them she knew that the soul of every Mass was the oblation that lived in her Son's Heart. She understood too that when, this world having reached its term, the last Mass would have been said, Jesus' interior oblation would continue for ever, not now as supplication but as adoration and thanksgiving—as the eternal cult expressed even now at Mass by the *Sanctus* in honor of the thrice-holy God.

How did Mary unite herself to the oblation of Jesus, the principal priest She united herself to it, as we shall explain later, as universal Mediatrix and Co-Redemptrix. She continued to unite herself to it as at the foot of the Cross—in a spirit of adoring reparation, in petition and thanksgiving.

Model of victim-souls, she offered up the anguish she suffered at those denials of the divinity of Jesus which prompted St. John to write his fourth Gospel. She offered thanks for the institution of the Blessed

Eucharist and for all the benefits of which It is the source. She prayed for the conversion of sinners, for the progress of the good, for the help the Apostles needed in their work and their sufferings.

In all that Mary is our model, teaching us how to become adorers in spirit and in truth.

What shall we say of Mary's communions? The principal condition for a fervent communion is to hunger for the Eucharist. The saints hungered for It. When Holy Communion was denied St. Catherine of Siena, her desires obtained that a portion of the large Host broke off unknown to the celebrant and was carried miraculously to the saint. But Mary's hunger for the Eucharist was incomparably greater and more intense than that of the saints. Let us contemplate reverently the strong loving desire which drew Mary to Jesus in the Blessed Sacrament.

Every soul is drawn towards God, for He is the Sovereign Good for whom we have been made. But the consequences of sin—original and actual—and of innumerable imperfections make God appear unattractive in our eyes and weaken our inborn desire for union with Him. Mary's soul, however, knew nothing of the consequences of sins and imperfections; nothing ever checked the Godwards tendency of her wonderful charity. Forgetting herself, Mary turned firmly towards God, with a firmness that grew daily as did her merits. The Holy Ghost dwelling in her moved her to give herself to God and to be united to Him. Her love of God, like an intense thirst, was accompanied by a sweet suffering which ceased only when she died of love and entered on the union of eternity. Such was her desire of the Eucharist.

Jesus for His part desired most ardently to consummate Mary's holiness, to communicate to her the overflowing riches of His Sacred Heart. If He could suffer in glory, He would suffer from the resistance we offer to the same desire He has in our regard. But He found no resistance in Mary. And so He was able to communicate Himself to her in the most intimate way possible for two lives to be fused into one on earth: Jesus' union with Mary was a reflection of the sanctifying union of the Word with the Sacred Humanity, an image of the communion of the Three Divine Persons in the one infinite Truth and the one limitless Goodness.

Mary became again the pure living tabernacle of the Lord when she communicated—a tabernacle which knew and loved; one a thousand times more precious than any golden ciborium; a true tower of ivory, house of gold, and ark of the alliance.

What were the effects of Mary's communion? They surpassed anything St. Teresa recounts of transforming union in the Seventh Mansion of the Interior Castle. Transforming union has been compared, in its power to transform the soul in some way into God by knowledge and love, to the union of fire with a piece of iron, or that of light with the air it illumines. Rays of supernatural warmth and light came forth from the soul of Jesus and communicated themselves to Mary's intellect and will. Mary could not take the credit to herself for the sublime effects they produced in her. Rather did she give praise on their account to Him who was their principle and end: "He that eateth me, the same also shall live by me;" he who eats my flesh lives by me and for me, just as I live by my Father and for my Father.

Each of Mary's communions surpassed the preceding one in fervour and, producing in her a great increase of charity, disposed her to receive her next communion with still greater fruit. Mary's soul moved ever more swiftly Godwards the nearer she approached to God; that was her law of spiritual gravitation. She was, as it were, a mirror which reflected back on Jesus the light and warmth which she received from Him; concentrated them also, so as to direct them towards souls.

In everything she was the perfect model of Eucharistic devotion. If we turn to her she will teach us how to adore and to make reparation; she will teach us what should be our desire of the Blessed Eucharist. From here we can learn how to pray at Holy Mass for the great intentions of the Church, and how to thank God for the graces without number He has bestowed on us and on mankind.

Article 6

Mary's Intellectual Endowments and her Principal Virtues

To understand Mary's fullness of grace, especially towards the end of her life on earth, it is necessary to examine the perfection of her intellect. We must consider her faith, enlightened by the gifts of Wisdom, Understanding and Knowledge. It will be necessary then to pass on to a consideration of some of her principal virtues, which, through their connection with her charity, were in her soul in a degree proportionate to her fullness of grace. To conclude this section we shall glance briefly at the gratuitous gifts of intellect which she received, particularly those of prophecy and the discernment of spirits.

Mary's Faith Enlightened by the Gifts

The natural perfection of Mary's soul resulted in very great powers of penetration in her intellect, as well as moral rectitude in her will and her lower faculties. These natural endowments continued to develop throughout the course of her life.

As regards her faith, it perceived its object in an exceptionally penetrating manner because of the revelation made to her at the Annunciation concerning the mysteries of the Incarnation and the Redemption, and because also of her daily intercourse with the Word made Flesh. Subjectively also her faith was remarkable, being strong, certain and prompt in its assent. In fact, Mary received the virtue of faith in the highest degree in which it was infused into any soul on earth, and the same must be said of her hope also. Jesus, having the beatific vision from the first instant of His conception, had neither faith nor hope: to Him belonged the full light of vision and full undelayed possession.

Hence, the sublimity of Mary's faith surpasses our understanding. She did not hesitate at the Annunciation but believed at once the very moment the mystery of the redemptive Incarnation was sufficiently proposed to her, so that St. Elisabeth can say soon after: "And blessed art thou that hast believed, because these things shall be accomplished that were spoken to thee by the Lord." In Bethlehem she sees her Son born in a stable and believes that He is the Creator of the world; she sees all the weakness of His infant body and believes in His omnipotence; when He commences to essay His first words she believes His infinite wisdom; when the Holy Family takes flight from Herod's anger she believes that Jesus is the King of Kings and Lord of Lords, as St. John would later say. At the Circumcision and the Presentation in the Temple her faith in the mystery of the Redemption expands. Her whole life on earth was passed in a dark brightness, the darkness arising not from human error and ignorance but from the very transcendence of the light itself—a darkness which was, in consequence, revealing of the heights of the mysteries contemplated by the blessed in Heaven.

She is at the foot of the Cross on Calvary, though all the Apostles, St. John only excepted, have fled; she stands erect there, firm in her faith that her Son is the Son of God, that He is the Lamb of God who is even then taking away the sins of the world, that though apparently defeated, He is Victor over Satan and sin, and that in three days He will conquer death by His resurrection. Mary's act of faith on Calvary was the greatest ever elicited on earth, for the hour was unspeakably dark and its object was the most difficult of all—that Jesus had won the greatest of victories by making the most complete of immolations.

Her faith was aided then by the gifts of the Holy Ghost. By the gift of Understanding she read far into the revealed mysteries, far into their inner meaning, their harmony, their appropriateness, their consequences. She was particularly favored in her understanding of the mysteries in which she herself had a part to play, such as the virginal conception of Christ, His Incarnation, and the whole economy of the Redemption. Brought as she had been into close contact with the Three Divine Persons, the mystery of the Blessed Trinity revealed more of its depths to her than to any other mere human being.

By the gift of Wisdom the Holy Ghost enabled her to judge the things of God through a certain connaturality or sympathy which is based on charity.[47] She knew therefore in an experimental manner how truly the great mysteries answer to our highest aspirations, and how grace continually awakens new desires in us so as to prepare the way for clearer light and more burning love. She relished the mysteries in the measure of her ever-growing charity, her humility, and her purity. In her were verified most strikingly the words "God gives His grace to the humble . . . Blessed are the pure of heart, for they shall see God." Even on earth the pure have some vision of their Father in Heaven.

By the gift of Knowledge the Holy Ghost taught her to judge temporal things, at times as symbols of eternal and divine things (as, for example, to see the heavens

---

47. Cf. IIa IIae, q. 45, a. 2.

telling the glory of God) or again in their nothingness and frailty so as to appreciate eternal life all the more by contrast.

Special Privileges of Her Intellect

Besides faith and the gifts of the Holy Ghost which all the faithful have as part of their spiritual organism, Mary, like many of the saints, had the *gratiae gratis datae,* or *charismata* which are given principally for the benefit of others rather than for the benefit of the person who receives them. These *charismata* are exterior signs having as purpose to confirm revelation or holiness, rather than fresh forms of sanctity. That is why they are distinct from grace, the infused virtues, and the gifts, all of which belong to a higher order.[48]

Regarding the *charismata,* theologians usually admit the principle: Mary received all privileges which it was becoming for her to receive, and which were not incompatible with her state, in a higher degree than the saints did. In other words, we cannot conceive of her as being inferior to the saints in the matter of *charismata,* seeing how much she surpassed them in the matter of holiness.

The principle is not, however, to be taken in a material sense. If, for example, certain saints have lived long months without food, if they have walked on the waters to come to another's aid, it does not follow that Mary did the same; it is enough if she received grace of a higher order in which such lower graces were contained and surpassed.[49] At the same time, in virtue of the principle just now enunciated, we must assert that she had certain *charismata,* either certainly or very probably.

First of all, she had by a special privilege a knowledge of the Scriptures greater than that of any of the

---

48. Cf. Ia IIae, q. III, a. 5.
49. Cf. E. Dublanchy, *Dict. de Théol. Cath.,* article *Marie,* cols. 2367-2368; 2409-2413.

saints, particularly in what concerned the Messiah, the redemptive Incarnation, the Blessed Trinity, the life of grace and of the virtues, and the life of eternity. And even though Mary did not receive the commission to share in the official ministry of the Church, she must have enlightened St. John and St. Luke concerning the infancy and the hidden life of Jesus.[50]

She must have known in a clear and penetrating manner all that was useful about objects of the natural order. Though she need not have known the chemical formula of such things as salt or water, it would still be possible for her to know their natural properties, and still more their higher symbolism. For Mary's knowledge of natural objects was of the kind which throws light upon the great religious and moral truths, such as the existence of God, His universal Providence extending to the minutest details, the spirituality and immortality of the soul, free will and moral responsibility, the principles and conclusions of the moral law, the relation between nature and grace. She saw clearly the finality of nature, the order of creation, and the subordination of every created cause to the First Cause. She saw that every good thing comes from God, even the free determination of our salutary and meritorious acts; she saw too that no one person would be better than another were he not more loved by God—a principle which is at the root of all humility and thanksgiving.

The knowledge which Mary had while still on earth had limits, especially at the beginning. She did not, for example, understand the full import of what Jesus said about His Father's business when she found Him in the Temple. But, as has been often said, the limits were limits, not gaps. Hence she was in no sense ignorant, for the limits did not deprive her of the knowl-

---

50. Cajetan remarks in his commentary on the IIIa, q. 27, a. 5: "Posset tamen dici quod non publica doctrina, sed familiari instructione, quam constat mulieribus non esse prohibitam, B. Virgo aliqua particularia facta explicavit Apostolis." This she did better and more frequently than Mary Magdalen, who obtained the title *Apostolorum apostola* through having announced the Resurrection to the Apostles.

edge of anything she should have known at the time. God's Mother knew at every stage of her life all that it was becoming for her to know.

Nor was she subject to error. She was never precipitate in judging; if she had not sufficient light she suspended her judgement; if she was not sure about a thing she was satisfied to affirm that it was likely or probable. For example, when she thought it likely that Jesus was not in the company of her friends and relatives on the occasion when she lost Him, her belief was a very likely one indeed—though in point of fact it was not true—and in looking on it as likely Mary did not err.

We have seen earlier (Chapter II, art. 5) that it is very probable that she had infused knowledge from the time she was in her mother's womb. We have seen too that it is equally probable that she was never deprived of it in the course of her life, and that many theologians hold that she had the use of it even during her sleeping hours.

Among Mary's gratuitous gifts we must include that of prophecy. An example of its exercise can be found in the *Magnificat:* "For behold from henceforth all generations shall call me blessed." The realization of this prophecy in the course of ages is as evident as is the meaning of the words themselves. It is more than likely that this was not the only occasion on which Mary used her prophetic gift since prophecy is so common among the saints, as for example St. John Bosco and the Cure of Ars.[51]

Finally, she had, like so many saints, the gift of discernment of spirits, by which to recognise the spirit of

---

51. For this same reason many theologians teach that Mary had, particularly after the Ascension, the gift of miraculous healing and that she used it to lighten the sorrows of the afflicted and to help the unfortunate who had recourse to her or whom she met. She was on earth the consoler of the afflicted in such a manner as to manifest her great sanctity. This was the opinion of St. Albert the Great, St. Antoninus, and Suarez, and is common in most of the present-day manuals of Mariology.

God and to distinguish it from diabolical illusion and natural exaltation. It enabled her also to read the secrets of hearts, especially when someone came to ask counsel of her. Thus her advice was always sound, opportune and practical.

Many theologians hold that Mary had the gift of tongues when she travelled in foreign countries—in Egypt, for example, and also in Ephesus.[52] There is still greater reason for believing that she had this gift after the Assumption, for in her apparitions at Lourdes and La Salette and elsewhere she spoke the dialect of the district—the only one understood by those to whom she appeared.

The question has been asked if Mary enjoyed on earth—even for a few instants—the face to face vision of the divine essence as the blessed in Heaven do. On one point theologians are unanimous against Vega and Franciscus Verra: unlike her Divine Son, she had not that vision in a permanent way on earth, for if she had it permanently she would not have had the virtue of faith. But it is more difficult to say whether or not she enjoyed the beatific vision from time to time. It is true that she must have had an intellectual vision of the Trinity higher than that described by St. Teresa in the Seventh Mansion. But the vision of which St. Teresa speaks does not transcend faith, and is therefore immeasurably inferior to that of the blessed.

Some light is thrown on the problem by what we know of St. Paul. St. Augustine and St. Thomas[53] teach that it is probable that St. Paul enjoyed the beatific vision momentarily when, in his own words, he was "caught up to the third Heaven . . . and heard secret words which it is not given to man to utter" (*2 Cor.* 12:2). The two great doctors both mention that according to the Jews the third Heaven was not merely the higher air,

---

52. Such was the teaching of St. Albert the Great, St. Antoninus, Gerson, Suarez, Cornelius a Lapide. Many modern theologians are of the same opinion.
53. IIa IIae, q. 175, a. 3.

but the spiritual Heaven inhabited by God, where He is seen face to face by the angels—Paradise, as St. Paul says in the same context. Hence they conclude that St. Paul, having been called to be the Doctor of the Gentiles and of grace, was probably favored by a brief moment of the beatific vision, since grace cannot be understood fully without having seen the glory of which it is the beginning. The authority of two such doctors, themselves favored with mystical graces and thus especially competent to speak of such matters, is sufficient to constitute serious probability. It must, however, be admitted that neither Estius nor Cornelius a Lapide accepts such an exegesis of St. Paul's text. Modern commentators tend to be non-committal.

To return to Our Lady, we agree entirely with Fr Hugon when he states that if it is probable that St. Paul enjoyed the beatific vision momentarily, it is difficult to see why the same should not be said of Our Blessed Lady,[54] for her divine maternity, her fullness of grace, and her freedom from every stain disposed her more perfectly than any saint for the beatitude of eternity. Hence, even if it is not certain that she had moments of the beatific vision, it remains very probable.[55]

This brief survey will suffice to give some idea of the rich intellectual gifts which Mary enjoyed on earth.

Mary's Principal Virtues

We have spoken already of her faith. A few words may now be said of her hope and her charity, as well as of the cardinal virtues and the virtues of humility and meekness.

Her hope, by which she tended to the possession of

---

54. *Marie, pleine de grâce,* 5th edit., 1926, pp. 106 sqq.
55. Cf. E. Dublanchy, *Dict. Théol. Cath.,* article *Marie,* col. 2410: "Probably conferred on Moses and St. Paul, the favor should be attributed to Mary also on the principle which allows us to attribute to her as Mother of God and Co-Redemptrix or universal Mediatrix every grace conferred on the other saints and in keeping with her dignity."

God whom she did not as yet fully possess, was a perfect confidence and trust which relied not on self but on the divine mercy and omnipotence. It was therefore sure.[56] And its sureness was increased by the gift of Piety. For Piety awakens in us a filial attitude to God, and by it the Holy Ghost "giveth testimony to our spirit that we are the sons of God" (*Rom.* 8:16) and assures us that we can count on His assistance. It was increased also by the fact that Mary was confirmed in grace and preserved free from every shortcoming—lack of confidence as well as presumption.

Some of the occasions for the exercise of hope in Mary's life spring at once to the mind. She exercised it when, yet a child, she awaited the coming of the Messiah and the salvation of all peoples; again, when she awaited the time that the secret of the virginal conception would be revealed to St. Joseph; again, when she fled into Egypt; again—and most of all— when on Calvary all seemed lost, but she awaited the victory which her Son had foretold He would win over death. Finally, her confidence, her unshaken hope, sustained the Apostles in their ceaseless labours for the spread of the Gospel and the conversion of the pagan world.

Her charity—her love of God in Himself and of souls for His sake—surpassed even in its beginnings the charity of all the saints combined, for it was of the same degree as her fullness of grace. Mary was always most intimately united to the Father as His best-beloved daughter, to the Son as His Virgin Mother, and to the Holy Ghost in a mystic marriage more perfect than the world had ever known. She was, in a way beyond all power of understanding, a living temple of the Trinity, loved by God more than all creatures, and corresponding perfectly with that love by consecrating herself fully to Him in the instant of her conception,

---

56. Cf. IIa, IIae, q. 18, a. 4.

and by living thenceforth in the most complete conformity to His Will.

No disordered passion, no vain fear, no distraction, checked the surge of her love for God. Her love for souls was of the same intensity, she offered her Son and herself unceasingly for souls.

The pages of the Gospel call many occasions to mind when her charity must have burned with a special flame—the Annunciation, the finding of Jesus after the three days' loss, Calvary. . . . Well may the Church apply to Mary the words of Ecclesiasticus (*Eccl.* 24:24): "I am the mother of fair love, and of fear, and of knowledge, and of holy hope."

The moral infused virtues are in all souls in the state of grace in the degree of their charity: prudence in the intellect, to make their judgement right in accordance with God's law; justice in their will to prompt them to give every one his due; fortitude and temperance in their sensitive nature to bring it into conformity with reason and faith. The acquired virtues—which bear the same names—facilitate the exercise of the corresponding infused virtues.

Mary's prudence directed all her actions undeviatingly towards her supernatural destiny. All her actions were deliberate and meritorious. Thus the Church calls her the Virgin most prudent. Aided by the gift of Counsel she exercised prudence in a notable manner at the Annunciation when, troubled at the angel's word, she wondered what his salutation could mean, and again when she asked "How shall this be done, because I know not man?" Nor was her prudence less when, the angel having explained his mission, she accepted God's will: "Behold the handmaid of the Lord; be it done to me according to thy word."

She practiced justice in its highest form—that is to say, justice in regard to God, which is the virtue of religion aided by the gift of Piety—when she consecrated herself to God in the first instant of her being.

She practiced it also by her vow of virginity, her presentation of Jesus to His Father in the Temple, and her final offering of Him on the Cross. On Calvary she offered the greatest act of the virtue of religion in union with Jesus, the perfect sacrifice and the holocaust of infinite value.

Justice was always wedded to mercy in Mary. As did her Son, she forgave all the wrongs done to her and showed the greatest compassion for sinners. Then, as now, she was the Mother of Mercy, Our Lady of Perpetual Succour. The words of the psalmist find in her their realisation: "The earth is full of the mercy of God."

Fortitude, that firmness of soul which can withstand the greatest dangers, the most difficult tasks, and the cruellest afflictions, was found in Mary in a no less eminent degree than the other virtues. At the foot of the Cross she did not flinch nor weaken, but stood courageously, as St. John tells us. Cajetan wrote a special tract, *De spasmo Virginis,* refuting the idea that Mary fainted on the road to Calvary. In this he was at one with Medina, Toletus, Suarez and with theologians generally, who all agree that Mary did not collapse under her grief. By her courageous bearing of trials Mary merited to be called Queen of Martyrs. She shared more intimately in Jesus' suffering by her inner union with Him than did all the martyrs by their exterior afflictions. This thought is called to mind by the Church on the Feast of the Compassion of Our Lady and the Feast of the Seven Dolours, particularly in the *Stabat Mater:*

Fac ut portem Christi mortem, *Passionis fac consortem* *Et plagas recolere.*	Let me to my latest breath, In my body bear the death Of that dying Son of thine.
Fac me plagis vulnerari,	Wounded with His every wound,

Fac me cruce inebriari,   Steep my soul till it hath
Et cruore Filii   swoon'd
                                  In His very blood away.
                                       —*Fr. Caswall.*

Temperance in its different forms, especially in that of perfect virginity, appeared in her angelic purity. In Mary the soul reigned over the body, the higher faculties over the senses. The image of God was reflected in her as in a mirror.

Her humility never had to struggle against the slightest movement of pride or vanity. She recognized that of herself she was nothing and could do nothing in the supernatural order. Therefore she bowed down before the Divine Majesty and before all that there was of God in creation. She placed all her greatness in God alone, realising thus the words of the Missal: *Deus humilium celsitudo.*

At the Annunciation she speaks of herself as the handmaid of the Lord, and in the *Magnificat* she thanks the Most High for having regarded her lowliness. On the day of the Purification she submits to a law which did not bind her. Her whole life long, humility was manifested in her bearing, her modesty, her voluntary poverty, in the lowly tasks she performed—and all that, even though she had received graces as no other mere human ever did.

The Liturgy reminds us too of her meekness: *Virgo singularis, inter omnes mitis.* She uttered no word of reproach against those who crucified Jesus, but in union with Him she forgave them and prayed for them. Here we have meekness at its highest united to consummate fortitude.

Such are, then, the intellectual endowments and the principal virtues with which Mary was adorned. They made her a model of the contemplative life, one characterised by devotion to the Incarnate Word, and, through participation in His redemptive work, one in whom we find the most universal of all hidden apostolates.[57]

What we have said in this chapter about Mary's principal virtues and her intellectual endowments shows in a concrete way the general plan of her spiritual progress. It remains to speak in the next chapter of her final fullness of grace at the moment of her death and of her entry into Heaven. We shall, then, have followed the stages of her spiritual life from her Immaculate Conception to her final glorification, a life which in its progress resembles a river rising at a great height and causing the fertility of the regions through which it passes, before it plunges at length into the mighty ocean.

---

57. For a treatment of Mary's virtues cf. Justin de Miéchow, O.P.; R. Bernard, O.P., *Le Mystère de Marie,* Paris, 1933; Rambaud, O.P., *Douce Vierge Marie,* Lyons, 1939; Journet in *Notre Dame des Sept Douleurs;* Lallement and Sertillanges in *Mater Misericordiae.*

∽ Chapter 4 ∽

The Final Plenitude of Mary's Grace

T HE plan of this chapter will be: to speak first of Mary's fullness of grace at the time of her death; then to recall the teaching of the Church concerning her Assumption;* finally to treat of her fullness of grace as it unfolded itself in Heaven.

Article 1

Mary's Fullness of Grace at the Moment of Death

Bossuet remarks[1] that Mary was left in the world after Jesus to console the Church. This she did by her prayers and ever-increasing merits which were the support of the Apostles in their labours and trials as well as the hidden source of the fecundity of all they did for souls.

We have seen already that in Mary's case death was not a consequence of original sin, but simply of human nature as such. Man was not made immortal at the beginning otherwise than by a special privilege. The Incarnate Word willed to take passible flesh.[2] Mary's flesh was passible too. Thus the deaths of Jesus and Mary were consequences of the inherent weakness of human nature left to itself and unsustained by any preternatural gift. Jesus, however, mastered death by accepting it for our salvation. Mary united herself to Him in His death, making for us the sacrifice of His life in the most generous martyrdom of heart the world has ever known after that of Our Saviour. And when, later on, the hour of her own death arrived, the sacrifice of her life had been already made. It remained but to renew it in that most perfect form which tradition speaks of as the death of love, a death, that is to say, in which the soul dies not simply in grace or in God's love, but *of* a calm and supremely strong love which draws the soul, now ripe for Heaven, away from the body to be united to God in immediate and eternal vision.

Mary's last moments are described by St. John Damascene[3] in the words "She died an extremely peaceful death." St. Francis de Sales' chapters in his treatise on the Love of God (ch. 13 and 14) are an eloquent commentary on the words of St. John Damascene:

"The Blessed Virgin, Mother of God, died of love for her Son. . . . It is impossible to conceive of her death as having been anything except a death of love, which is the most noble of all deaths and the fitting crown of the most noble of all lives. . . . If the early Christians were said to have but one heart and one soul because of their perfect mutual love, if St. Paul lived no longer for himself but Christ lived in him because of the intense union of his heart with the heart of his Master . . . how much more true is it that the Blessed Virgin and her Son had but one soul, one heart, and one life . . . so that her Son lived in her. Mother most loving and most loved that could be . . . of a love incomparably higher than that of angels and men in the measure in which the titles of only mother and only Son arc higher than all names that are united in love.

But if this mother lived by the life of her Son, she died also by His death; for as the life is, so is the death. . . . Retaining in her memory all the most lovable mysteries of the life and death of her Son, and receiving always the most ardent inspirations which her Son, the Sun of Justice, poured out on men in the noonday ardor of His charity . . . she was at length con-

---

3. *Homiliae duae de dormitione Virginis Mariae.* Cf. also St. Brigid of Sweden, *Revelations,* Bk. VI, c. 62.

sumed by the sacred fire of this charity, as a holocaust
of sweetness. And thus she died, her soul ravished and
transported in the arms of the love of Jesus. . . .

She died of a most sweet and tranquil love. . . . The
love of God increased every moment in the virginal
heart of our glorious Lady, but in a sweet, peaceful,
and continuous way, without agitation, nor shocks, nor
any violence . . . like a great river which, finding no
obstacles in the level plain, flows along effortlessly.

Just as iron, if not hindered, is drawn strongly but
sweetly by the magnet, and the attraction increases
according as it is drawn more close to it, so the Blessed
Virgin, being in no way hindered in the operation of
the love of her Son, united herself to Him in an incomparable union by sweet, peaceful and effortless
ecstasies. . . . So that the death of the Virgin was more
peaceful than we can conceive, her Son drawing her
gently by the odor of His ointments. . . . Love had
caused Mary the pangs of death on Calvary; it was
only just, then, that death should cause her the highest delights of love."

Bossuet, in his turn, voices the same sentiments in
his first sermon for the Feast of the Assumption.

"If to love Jesus and to be loved by Jesus are two
things which draw down the divine blessing on souls,
what a sea of graces must have inundated the soul of
Mary. Who can describe the impetuosity of that mutual
love in which all that is tender in nature concurred
with all that is efficacious in grace? Jesus never tired
of seeing Himself loved by His Mother: Mary never
thought she had had enough of the love of her Son.
She asked no grace from her Son except that of loving Him, and that fact drew down more graces on her.

Compare, if you can, with her love the holy impa-
tience she experienced to be united to her Son. . . . St.
Paul wished to burst at once the bond of the flesh so
as to be with his Master at the right hand of the

Father, and how much greater must have been the longing of a maternal heart! The absence of a year was enough to pierce the heart of the mother of Tobias with sorrow, and what must have been the regret of Mary when she felt herself so long separated from a Son she loved so well! When she saw St. Stephen and so many others depart from this world she must well have asked her Son why He wished to leave her the last of all. He had brought her to the foot of the Cross to see Him suffer, and would He delay to allow her to see Him enthroned? If only He would allow her love its way, it would soon withdraw her soul from her body to unite it to Him in whom she lived.

That love was so ardent, so strong, so inflamed, that not a desire for Heaven sprang from it which was not capable of drawing with it Mary's soul.

Thus, Mary yielded her holy and blessed soul peacefully and without violence into the hands of her Son. Just as the least touch gathers the ripe fruit, so was gathered her blessed soul, to be at once carried to Heaven; thus the divine Virgin died in a movement of the love of God."

That holy death reveals the final fullness of Mary's grace, a fullness which corresponded wonderfully to that initial fullness which had not ceased to grow from the moment of the Immaculate Conception. It disposed her for the consummated fullness of Heaven which is always proportionate to the merits acquired at the moment of death.

Article 2

The Assumption of the Blessed Virgin

What is meant by the Assumption? The whole Church understands by the term that the Blessed Virgin, soon after her death and glorious resurrection, was taken up body and soul to Heaven to be forever throned above the angels and saints. The term Assumption is used rather than Ascension since, unlike Jesus who ascended to Heaven by His own power, Mary was lifted up by God to the degree of glory for which she had been predestined.

Was the Assumption capable of being perceived by the senses, and if there were witnesses—the Apostles and St. John in particular—had they ocular evidence of it? Certainly there was something of the sense-perceptible order about the Assumption, since it was the taking up of Mary's body to Heaven. But the term of that taking up, that is, the entry to Heaven and the exaltation of Mary above all the saints, was invisible and inaccessible to the senses.

It can be admitted that did certain witnesses find the tomb of the Mother of God empty after her burial, and did they later witness her resurrection and her being raised up in the skies, they would have been able to presume that she entered Heaven and that Our Blessed Lord had associated her with the glory of His Ascension. But a presumption is not certitude. Mary's body could have been transported, for all their evidence proved, into a place not visible to human eyes— to the place, for example, in which Jesus' risen body was between His different apparitions.

But if a presumption is not certitude, how was Our Lady's entry into Heaven ever known with certainty? For that a divine revelation was required. St. Thomas remarks that there was such a revelation in the case of the Ascension[4] made through the intermediary of

4. IIIa, q. 55, a. 2, ad 2.

the angels who said: "Ye men of Galilee, why stand
you looking up to Heaven? This Jesus who is taken up
from you to Heaven, shall so come, as you have seen
him going into Heaven." (*Acts* 1:2).

Besides, without a divine revelation, the Assumption
would not be capable of being defined a dogma of faith,
since the motive of faith is the authority of God in revelation. A private revelation would not however be sufficient. Private revelations—those made to St. Joan of
Arc, to St. Bernadette, to the little shepherds of La
Salette, are examples of private revelations—could
become well known and public in that sense. But they
are not public in the sense of being part of the common
deposit of revelation and proposed infallibly by the
Church to all the faithful. Neither would a revelation
of the kind made to St. Margaret Mary be sufficient.
For her revelations were private too, and did no more
than to draw attention to certain practical consequences
of what was already known to be an object of faith—
the already accepted truth that the Sacred Heart of
Jesus is entitled to adoration or the cult of latria.

Hence, that the Assumption should have been known
as certain and capable of being proposed to the whole
Church for acceptance, a public revelation must have
been made to the Apostles, or at least to one of them—
to St. John, for example. Note that this revelation must
have been made to an Apostle since the deposit of common and public revelation was completed with the death
of the last Apostle. It may have been made explicitly
or implicitly. In this latter case its message would have
become more explicit in the course of time.

Let us now see what we have to learn from Tradition, and also the theological arguments which have
been commonly invoked, at least since the 7th century.

1st—The documents of Tradition show that the privilege was at least implicitly revealed.

It is not possible to prove directly from Sacred Scripture nor from primitive documents that the privilege of

the Assumption was revealed explicitly to any of the Apostles, for no text of scripture affirms it explicitly, and there is a similar absence of explicit testimony in the primitive documents. But it can be proved indirectly from later documents that there was at least an implicit revelation since there are certain facts, dating from the 7th century, which are explicable in no other way.

From the 7th century, almost the whole Church, east and west, celebrated the Feast of the Assumption. Pope Sergius (687-707) ordered a solemn procession on that day.[5] Many theologians and liturgists contend that it existed already before the time of St. Gregory the Great (d. 604) and they quote in support of their opinion the Collect of the Mass of the Assumption contained in the Sacramentary known as Gregorian (though it is probably later in date) where we read the words: "Nec tamen mortis nexibus deprimi potuit."[6] St. Gregory of Tours seems to imply that the Feast was celebrated in Gaul in the 6th century.[7] At any rate, it was certainly celebrated there in the 7th century as is proved by the *Missale Gothicum* and the *Missale Gallicanum vetus,* which date from the beginning of that century and contain very beautiful prayers for the Feast. *(P. L., t. LXXII, col. 245-246.)*

In the East the historian Nicephorus Callistus[8] recounts that the Emperor Maurice (582-602), contemporary and friend of St. Gregory the Great, ordered the solemn celebration of the Feast on August 15th. The earliest testimony to the traditional faith of the East appears to be that of Saint Modestus, Patriarch of Jerusalem (d. 634), in his *Encomium in dormitionem Deiparae (P. G., t. LXXXVI, col. 3288 sqq.).* His account of the matter is that the Apostles were led to the

---

5. *Liber Pontificalis, P. L.,* t. CXXVIII, c. 898; in Duchesne's edit., t. I, p. 376.

6. *P. L.,* t. LXXVIII, col. 133.

7. "Dominus susceptum corpus (Virginis) sanctum in nube deferre jussit in paradisum ubi, nunc, resumpta anima, cum electis eius exultans, aeternitatis bonis nullo occasuris fine perfruitur." *(De gloria martyrum, c.* iv; *P. L.,* t. LXXI, col. 708.)

8. *H. E.,* l. XVII, c. xxviii; *P. G.,* t. CXLVII, col. 292.

Blessed Virgin by a divine inspiration and were present at the Assumption. After him, mention must be made of St. Andrew of Crete (d. 720), monk in Jerusalem and later Archbishop of Crete, the author of the homilies *In dormitionem Deiparae,*[9] of St. Germanus, Patriarch of Constantinople (d. 733), author of *In sanctam Dei Genitricis dormitionem,*[10] and finally of St. John Damascene (d. 760), author of *In dormitionem beatae Mariae Virginis.*[11]

There is no shortage of testimonies from the 8th century on. Those commonly quoted are Notker of St. Gall, Fulbert of Chartres, St. Peter Damien, St. Anselm, Hildebert, Peter Abelard, St. Bernard, Richard of St. Victor, St. Albert the Great, St. Bonaventure and St. Thomas.[12] The period between the 7th and the 9th centuries witnessed the development of the liturgy, theology, and preaching of the Assumption. Pope Leo IV instituted the octave of the Feast around the year 847. Authors then and in the succeeding periods regarded the object of the Feast not as a pious belief peculiar to this or that country, but as an integral part of the general tradition which went back in the Church to the earliest times. And not only the authors, but the Church herself voiced the same doctrine: the simple fact that the Church celebrated the Feast universally in East and West, usually on the 15th of August, shows that she considered the privilege of the Assumption to be a certain truth taught by her ordinary *magisterium,* that is to say, by all the bishops in union with the supreme pastor. For the faith of the Church is manifested in her prayer: *Lex orandi, lex credendi.* The doctrine of the Assumption has not yet been solemnly defined, but it is commonly asserted that it would be at least temerarious

---

9. *P. G.,* t. XCVII, col. 1053 sqq., 1081 sqq.
10. *P. G.,* t. XCVIII, col. 345 sqq.
11. *P. G.,* t. XCVI, col. 716.
12. Cf. Merkelbach, *Mariologia,* pp. 277 sqq.

or erroneous to deny it.[13] When some few authors proposed to change the Feast of the 15th of August, Benedict XIV answered: *Ecclesiam hanc amplexam esse
sententiam.*[14]

The attitude of the Church in regard to the doctrine
is not therefore simply one of tolerance: she proposes
it positively in the liturgy and in preaching both in the
East and the West. This universal agreement of the
whole Church in celebrating the solemn Feast shows
that her ordinary *magisterium* is at work. But the ordinary *magisterium* presupposes at least that the doctrine has been implicitly revealed: otherwise, as we
have seen, there could be no certainty that Mary had
entered Heaven. And we may go further still and assert
that it is probable that the revelation made to the Apostles, or to one of them, was even explicit, since otherwise it is hard to explain the universal tradition in the
East and the West from the 7th century at the latest,
which manifests itself in the celebration of the Feast.[15]
For if the revelation had been only implicit at the beginning, how could it happen that the different bishops
and theologians in the different parts of the Church,
both East and West, would agree that it was implicitly
revealed? For such agreement much preliminary work
and many preliminary councils would be required, of
which there is absolutely no record. Neither is there
any record of private revelations such as are sometimes
made in order to set the Church's official investigations
of the deposit of revelation in motion.

Up to the 6th century this privilege of Mary's was
hidden behind a veil of silence, lest it be misunder-
stood through an unfortunate confusion with the fables

---

13. The doctrine has been defined since this was written. (Translator's note.)
14. *De Canoniz. Sanct.*, l. I, c. 42, no. 151.
15. This is the opinion of Dom P. Renaudin, *La Doctrine de la Assumption, sa définibilité,* Paris, 1913, pp. 119 sqq.; of J. Bellamy, *Dict. Théol.,* art. *Assumption,* col.
2139 sqq. and many other authors including P. Terrien. Other theologians are
satisfied to assert that there was an implicit revelation, though not denying the
probability of an explicit one, transmitted orally and by the liturgy.

concerning pagan goddesses. The principal contribution of the early centuries of the Church to Mariology was to establish her great title, "Mother of God," and eventually to define it in the Council of Ephesus.

Thus, we may conclude that everything tends to indicate that the privilege of the Assumption was explicitly revealed to the Apostles, or at least to one of them, and that it was transmitted subsequently by the oral tradition of the Liturgy; otherwise there is no explanation of the universal Feast of the Assumption, found so clearly from the 7th century on, by which time the Assumption itself was already the object of the ordinary *magisterium* of the Church.

2nd—The theological reasons usually adduced show that the Assumption is at least implicitly revealed.

These theological arguments, as well as the scriptural texts on which they are built, may be considered in two ways: abstractly—from which point of view many of them are mere arguments *ex convenientia* and are not demonstrative—and in the concrete—that is to say, as expressing concrete facts, the complexity and richness of which is learned from tradition. It is well to note too that even the arguments *ex convenientia* may be considered from two points of view: either purely theoretically or as being themselves at least implicitly revealed and as having influenced the divine choice.

In this section we shall insist on two arguments which, taken as expressing Tradition, show that the privilege of the Assumption is implicitly revealed.[16] As for the eminent dignity of the Mother of God, though this is the root reason of all Mary's privileges, it is not the proximate cause of her Assumption. Thus it seems to yield only an argument *ex convenientia* which is not demonstrative.[17] The first of these two

---

16. Cf. Merkelbach, op. cit., pp. 279 sqq., and Friethoff, O.P., *De Doctrina Assumptionis corporalis B. Mariae Virginis rationibus theologicis illustrata, Angelicum,* 1938, pp. 13 sqq.
17. Cf. Friethoff, *loc. cit.*

arguments runs as follows:

Mary received fullness of grace and was blessed by God among women in an exceptional way. But this exceptional blessing negatives the divine malediction to bring forth children in pain and to return to dust (*Gen.* 3:16-19). Mary was therefore preserved through it from corruption in her body: her body would not return to dust but would be resuscitated in an anticipated resurrection. Since the two premisses of this argument are revealed, the conclusion is, according to the teaching of most theologians, capable of being defined.

A thing to be noted in this argument is that the reasoning process in it is not precisely illative, but rather explicative since the divine malediction contains the "into dust thou shalt return" of Genesis not as a cause contains an effect but as a whole contains its parts: "Into dust thou shalt return" is a part of the divine malediction. Thus Mary, blessed among women, and not falling under the malediction, would not suffer the corruption of the tomb. The hour of the resurrection would be anticipated for her, and her glorious resurrection would be followed by the Assumption or elevation of her glorified body to Heaven. It is, then, clear that the privilege of the Assumption is contained implicitly revealed in the plenitude of grace and the exceptional blessing with which Mary was favored.

The second argument is no less cogent. It was put forward by the many fathers of the Vatican Council who asked for the definition of the dogma of the Assumption and was indicated by Pius IX in the Bull *Ineffabilis Deus*.[18] The argument may be formulated thus:

---

18. For the Vatican Fathers cf. Conc. Vitac. documentorum collectio, Paderborn, 1872: "Quum juxta Apostolicam doctrinam, *Rom.* 5:8; *1 Cor.,* 15: 24, 26, 54, 57; *Heb.* 2:14-15, aliisque locis traditam, *triplici victoria* de peccato et de peccatorum fructibus, concupiscentia et morte, *veluti ex partibus integrantibus, constituatur ille triumphus, quem de Satana,* antiquo serpente, *Christus retulit;* quumque *Gen.* 3:15, Deipara exhibeatur singulariter associata Filio suo in suo triumpho ; accedente unanimi sanctorum patrum suffragio non dubitamus quin in praefato oraculo *eadem beata Virgo triplici illa victoria praesignificetur illustris,* adeoque non secus ac de peccato per immaculatam Conceptionem et de concupiscentia per

Christ's perfect victory over Satan included victory over sin and death. But Mary, the Mother of God, was most intimately associated with Jesus on Calvary in His victory over Satan. Hence she was associated with Him in His victory over death by her anticipated resurrection and her Assumption.

In this argument, as in the first one, the premisses are both revealed, and the argument itself is explicative rather than illative: it turns on Christ's perfect victory which is a whole containing as its parts victory over sin and victory over death.

The major premiss is known to be revealed, as the Fathers of the Vatican Council stated, from many texts in the Epistles of St. Paul. Among texts from other books of the New Testament, we may mention a few from St. John's gospel. Jesus is "the Lamb of God . . . who taketh away the sin of the world" (*John* 1:29); He said of Himself "I have overcome the world" (*John* 16:33); shortly before His Passion He said "Now is the judgement of the world: now shall the prince of this world be cast out. And I, if I be lifted up from the earth, will draw all things to myself." (*John* 12:31-32). The sacrifice of the Cross offered in love, the acceptance of humiliation and a most painful death—these were the victory over Satan and sin. But death is a consequence of sin. Hence, He who had conquered Satan and sin on the Cross would conquer death by His glorious resurrection.

The minor premiss is revealed also—that is, that Mary, Mother of God, was associated as closely as possible on Calvary with Jesus' perfect victory over Satan. It is announced mysteriously in Genesis in the words addressed to Satan: "I will put enmities between thee

---

virginalem Maternitatem, sic etiam *de inimica morte* singularem triumphum relatura, per acceleratam similitudinem Filii sui resurrectionis, ibidem praenuntiata fuerit." In the Bull *Ineffabilis* we read: ". . . sempiternas contra venenosum serpentum inimicitias exercens, ac de ipso *plenissime triumphans* and again ". . . Numquam fuit maledicto obnoxia, ergo concepta immaculata" and victorious in consequence over death too.

and the woman, and thy seed and her seed: she shall crush thy head. . . ." And though that text alone would not suffice to establish the point, we have in addition Mary's words at the Annunciation" "Behold the handmaid of the Lord; be it done to me according to Thy word . . ." uttered when she consented to be the Mother of the Redeemer. But she would not have been a worthy mother unless her will were perfectly conformed to the will of Him who was to offer Himself for us. Besides, Simeon told her of the sufferings to be borne: "And thy own soul a sword shall pierce. . . ." Last of all we read in St. John's gospel: "There stood by the Cross of Jesus, his mother, and his mother's sister." She shared in His sufferings, therefore, in the measure of her love for Him: so fully did she share that she is called Co-Redemptrix.[19]

There is a very intimate connection between compassion and motherhood, for the deepest compassion is that of a mother, and Mary would not have been a worthy mother of the Redeemer had she been lacking in conformity of will with His redemptive oblation.

Since, therefore, Mary was associated very intimately with Jesus in His perfect victory over Satan, it follows that she was associated also with Him in the different parts of His triumph, that is to say, in His victory over sin and over death, sin's consequence.

It could, perhaps, be objected that it would be enough were Mary associated in His victory over death by her final resurrection on the Last Day. To which the answer

---

19. Cf. Denz. 3034. Pius X wrote in his Encyclical, *Ad diem ilium,* Feb. 2nd, 1904, quoting Eadmer, the disciple of St. Anselm: "Ex hac autem Mariam inter et Christum communione dolorum et voluntatis "promeruit" illa "ut reparatrix perditi orbis dignissime fieret." Quoniam universis sanctitate praestat conjunctioneque cum Christo atque a Christo ascita in humanae salutis opus, *de congruo,* ut aiunt, promeret, nobis, quae Christus *de condigno* promeruit." Cf. also Benedict XV in the Apostolic Letter, *Inter Sodalicia,* March 22nd, 1918: "Ita (B.M.V.) Filium immolavit, ut dici merito queat, ipsam cum Christo humanum genus redemisse" and Pius XI in the Apostolic Letter *Explorata res,* February 2nd, 1923: "Virgo perdolens redemptionis opus cum Christo participavit."

The Holy Office approved the invocation of Mary as Co-Redemptrix of the human race on June 26th, 1913, and January 22nd, 1914; cf. Denz. 3034, note.

can be given that Mary was more closely associated than anyone else with Jesus in His perfect victory— or in the perfection of His victory—over Satan, and that perfect victory included exemption from bodily corruption, and, in consequence, anticipated resurrection and assumption into Heaven. As we read in the Collect of the Mass of the Assumption: "Mortem subiit temporalem, nec tamen mortis nexibus deprimi potuit. . . ." She died; but she was not retained captive by the bonds of death—a privilege accorded to no other saint, for even though the bodies of some saints are miraculously preserved from corruption, they are still in the bonds of death.

These two great theological arguments taken respectively from Mary's fullness of grace united to her special blessing, and her association with Jesus in His perfect victory, prove that the Assumption is implicitly revealed and capable of definition as an article of faith.

There are other theological arguments too which confirm the same conclusion, at least by way of proof *ex convenientia*. The love of Jesus for Mary can be appealed to as a reason why she should have been accorded the privilege. The excellent virginity of Mary seems to demand that her body, free from all stain of sin, should be free from the bonds of death, the consequence of sin. The Immaculate Conception calls for it also since death is a consequence of original sin from which Mary was preserved. It may also be added that there are no relics of Our Lady, which is a probable indication of her Assumption, body and soul, into Heaven.

Since the Assumption is contained at least implicitly in Revelation, it can be defined as an article of faith. The opportuneness of its definition is manifest, as Dom Renaudin says.[20] For, from the doctrinal point of view, the Assumption of the Blessed Virgin along

---

20. *La Doctrine de l'Assomption, sa définibilité*, Paris, 1913, pp. 204-217.

with the Ascension of Our Blessed Lord, crowns our faith in the objective completion of the work of the Redemption, and gives our hope a new guarantee. For their part, the faithful will derive from a solemn definition of the Assumption the advantage of being able to go beyond their adherence to the infallibility of the ordinary *magisterium* of the Church who has instituted the Feast, and to adhere immediately to the dogma on the authority of God who revealed it, in which dogma they will find an arm against all those errors of our times—whether materialism, rationalism, or liberal Protestantism—which agree in minimising the faith in every possible way rather than to recognise that the gifts of God surpass our ideas of them. From the point of view of heretics and schismatics, the solemn definition will be a help rather than a hindrance, for it will make more manifest the power and goodness of Mary who has been given to men to lead them along the way of salvation. Finally, the just man lives by his faith. Hence he finds in the solemn definition of a revealed truth a form of spiritual nourishment which increases his faith, and strengthens his hope, and makes his charity more fervent.

Article 3

The Final Plenitude of Grace in Heaven

In this article we shall consider Mary's eternal beatitude: the beatific vision; the love of God and the joy which results from it; her elevation above the choirs of angels; her participation in Christ's Kingship and the consequences which follow from it.

Mary's Essential Beatitude

Mary's essential beatitude surpasses in intensity and extension that conferred on all the other blessed. This doctrine is theologically certain. Heavenly glory, or essential beatitude, is proportioned to the degree of grace or charity which precedes entry to Heaven. But Mary's initial fullness of grace surpassed the fmal grace of the highest saints and angels; and we have seen that it is probable, if not certain, that it surpassed their final graces united. It follows that Mary's essential beatitude surpasses that of all the saints taken together. In other words, Mary's beatific vision penetrates more deeply into the divine essence seen face to face than that of all the other blessed—exception being, of course, made for the beatified soul of Jesus.

It is true that the natural intellectual powers of the angels are greater than those of Mary, or even the human powers of Jesus. Nevertheless Mary's intuitive gaze of the divine essence is more piercing than theirs because of the much more intense *lumen gloriae* (light of glory) with which she is enriched. The object of the beatific vision being essentially supernatural, greater natural powers confer no greater advantage in knowing it. In much the same way an unlettered Christian can have a greater infused faith and charity than a highly endowed and qualified theologian.

Not only does Mary know more of the essence of God in Heaven, but she knows more too of His wisdom, His love, His power, and she sees better the range of their extent both in the order of possible and of existing realities. Besides, since the blessed in Heaven see more things in God according as their mission is a more universal one, Mary, as Mother of God, Universal Mediatrix, Co-Redemptrix, Queen of Angels, Saints, and the whole universe, sees much more in God, *in Verbo,* than do the other blessed. Higher than her in glory is only her Divine Son. His human mind reads into the divine essence deeper than hers. He knows certain secrets which are hidden from her, for they pertain to Him only, the Saviour, the High Priest and the Universal King.

Mary comes immediately after Jesus in heavenly

glory. That is why the liturgy affirms, on the Feast of the 15th of August, that she has been lifted up above the choirs of angels, and that she is at the right hand of her Son. (*Ps.* 44:10). According to St. Albert the Great,[21] she constituted among the blessed an order apart, higher than the seraphim as they are higher than the cherubim: for the queen is as much higher than the first of her servants as they are higher than the last of their fellows.

Being Mother of God she participates more than anyone else in the glory of her Son. And since the divinity of Jesus is absolutely evident in Heaven, it is clear to the blessed that Mary belongs to the hypostatic order, that she has a special affinity to the divine Persons, and that she shares in a unique way in Jesus' universal kingship over all creatures. This is the doctrine of so many of the liturgical prayers: *Ave Regina Coelorum* . . . *Regina Coeli* . . . *Salve Regina.* It is found also in the Litanies: Queen of Angels . . . Queen of all saints. . . . And it is affirmed also in the passage we quoted earlier from the Bull *Ineffabilis Deus.* It is taught explicitly by St. Germanus of Constantinople,[22] St. Modestus,[23] St. John Damascene,[24] St. Anselm (Orat. I), St. Bernard,[25] St. Albert the Great,[26] St. Thomas Aquinas,[27] and all the doctors.

Mary's Accidental Beatitude

To Mary's accidental beatitude contribute her more intimate knowledge of the glorious Humanity of Jesus, the exercise of her universal mediation and of her motherly mercy, and the cult of hyperdulia which she

---

21. *Mariale,* q. 151.
22. *Hom. II in Dorm.*
23. *Enc. in Dorm.*
24. *Hom. I, II, III, in Dorm.; De Fide orth.,* IV, 14.
25. He speaks very frequently of Mary as *Regina* and *Domina.*
26. *Mariale,* q. 151.
27. In III *Sent.,* dist. 22, Q. 3, a. 3, q. 3, ad 3.

receives as Mother of God. She enjoys also in an eminent way the triple aureola of the martyrs, the confessors, and the virgins, for she suffered more than the martyrs during the Passion of her Son, she instructed the Apostles themselves in a private and intimate way, and she preserved virginity of soul and body in all its perfection. The glory of her body—which is a reflection of that of her soul—is of the same eminent degree.

Under all these respects Mary is raised above all the saints and angels, and it becomes increasingly evident that the reason and root cause of all her privileges is her eminent dignity as Mother of God.

PART II

Mary, Mother of all Men

Her Universal Mediation and Our Interior Life

INTRODUCTION TO PART II

Having considered the Blessed Virgin as Mother of God, and the fulness of grace which was given her that she might be God's worthy mother, it remains to speak of her relations with men. Tradition attributes to Mary three titles, Mother of the Redeemer, Mother of all men, and Mediatrix, to express her relations with men as yet on their way to eternity. In regard to the blessed she has especially the title, Universal Queen.

Theology teaches us that these titles correspond to those of Christ the Redeemer.[1] He performed His redemptive work as Head of the humanity He was to regenerate, as First Mediator Who has the power by His priesthood to sacrifice and to sanctify, and to exercise teaching authority, and finally as Universal King, Who legislates for all men, judges the living and the dead, and governs all creatures not excluding the angels. Mary, in her quality of Mother of the Redeemer, is associated with Jesus in those three roles. She is associated with Him as Head of the Church by being spiritual Mother of all men; she is associated with Him as First Mediator by being a secondary and subordinate mediatrix; and she is associated with Him as Universal King by being Queen of the universe. That is Mary's triple mission to men which we are about to consider in this part of the book.

We shall speak first of Mary as Mother of the Redeemer and as Mother of all men; then of her universal mediation on earth and in heaven; finally of her universal queenship.

All these titles, but especially that of Mother of God, are the justification of the cult of hyperdulia of which we shall speak in the last place. At no time shall we

---

1. Cf. Merkelbach, Mariologia, p. 295.

endeavor to put forward original views, or those of individual authors—nor have we done that in the earlier part of the book—but rather will it be our aim to expose the common teaching of the Church, transmitted by the Fathers and explained by theologians. It is only on such a foundation that one can safely build.

Because of the method we have chosen, a superficial reader may think our treatment of the different questions banal or elementary. But it is well to recall that the most elementary philosophical truths, such as the principles of causality and finality, and the most elementary religious truths, such as those contained in the Our Father, are found to be the most profound and vital when they are examined carefully and put into practice. In the present matter as elsewhere it is necessary to advance from what is known and certain to what is less well known, from what is easy to what is difficult; were one to embark on a premature consideration of more difficult problems, especially if they were presented in the form of dramatic and striking paradoxes, the result might be—as has happened to so many heretics—to end up by denying evident truths and obvious conclusions. The history of theology and philosophy shows that this is no fictitious danger. Finally it should not be forgotten that though in human matters, where truth and falsity, good and evil, are jumbled together, simplicity is superficiality and exposes one to error; in the things of God, where there is but the true and the good, simplicity alone will reveal the greatest heights and the most secret depths.[2]

---

2. For a treatment of the place of Our Lady in the interior life cf. M. V. Bernadot, O.P., *Notre Dame dans ma Vie;* Morineau, *L'Annlée Mariale;* Boulenger, O.P., *Le Dieu de Marie dans le Saint Rosaire;* Marie de Sainte-Thérèse, *L'Union Mystique à Marie;* Neubert, *La Doctrine Mariale du P. Chaminade;* all of which are published by La Vie Spirituelle.

ᴄᴏChapter 1ᴄᴏ

The Mother of the Redeemer and of all Men

These two titles are evidently connected. We shall consider them in the order indicated.

Article 1

The Mother of the Saviour Associated with His Redemptive Work

The Church calls Mary Mother of the Saviour as well as Mother of God. In the Litany of Loreto, for example, after the invocations, "Holy Mother of God," and "Mother of the Creator," we find the other, "Mother of the Saviour, pray for us." Though some have thought the contrary,[1] the fact of these two titles is no reason for believing that Mariology labors under the defect of a duality of distinct principles: "Mother of God" and "Mother of the Saviour, who is associated with His redemptive work." Mariology is a unity, for Mary is "Mother of God the Redeemer or the Saviour." In much the same way the two mysteries of the Incarnation and the Redemption do not take away from the unity of Christology, for its central point is the redemptive Incarnation. The motive of the Incarnation is sufficiently indicated in the Creed which says that the Son of God came down from Heaven for our salvation.

Let us now see how Mary became Mother of the Saviour by her consent, and how, as Mother of the Saviour, she was to be associated with His redemptive work.

---

1. Rev. Professor Bittremieux in *De supremo principlo Mariologiae, Eph. theol. Lovan.,* 1931, though he does not deny that in a sense Mariology can be reduced to one principle, insists rather on duality. As against this cf. Merkelbach, *Mariologia,* pp. 91 sqq.

Mary Became Mother of the Saviour by Her Consent

Mary gave her consent to the redemptive Incarnation when, on the day of the Annunciation, the angel said to her: "Thou shalt conceive in thy womb, and shalt bring forth a son; and thou shalt call his name Jesus"—the name to be given to her Son meaning "saviour." Mary was not ignorant of the Messianic prophecies—most particularly those of Isaias—which foretold the redemptive sufferings of the promised Saviour. Thus, when she uttered her fiat she accepted in advance for herself and for her Son all the sufferings which the redemption would involve.

She learned something still more explicit about them a few days later when Simeon spoke to her: "Behold this child is set for the fall, and for the resurrection of many in Israel, and for a sign which shall be contradicted; And thy own soul a sword shall pierce." A little earlier he had spoken of Jesus as . . . thy salvation, which thou hast prepared before the face of all peoples." Mary, we are told, kept all these words in her heart. The divine plan became gradually clearer to her contemplative faith, lit up as it was by the illumination of the gift of understanding.

Mary therefore became freely Mother of the Redeemer in His role of Redeemer; she grew in her appreciation of the fact that the Son of God became Man for our salvation. She united herself to Jesus as only a mother, and a very holy mother, could in perfect oneness of love for God and souls. That was her way of fulfilling the great precept of the law—and what more perfect way could there be? Tradition is clear on Mary's union with the Redeemer; it never tires of repeating that as Eve was united to the first man in the work of perdition Mary was united to the Redeemer in the work of redemption.

Mother of the Redeemer, she grew too in her appreciation of the manner of our redemption. It was sufficient for her to call to mind and meditate on the prophecies which all knew so well. (*Isaias* 53:1-12) announced the sufferings and humiliations of the Messiah, saying that they would be borne to expiate our sins by Him Who is innocence itself, and that by His Death He would justify many. She knew too David's psalm (*Ps.* 21) "O God, my God, why has thou forsaken me?" describing the prayer of the Just One, His cry of anguish in His abandonment, and His confidence in Jahve, His apostolate and its effects in Israel and among the gentiles. There was finally Daniel's prophecy of the Son of Man (*Dan.* 7:13-14) and of the power that would be given Him: "And he gave him power, and glory, and a kingdom: and all peoples, tribes, and tongues shall serve him: his power is an everlasting power that shall not be taken away: and his kingdom, that shall not be destroyed." All Tradition has seen the Messiah promised as Redeemer in the Man of Sorrows of Isaias and the Son of Man of Daniel.

Mary, who was not ignorant of these prophecies, became therefore Mother of the Redeemer in His role of Redeemer at the Annunciation. From her consent "Be it done to me according to thy word" follows all the rest of her life, just as all Jesus' life followed from the consent He gave to His Father's will on entering the world: "Holocausts for sin did not please thee. Then said I: Behold I come to do thy will, O God." (*Heb.* 10:6-9). The Fathers could say that our salvation depended on Mary's consent, and that she conceived her Son spiritually before she conceived Him corporeally.[2]

It may be objected that a divine decree such as that of the Incarnation could not depend on the consent of a creature who was free not to give it. To this theology answers that God has efficaciously willed and infal-

---

2. Cf. St. Augustine, *De Virg.*, c. 3, 31; St. Gregory the Great, *Hom.* 38 *in Evang.*; St. Leo the Great, *Sermo 20 in Nat. Dom.*, c. 1; St. Bernard, *Hom. IV super Missus est;* St. Laurence Justinian, *Serm. de Ann.*

libly foreseen everything that will happen in the course
of time. Therefore, He willed efficaciously and foresaw
infallibly Mary's consent to the realization of the mystery of the Incarnation. From all eternity God, who
works with strength and gentleness, decided to give
Mary the efficacious grace which would move her to
consent freely and meritoriously. Just as He makes the
trees to bear their blossoms, so He makes our wills to
produce their free acts; and far from doing them any
violence He is the author of their freedom, for that too
is a reality, a form of being. The "how" of all this is
the secret of God Omnipotent. Just as Mary conceived
the Saviour by the operation of the Holy Ghost without losing her virginity, so she uttered her fiat infallibly under the motion of efficacious grace without
prejudice to her complete liberty—rather did her will,
under the divine motion, flower spontaneously into the
free consent she gave in the name of all mankind.

Mary's fiat belonged entirely to God as First Cause
and entirely to Mary as secondary cause. In it we find
a perfect example of what St. Thomas speaks of
(Ia, q. 19, a. 8): "Since the will of God is supremely
efficacious it follows that not only do the things that
God wills (efficaciously) happen, but that they happen
in the way in which He wills. But it is His will that
some things should happen of necessity and others
freely." By her fiat, then, Mary became voluntarily the
Mother of the Redeemer.

Tradition recognizes that Mary consented to be
Mother of the Redeemer in His redemptive role by calling her the New Eve. The first Eve, by consenting to
temptation, led the first man to commit the sin which
lost original justice for mankind. Mary is the New Eve
by her consent to be the Mother of the Redeemer for
the sake of the work of redemption.

Some non-Catholics have objected that Mary's parents could equally well have been entitled father or
mother of the Redeemer and regarded as associated

with Him in the work of redemption. It is not hard to find an answer to this objection. Mary alone received the light required for the consent of which we speak. Her parents did not know that the Messiah would be born of their family. St. Anne could not foresee that her child would be the mother of the Messiah.

How Was the Mother of the Redeemer to be Associated with His Work?

According to what the Fathers of the Church tell us about Mary as the New Eve whom many saw foretold in the words of Genesis, it is common and certain doctrine, and even *fidei proxima,* that the Blessed Virgin, Mother of the Redeemer, is associated with Him in the work of redemption as secondary and subordinate cause, just as Eve was associated with Adam in the work of man's ruin.[3]

The doctrine of Mary as the second Eve was universally accepted in the 2nd century. The Fathers who taught it then did not regard it as the fruit of personal speculation but as the traditional doctrine of the Church supported by the words of St. Paul which describe Jesus as the second Adam and oppose Him to the first as the Author of salvation to the author of the fall. (*1 Cor.* 15:45 sqq.; *Rom.* 5:12 sqq.; *1 Cor.* 15: 20-23). They fitted St. Paul's words into the context of Genesis' account of the fall, the promise of the redemption, and the victory over the demon, as well as St. Luke's account of Mary's consent at the Annunciation. It is necessary therefore to regard the doctrine of Mary as the second Eve, associated with the redemptive work of her Son, as a divinoapostolic tradition.[4]

The Fathers who speak most explicitly of this mat-

3. Many Fathers, followed by many theologians, have noted that if Eve alone had sinned there would have been no original sin, and if Mary alone had given her consent without Jesus there would have been no redemption.
4. Cf. Merkelbach, *Mariologia,* pp. 74-89.

ter are St. Justin,[5] St. Irenaeus,[6] Tertullian,[7] St. Cyprian,[8] Origen,[9] St. Cyril of Jerusalem,[10] St. Ephrem,[11] St. Epiphanius,[12] St. John Chrysostom,[13] St. Proclus,[14] St. Jerome,[15] St. Ambrose,[16] St. Augustine,[17] St. Basil,[18] St. Germanus of Constantinople,[19] St. John Damascene,[20] St. Anselm,[21] St. Bernard.[22] In later times the theologians of the middle ages and of our own day have maintained the same doctrine.[23]

What, according to Tradition, is the sense in which Mary, the New Eve, was associated with the work of redemption?

It was not merely by having conceived the Redeemer physically, by having given Him birth and nourished Him, but rather was her association moral, through her free, salutary, and meritorious acts. Eve contributed morally to the fall by yielding to the temptation of the devil, by disobedience, and by leading up to Adam's sin; Mary, on the contrary, co-operated morally in our redemption by her faith in Gabriel's words, and by her free consent to the mystery of the redemptive Incarnation and to all the sufferings it entailed for her Son and for herself.

Clearly, Mary is not the principal and perfective cause

---

5. *Dial. cum Tryphone,* c. 100—written about 160 A.D.
6. *Adv. Haer.,* Bk. III, c. 19, 21-23; Bk. IV, c. 33; Bk. V, c. 19—written before the end of the 2nd century.
7. *Liber de Carne Christi,* c. 17—written about 210-212 A.D.
8. *Lib. II ad Quirinum.*
9. *Hom. 8 in Luc.*
10. *Cat.* XII, 5, 15.
11. Edit. Assemani, t. II, syr. lat., pp. 318-329; edit. Lamy, t. 1, p. 593; t. II, p. 524.
12. *Panarion,* haer. lxxxiii, 18.
13. *Hom. in Pasch.,* n. 2; in *Ps.* xliv.
14. *Or. I in laud. S.M.*
15. *Ep.* 22 *ad Eustochium,* n. 21.
16. *Ep.* 63 *ad Eccl. Vercel.,* n. 33.
17. *De agone christiano,* 22.
18. Or. 3, n. 4.
19. *Hom. II in Dorm.*
20. *Hom. I in Dorm.*
21. *Or.* 51 *and* 52.
22. *Sermo in Dom. infra Oct. Ass.; in Nat. B. V. de Aquaeductu;* 12 *Praer.*
23. Hugo a S. Charo, *Postillae in Luc.* I, 26-28; Richardus a S. Laurentio, *De Laud. B. M. V.,* I. 1, c. 1; S. Albertus Magnus, *Mariale,* q. 29, 3; St. Bonaventure, *De donis Sp. Sti.,* coll. 6, n. 16; *Sermo III de Ass. B. M. V.;* St. Thomas, *Opusc. VI Exp. Salut. Ang.*

of the Redemption: she could not redeem us in justice, *de condigno,* since for that a theandric act of infmite value which could belong only to an incarnate Divine Person was required. But she is really a secondary cause of salvation, dispositive, and subordinate to Jesus. She is said to be subordinated to Jesus not merely in the sense that she is inferior to Him, but also in the sense that she concurred in saving us by a grace which proceeded from His merits, and therefore acted in Him, with Him, and by Him. We must never forget that Jesus is the Universal Mediator. He redeemed Mary by preserving her from original sin. Similarly, it is through Him that she contributed to saving us. She is not the perfective cause of salvation, but a dispositive one, disposing us to undergo the action of her Son, who it is achieves our salvation and is our Redeemer.

Mary's association with Jesus in the redemption is therefore not like that of the Apostles, but is something still more intimate. That is what St. Albert the Great formulated so happily when he said: "The Blessed Virgin Mary was chosen by God not to be His minister but to be His consort and His helper—*in consortium et adjutorium*—according to the words of Genesis: Let us make him a help like to himself." (*Mariale,* q. 42).

We can now see that the unity of Mariology does not suffer from the defect of having two distinct principles. There is one principle which dominates it: Mary is Mother of God the Redeemer and is by that fact associated to His work. In the same way, the two mysteries of the Incarnation and the Redemption do not constitute a duality so as to take from the unity of Christology, for they find themselves united in the idea of the redemptive Incarnation; and their union in it is expressed in the Creed in the words ". . . qui propter nos homines et propter nostram salutem descendit de caelis, et incarnatus est."

Jesus' natural sonship of God or His grace of hypostatic union is greater than His fulness of created grace and our redemption. In the same way Mary's motherhood of God is greater than her fulness of grace which overflows on us, as has been shown in the first chapter of this book. The unity of theological knowledge contributes to its certainty, since, because of its unity, it uses subordinated and not co-ordinated principles. All the different treatises, too, which go to make it up are subordinated in their totality to some supreme truth.

Article 2
The Mother of All Men

Tradition ascribes to Mary the titles Mother of Divine Grace, Mother most amiable, Mother most admirable, Mother of Mercy. The Fathers have often spoken of Mary as Mother of all Christians, and even as Mother of all men. In what sense is this maternity to be understood? When did Mary become our Mother? How does her maternity affect all the faithful, even those who are not in the state of grace, and all men, even those who have not the true faith? These are the questions we shall try to answer in this section.

In what sense is Mary our Mother?

Evidently Mary is not our mother in the ordinary sense of the term since she did not give us natural life. Considering our natural life, it is Eve who deserves to be called the mother of all men. Mary is our mother rather in a spiritual sense and through adoption, for, by her union with Jesus the Redeemer, she has communicated to us the supernatural life of grace. She is very much more than a sister in grace: we say, on the analogy of natural life, that she has given us birth to a divine form of life. St. Paul could say, speaking to the Corinthians, "In Christ Jesus, by the gospel, I have begotten you." (*1 Cor.* 4:15). With still more truth can we speak of Mary's spiritual maternity—a maternity which is source of a life destined to endure not sixty or eighty years, but all eternity.

Mary's maternity is adoptive, as is God's fatherhood of the just. It is, however, much more intimate and fruitful than in ordinary human adoption. Human adoption constitutes a person legally the child and heir of another. But all this is in the legal order; and even though it is a sign of the affection bestowed on the adopted child, it does not produce any interior change in it. Divine adoption, on the contrary, produces sanctifying grace in the soul of the just, thereby making it to participate in the divine nature and to have within itself the germ of eternal life. The soul which is endowed thus with grace is agreeable in God's eyes and is His child, called to know Him face to face and to love Him for all eternity. St. John speaks of this in his prologue when he describes those who believe in the Son of God made man as "Who are born, not of blood, nor of the will of the flesh, nor of the will of man, but of God." (*John* 1:13). Mary's maternity participates in the fruitfulness or fecundity of the divine Paternity: in union with the Redeemer, she has truly and really communicated to us grace, the germ of eternal life. She can therefore be called Mother of grace, Mother of mercy. That is what the Fathers meant when they called her the New Eve, and said that she had co-operated voluntarily in our salvation as Eve had co-operated in our fall.

The points of doctrine just outlined are found in the Church's preaching from the 2nd century on. The references are the same as those given a short while ago in connection with the doctrine of the New Eve. St. Ephrem, in the 4th century, is a particularly eloquent witness. He calls Mary "Mother of life and of salvation, Mother of the living and of all men" since she gave us the Saviour and united herself to Him on Calvary.[24] Similar expressions are found in St. Germanus of Constantinople,[25] St. Peter Chrysologus,[26] Eadmer,[27] St. Bernard,[28] Richard of St. Laurence,[29] St. Albert the Great[30] who calls Mary "Mater misericordiae, Mater regenerations, totius humani generis mater spiritualis", and in St. Bonaventure.[31]

Every day the liturgy repeats: "Hail holy Queen, Mother of mercy . . . Show thyself a mother . . . Hail, Mother of mercy, Mother of God and Mother of pardon, Mother of hope and Mother of grace."

When did Mary become our Mother?

The different texts we have quoted indicate that Mary became our mother by consenting freely to be the Mother of the Saviour, the Author of grace and of our spiritual regeneration. By that act she conceived us spiritually and would have been our adoptive mother as its result even had she died before her Son. But that was not to be. Instead she lived on to unite herself to Jesus in the sacrifice of the Cross and by that great act of faith, hope and love of God and souls, she became our mother in a still more perfect way and contributed more directly, more intimately, and more profoundly to our salvation. Besides, it was on Calvary that Jesus proclaimed Mary our mother, when He addressed to Mary the words: "Woman, behold thy son", and to St. John, who personified all the redeemed, the words: "Behold thy mother." Tradition has always understood the words in that sense: they do not refer to a grace peculiar to St. John alone, but go beyond

24. *Opera S. Ephraem Syr.*, edit. Assemani t. II, syr. lat., pp. 324, 327; III, 607.
25. *Sermo in Dorm., Deip.*, 2 and 5.
26. *Serm.* 140 and 142.
27. *De Exc. V.M.*, c. xi, 5.
28. *Sermo de Aquaeductu*, n. 4 sqq.
29. *De Laud. B. M. V.*, l. VI, c. 1, n. 12; l. IV, c. 14, n. 1.
30. *Mariale*, q. 29, n. 3; qq. 42, 43.
31. *Serm. VI in Ass. B. M. V.*, and in *I Sen.*, d. 48, a. 2, q. 2, dub. 4.

him to all who are to be regenerated by the Cross.[32]

The words of the dying Saviour, like sacramental words, produce what they signify: in Mary's soul they produced a great increase of charity and of maternal love for us; in John a profound filial affection, full of reverence for the Mother of God. There is the origin of devotion to Mary.

Mary continues to exercise her motherly functions in our regard by watching over us so that we grow in charity and persevere in it, by interceding for us and by distributing to us all the graces we receive.

What is the Extension of Mary's Maternity?

She is first of all Mother of the faithful, of those who believe in her Son and receive through Him the life of grace. But she is also Mother of all men, since she gave the world the Saviour of all men and since she united herself to the oblation of her Son Who offered His precious blood for all. This is what has been affirmed by Popes Leo XIII, Benedict XV, and Pius XI.[33]

She is not the Mother of all men in a general way, as may be affirmed of Eve in the natural order, but of each man in particular, for she intercedes for each and obtains for each all the graces he receives. Jesus says of Himself that He is the Good Shepherd who "calleth his own sheep by name." (*John* 10:3). Something the

---

32. This explanation, suggested by Origen in the 3rd cent., *Praef. in Joan., I, 6,* is explicitly advanced by many authors, especially from the 12th century on, from which time it became common. It has been regarded in different papal documents as the common belief of the Church. Cf. Benedict XIV, Bull *Gloriosae Dominae,* Sept. 27th, 1748; Gregory XVI, Bull Praestantissimum; Leo XIII, enc. *Octobri Mense,* 22nd Sept., 1891; *Adjutricem,* 5th Sept., 1895; *Augustissimae Virginis,* 12th Sept., 1897; Pius X, *Ad diem ilium,* Feb. 2nd, 1904; Benedict XV, *litt. ap. Inter Sodalicia,* Mar. 22nd, 1918; Pius XI, *litt. ap. Explorata res,* Feb. 2nd, 1923; enc. *Rerum Ecclesiae,* Feb. 21st, 1926.

33. Leo XIII calls Mary mother not only of christians, but of the whole human race: enc. *Octobri Mense,* Sept. 22nd, 1891; ep. *Amantissimae voluntatis,* April 14th, 1895; enc. *Adjutricem populi,* Sept. 25th, 1895; Benedict XV calls her mother of all men: *litt. ap. Inter sodalicia,* March 22nd, 1918; for Pius XI cf. *litt. ap. Explorata res,* Feb. 2nd, 1923; enc. *Rerum Ecclesiae,* Feb. 21st, 1926.

same may be said of Mary who is the mother of each individual man.

However, Mary is not Mother of the faithful and of infidels, of the just and sinners, in exactly the same way. The distinctions which are made in regard to the members of Christ's Mystical Body must be made here also.[34] Mary is Mother of infidels in that she is destined to engender them to grace, and in that she obtains for them the actual graces which dispose them for the faith and for justification. She is Mother of the faithful who are in the state of mortal sin, in that she watches over them by obtaining for them the graces necessary for acts of faith and hope, and for disposing themselves for justification. Of those who have died in the state of mortal sin, she is no longer the mother: she *was* their mother. She is fully the Mother of the just, since they have received sanctifying grace and charity through her. She cares for them with tender solicitude so that they may continue in grace and grow in charity. She is in an eminent way the Mother of the blessed who can no longer lose the life of grace.

All this makes clear the meaning of what the Church sings every day at Compline: Hail, Holy Queen, Mother of mercy; Hail, our life, our sweetness, and our hope. To thee do we cry, poor banished children of Eve. To thee do we send up our sighs in this vale of tears. . .

St. Grignon de Montfort has explained the consequences of this doctrine very beautifully in his *Treatise on True Devotion to the Blessed Virgin,* ch. 1, art. 1, no. 2: God wishes to make use of Mary for the sanctification of souls. He sums up thus in the *Secret of Mary* (First Part: Why Mary is necessary for us):

"She it is who has given life to the Author of grace, and on that account she is called Mother of grace. In giving her His Son, God the Father, from whom all

---

34. Cf. IIIa, q. 8, a. 3.

good things descend, gave her all graces: as St. Bernard
says, God's will is given her in Him and with Him.

"God has chosen her to be treasurer and dispensatrix of all His graces. All His graces and all His gifts
pass by her hands. . . . Since Mary has formed the
Head of the predestined, Jesus Christ, it pertains to
her to form also the members of the Head, who are
the true christians. . . . She has received from God a
special power to nourish souls and to make them grow
in Him. St. Augustine goes so far as to say that the
predestined in this world are enclosed in Mary's womb
and that they come to the light only when their good
Mother brings them forth to eternal life. It is to her
that the Holy Ghost has said 'Take root in my elect'
(*Eccl.* 24:13)—roots of profound humility, of ardent charity and of all the virtues.

"Mary is called by St. Augustine, and is in fact, the
living mould of *God—forma Dei.* In her was the Man-
God formed . . . and in her alone can man become
deiform. Whoever is in this mould and allows himself
to be shaped there, takes on the appearance of Jesus
Christ, true God, in a manner adapted to his human
weakness, without excess of pain and labor. This is a
sure way, without danger of illusion, for Satan never
had and never will have power over Mary, holy and
immaculate, stainless and sinless.

"What a difference there is between a soul formed
in Jesus by the method of those who, like sculptors,
rely on their art and their industry, and a soul which,
relying in nothing on itself, and freed from all attach-
ments and submissive in all things, throws itself into
Mary's hands, there to be shaped by the action of the
Holy Ghost. What stains, what defects, what darkness,
what illusions, what an amount of the merely natural
there is in the first soul, and how the second one is
pure, divine, and like to Jesus. . . !

"A thousand times happy is the soul to whom the
Holy Ghost reveals the secret of Mary and to whom

He opens this enclosed garden. That soul will find God alone in that most lovable creature—God infinitely holy and infinitely condescending, yet proportioned to its weakness. . . . God lives in her and, far from causing souls to rest in herself, she leads them to God and unites them to Him."

Thus christian doctrine becomes the object of a penetrating faith for St. Grignon de Montfort, of a contemplation which issues in a true and strong charity.

Mary, Exemplary Cause of the Elect

Jesus is our model. His predestination to natural divine sonship is the exemplary cause of our predestination to adoptive sonship for "whom he foreknew he also predestined to be made conformable to the image of his Son; that he might be the first-born among many brethren." (*Rom.* 8:29). Similarly Mary our Mother, associated with her Son, is the exemplary cause of the life of the elect. It is in that sense that St. Augustine and St. Grignon de Montfort after him say that she is the mould or the model according to which God forms the elect. One must be marked with Mary's seal and reproduce her characteristics to have a place among those loved by Our Lord—which is the reason why theologians teach commonly that a true devotion to Mary is one of the signs of predestination. Blessed Hugh of Saint-Cher even says that she is, as it were, the book of life,[35] or the mirror of that eternal book, since God has written in her the names of all the elect, just as He willed to form, in her and by her, Jesus Who is the First of the elect.

St. Grignon de Montfort writes:[36] "God the Son said to His Mother 'Let thy inheritance be in Israel.' (*Eccl.* 24:13). It is as if He had said: God, My Father, has given

---

35. *Comm. in Eccles.*, XXIV.
36. *Treatise of True Devotion to the Blessed Virgin*, ch. i, a. 1, no. 2.

Me for heritage all the nations of the earth, all men good and evil, predestined and reprobate; I shall lead some by a rod of gold and others by a rod of iron; I shall be the father and advocate of some, the just chastiser of others, and the judge of all; but you, My dear Mother, you shall have for your heritage only the predestined who are prefigured by Israel, and as their mother, you will give them birth, nourish and rear them; as their Queen you will lead, govern and protect them."

It is in that same sense that we must understand the words of St. Grignon de Montfort a little further on in the same work, when showing that Mary, like Jesus, makes her choice always in accordance with the divine good pleasure: "The Most High has made her His treasurer and the dispenser of His favors, to ennoble, raise up, and enrich whom she wills, to allow whom she wills to enter on the narrow way of Heaven, to make whom she wills pass through the narrow gate of life in spite of everything, and to give the throne, the sceptre, and the kingly crown to whom she will. To Mary alone has God given the keys of the cellars of divine love, and the power to enter on the highest and most secret ways of perfection and to lead others thereto."

Those words make clear the scope of Mary's spiritual maternity by which she forms the elect and leads them to the term of their predestination.

◌Chapter 2◌

Mary's Universal Mediation During her Earthly Existence

We shall see first of all in what this mediation consists and what are its principal characteristics. After that we shall examine the two ways in which Mary exercised her mediation during her life on earth, by her merits and her satisfaction.

Article 1

Mary's Universal Mediation in General

Our Holy Mother the Church approved during the pontificate of Benedict XV the proper Mass and Office of Mary, Mediatrix of all Graces.[1] Many theologians consider that the doctrine of Mary's universal mediation is sufficiently contained in the deposit of revelation to be one day proposed solemnly as an object of faith by the infallible Church. It is taught by the ordinary *magisterium* of the Church through the liturgy, through encyclical letters, through pastoral letters, in preaching, and in the works of theologians approved by the Church. Let us see first what is meant by this mediation and then enquire if it is affirmed by tradition and proved by theology.

What is meant by Mary's Universal Mediation?

St. Thomas says, speaking of the mediation of the Saviour (IIIa, q. 26, a. I): "It pertains to the office of a mediator between God and men to unite them." That

---

1. Cf. the decree of January 21st, 1921, of the Sacred Congregation of Rites: "De Festo Beatae Mariae Virginis Mediatricis omnium gratiarum."

is, as he explains in the following article, the mediator offers to God the prayers of men, and most particularly, sacrifice which is the principal act of the virtue of religion, and distributes as well to men God's sanctifying gifts, light from on high and grace. There is, thus, a double movement in mediation: one upwards in the form of prayer and sacrifice, and the other downwards in the form of God's gifts to men.

The office of mediator belongs fully only to Jesus, the Man-God, Who alone could reconcile us with God by offering Him, on behalf of men, the infinite sacrifice of the Cross, which is perpetuated in Holy Mass. He alone, as Head of Mankind, could merit for us in justice the grace of salvation and apply it to those who do not reject His saving action. It is as man that He is mediator, but as a Man in Whom humanity is united hypostatically to the Word and endowed with the fulness of grace, the grace of Headship, which overflows on men. As St. Paul puts it: "For there is one God, and one mediator of God and men, the man Christ Jesus: who gave Himself for a redemption for all, a testimony in due times." (*1 Tim.* 2:5-6).

But, St. Thomas adds (*loc. cit.*): "there is no reason why there should not be, after Christ, other secondary mediators between God and men, who co-operate in uniting them in a ministerial and dispositive manner." Such mediators dispose men for the action of the principal Mediator, or transmit it, but always in dependence on His merits.

The prophets and priests of the Old Testament were mediators of this kind, for they announced the Saviour to the chosen people by offering sacrifices which were types of the great sacrifice of the Cross. The priests of the New Testament may also be spoken of as mediators between God and men, for they are the ministers of the supreme Mediator, offering sacrifice in His Name, and administering the sacraments.

The question arises, is Mary, in subordination to and

in dependence on the merits of Christ, universal mediatrix for all men from the time of the coming of the
Saviour, in regard to obtaining and distributing all
graces, both in general and in particular? Does it not
appear that she is? Nor is her role precisely that of a
minister, but that of an associate in the redemptive
work, in the words of St. Albert already quoted.

Though non-catholics answer the question with a
denial, the christian sense of the faithful, formed for
years by the liturgy, which is one of the voices of the
ordinary magisterium of the Church, has no hesita-
tion in maintaining that, by the very fact of her being
Mother of the Redeemer, all the indications are that
Mary is universal mediatrix, for she finds herself placed
between God and men, and more particularly between
her Son and men.

Since she is a creature she is, of course, altogether
below God Incarnate. But at the same time she is
raised far above men by the grace of the divine maternity, which is of the hypostatic order, and by the fulness of grace which she received even from her
Immaculate Conception. Hence, the mediation attributed by the liturgy and the christian sense of the
faithful to Mary is, strictly speaking, subordinated to
that of Jesus and not co-ordinated; her mediation
depends completely on the merits of the Universal
Mediator. Nor is her mediation necessary (for that of
Jesus is superabundant and needs no complement): it
has however been willed by God as a kind of radiation of the Saviour's mediation, and of all radiations
the most perfect. The Church regards it as most useful and efficacious to obtain from God all that we need
to lead us directly or indirectly to salvation and perfection. Last of all, Mary's mediation is perpetual and
extends to all men, and to all graces without any
exception whatever.

The above is the precise sense in which universal
mediation is attributed to Mary in the liturgy, in the

Feast of Mary Mediatrix, and by the theologians who have recently treated the question at great length.

The Testimony of Tradition

Mary's mediation was affirmed in a general and implicit way from the earliest centuries by the use of the titles, the New Eve, the Mother of the Living. There is all the more reason for so understanding tradition in that the titles were attributed to her not solely because she gave birth physically to the Saviour but because she co-operated morally in His redemptive work, especially by uniting herself very intimately to the sacrifice of the Cross.[2] From the 4th century onwards, and notably in the 5th century, the Fathers affirm clearly that Mary intercedes for us, that all the benefits and helps to salvation come to us through her, by her intervention and her special protection. From the same time too she is called mediatrix between God and men or between Christ and us. Recent studies have thrown much light on this point.[3]

The antithesis between Eve, cause of death, and Mary, cause of salvation for all men is repeated by St. Cyril of Jerusalem,[4] St. Epiphanius,[5] St. Jerome,[6] St. John Chrysostom.[7] The following invocation of St. Ephrem deserves to be quoted in full: "Hail, most

2. Cf. St. Justin, *Dial.*, 100; *P. G.*, t. VI, col. 711; St. Irenaeus, *Contr. haer.*, III, xxii, 4; V, xix, I: *P. G.*, t. VII, col. 958 sqq., 1175; Tertullian, *De carne Christi*, 17; *P. L.*, t. II, col. 782.
3. Cf. Bittremieux, *De mediatione universali B. Mariae Virginis*, 1926; *Marialia*, 1936; Dublanchy in *Dict. de Théol. Cath.* also *Marie Médiatrice* in *La Vie Spirituelle*, 1921-22. Bover, S.J., *La Mediación universal de la Segunda Eva en la Tradición patristica*, Madrid, 1923-1924. Frietoff, O.P., *Maria alma socia Christi mediatoris*, 1936. Merkelbach, *Mariologia*, 1939, pp. 309-323. Génevois, O.P., *La maternité spirituelle de Marie en sainte Irenée, Revue Thomiste*, 1935. Galtier, S.J., *La Vierge qui nous régénère, Rech. de sc. rel.* 1914.
4. *Cat.*, XII, 5, 15.
5. *Haer.*, LXXVIII, 18; *P. G.*, t. XXII, col. 728.
6. *Epist.*, XXII, 21; *P. L.*, XXII, col. 408.
7. *Hom. in sanctum Pascha*, 2; *P. G.*, t. LV, col. 193 and *in Gen.*, III, hom. XVII, I; *P. G.*, t. LIII, col. 143.

excellent mediatrix of God and men, hail most efficacious reconciler of the whole world."[8]

St. Augustine speaks of Mary as mother of all the members of our Head, Jesus Christ. He tells us that by her charity she co-operated in the spiritual birth of all the faithful who are Christ's members.[9] St. Peter Chrysologus says that Mary is the mother of all the living by grace whereas Eve is the mother, by nature, of all the dying.[10] It is evident that he considers Mary as associated with the divine plan for our redemption.

From the 8th century we may quote the Venerable Bede.[11] St. Andrew of Crete calls Mary Mediatrix of grace, dispenser and cause of life.[12] St. Germanus of Constantinople says that no one has been saved without the co-operation of the Mother of God.[13] The title of mediatrix is given by St. John Damascene also, who asserts that we owe to her all the benefits conferred on us by Jesus.[14]

In the 9th century we find St. Peter Damien teaching that nothing is accomplished in the work of our redemption without her.[15] The teaching of St. Anselm,[16] Eadmer,[17] and St. Bernard in the 12th century is the same. St. Bernard speaks of Mary as: *gratiae inventrix, mediatrix, salutis restauratrix saeculorum.*[18]

From the middle of the 12th century the explicit affirmation of Mary's co-operation in our redemption becomes quite common. Her co-operation is looked on

8. *Opera omnia,* edit. Assemani, Rome, 1740, t. III, graecolat., col. 528 sqq., 531 sqq., 551; in Lamy's edit. II p. 547 and t. I, proleg., p. xlix.
9. *De sancta virginitate,* VI, 6; *P. L.,* t. XI, col. 399.
10. *Serm. 140 and 142, P. L.,* t. LII, col. 576, 579.
11. *Homil. I in fest. Annunc. and hom. I in fest. Visit.; P. L.,* t. XCIV. col. 9, 16.
12. *In Nativit. B. M., hom.* IV, and *in Dormit. S. M.,* III; *P. G.,* t. XCVII, cols. 813 and 1108.
13. *In dormit. B. M.; P. G.,* t. XCVIII, c. 349.
14. *In dormit. B. M., hom.* I, 3, 8, 12; II, 16; *P. G.,* t. XCVI, cols. 705, 713, 717, 744.
15. *Serm.* 45; *P. L.,* CXLIV, cols. 741, 743.
16. *Orat.* 47, 52; *P. L.,* t. CLVIII, cols. 945, 955, 964.
17. *De excellentia B. M.,* IX, XI; *P. L.,* t. CLIX, cols. 573, 578.
18. *Ep.* 174; *P. L.,* t. CLXXXII, col. 333; *Super Missus est, hom.* IV, 8; *P. L.,* t. CLXXXIII, c. 83.

as consummated by her consent to her sacrifice at the Annunciation, and its accomplishment on Calvary. Among names that may be cited are those of Arnold of Chartres, Richard of St. Victor, St. Albert the Great,[19] and Richard of Saint-Laurent. St. Thomas seems to be of the same opinion.[20] It is found quite explicitly in St. Bernadine of Siena, St. Antonine,[21] Suarez[22], Bossuet,[23] and St. Alphonsus. St. Grignon de Montfort is one of those who, in the 18th century, did the most to spread the doctrine by bringing out its practical conclusions.[24]

In the encyclical *Ad Diem Illum,* Pius X stated that Mary is the all-powerful mediatrix of the world before her Son: "Totius terrarum orbis potentissima apud Unigenitum Filium suum mediatrix et conciliatrix." The title of mediatrix has been consecrated by the institution of the feast of Mary, Mediatrix of all graces, on January 21st, 1921.

Theological Arguments

The theological arguments invoked by the Fathers and still more explicitly by theologians are principally the following:

Mary deserves the title of universal mediatrix, subordinated to the Redeemer, if she is an intermediary between Him and men, presenting to Him their prayers and obtaining benefits from Him for them. But

---

19. *Mariale,* q. 42. He terms Mary the *coadjutrix et socia Christi.*
20. He says that on the day of the Annunciation Mary gave her consent in the name of all humanity, *loco totius humanae naturae.* Cf. also his *Expos. Salut. Angelicae.*
21. He terms Mary *adjutrix nostrae redemptionis et mater nostrae spiritualis regenerationis. Summa Theol.,* part IV, tit. XV, c. xiv, 2.
22. In IIIam S. Thomae, t. II, disp. XXIII, sect. I, n. 4. He shows from tradition that Mary merited *de congruo* what Christ merited *de condigno.* This is also the teaching of John of Cartagena, Novatus, Chr. de Véga, Théophile Raynaud, etc.
23. *4th sermon for the Feast of the Annunciation.* Cf. also the index to his works under the word *Marie.*
24. *Treatise of True Devotion to the Blessed Virgin,* chs. I and II.

that is precisely Mary's role. For, though a creature, she reaches by her divine maternity to the frontiers of the divinity, and she has received a fulness of grace which is intended to overflow on us. She has, too, co-operated in saving us by consenting freely to be the Mother of the Saviour and by uniting herself as intimately as possible to His sacrifice. We shall see later that she has merited and made satisfaction for us, and we know from the teaching of the Church that she continues to intercede for us so as to obtain for us all graces that contribute to our salvation. These different offices pertain to the exercise of her maternity, as we have already seen.

Thus Jesus is the principal and perfect Mediator, in dependence on Whose merits—and they are superabundant and sufficient of themselves—Mary exercises her subordinate mediation.[25] But Mary's mediation has nevertheless been willed by God because of our weakness and because God wished to honor her by allowing her the exercise of causality in the order of salvation and sanctification.

The work of redemption proceeds therefore entirely from God as First Cause of grace, entirely from Jesus as principal and perfect Mediator, and entirely from Mary as subordinate mediatrix. These three causes are not partial and co-ordinate—as are three men who drag the same load—but total and subordinated: the second acts under the influence of the first, and the third under the influence of the second. An example which may make the point clear is that of the fruit which proceeds entirely from God the Author of nature, entirely from the tree, and entirely from the branch on which it grows. It does not proceed in its different parts from different causes: neither is our redemption the work in part of the Divinity, in part of the Human-

---

25. Jesus' merits needed no *complement* on the part of Mary; that is why she is compared in the mystical body to the neck which unites the head to the members. She is compared also with an aqueduct through which grace passes to us.

ity, and in part of Mary.[26] It is worth noting how becoming it is that Mary who was redeemed by the Saviour in a most excellent manner and preserved from all sin, original and actual, should co-operate in this way in our justification and our final perseverance.

Mary's mediation is of a much higher order than that of the saints, for she alone has given us the Saviour, she alone was so intimately united to the sacrifice of the Cross, she alone is universal mediatrix for all mankind and (as we shall see later) for all graces in particular—even for that grace which is of all the most particular, the grace of the present moment which assures our fidelity from instant to instant.

We shall grasp this universality better when we shall have seen that Mary merited *de congruo* everything that Jesus merited in strict justice, that she made satisfaction (*ex convenientia*) for us in union with Him, and that as regards the application of the fruits of the redemption, she continues to intercede for each one of us, and more particularly for those who invoke her, so that of all the particular graces granted to us, none are granted *de facto* without her intervention.

Article 2
Mary's Merits for Us

Nature and Extent of Her Merits

The exercise of her functions as universal mediatrix was not confined for Our Lady to the period of her

---

26. For the moment we are attributing to Mary only *moral causality* which, as we shall see, is exercised by merit, satisfaction and intercession. However, it is probable, as we shall show later, that she exercises a *physical instrumental causality* as well in the spiritual order for the transmission and production of the graces which we receive through her. This is no more than a simple probability, but we believe it cannot be denied without running the risk of diminishing Mary's influence, which must be greater than is commonly believed. Cf. *infra* pp. 194-206.

glory in heaven: she exercised them on earth, as far as the acquisition of grace was concerned, by co-operating in our redemption by her merits and her satisfaction. In that she followed the example of Jesus Who was Mediator during His life on earth, most of all by His death on Calvary: in fact, His mediation on earth was the foundation of His mediation in heaven, whence, by His intercession, He transmits to us the fruits of His sacrifice.

The Three Kinds of Merit

Merit in general means a right to a reward: the meritorious act confers a right to a reward even though it does not itself produce it. Supernatural merit—which presupposes habitual grace and charity—is a right to a supernatural reward. It is distinguished from satisfaction, which has as purpose to expiate the insult offered the Divine majesty by sin and to render God once more propitious. It is distinguished also from prayer, for even a sinner in the state of mortal sin can pray with the help of actual grace. Besides, unlike merit, prayer appeals not to the divine justice but to the divine mercy. Even when a person is in the state of grace the meritorious value of his prayer should be distinguished from its value considered precisely as prayer. Considered as prayer—that is, from the point of view of impetratory value—it can obtain grace, such as that of final perseverance, which cannot be merited in the strict sense of the term.

There are three kinds of merit. The highest kind, which was that of the Incarnate Word, is merit which is perfectly and fully worthy of a reward, *perfecte de condigno:* the act of charity of the God-Man, since it is the act of a divine Person, is at least equal in value to the reward, even when evaluated in strict justice. Even when the reward was not for Himself, but for us, Jesus could still merit it in strict justice since He was Head of the human race through the fulness of grace which had been given Him that we might all receive of it.

The second kind of merit is that of the person in the state of grace. It is a dogma of faith[27] that every person in the state of grace and endowed with the use of reason and free will, and who is as yet a member of the Church militant, can merit an increase of charity and of eternal life with a merit commonly termed *de condigno.* The force of the term (which may be translated literally "of worthiness") is that such a person is capable of performing acts which are really worthy of a supernatural reward, not in the sense that they are fully equal in value to it, but in the sense that they are proportionate to it since they proceed from habitual grace which is the germ or beginning of that eternal life which God has promised to those who keep His commandments. Merit *de condigno* is a right in distributive justice, though not in the full rigor of justice. The connection between merit *de condigno* and justice throws light on certain texts of scripture such as those in which eternal life is spoken of as a crown of justice (*2 Tim.* 4:8), a retribution made according to each one's work (*Rom.* 2:6-7), or the recompense of a labor which God could not pass over. (*Heb.* 6:19).

A person in the state of grace cannot, however, merit grace *de condigno* for another—for example, the conversion of a sinner or another's advance in charity. The reason is that Christ alone has been constituted Head of the human race to regenerate men and to lead them to salvation.[28] In other words the merit *de condigno* of the just, and even of Mary, is incommunicable. One person can, however, merit grace for another by a lower kind of merit—that known as *de congruo proprie,* or merit of becomingness. Merit *de congruo* is founded on charity or friendship with God

---

27. Council of Trent, Session VI, can. 32: Denz. 842.
28. Cf. Acts 4:12: "There is no other name under Heaven given to men, whereby we must be saved." Cf. also Ia IIae, q. 114, a. 6.

rather than on justice: theologians say that it is founded on the rights of friendship, *in jure amicabili*. St. Thomas explains it thus: "since a man in the state of grace does God's will, it is in keeping with the proprieties (or rights) of friendship that God should do his will in saving another person (for his sake)—although it can happen that at times there will be an obstacle on the side of the other person."[29] In this way, a good christian mother, for example can, by her good works, her love of God and of her neighbour, merit the conversion of her son *de congruo proprie*. St. Monica obtained the conversion of St. Augustine by that kind of merit as well as by her prayers: "The son of so many tears", said St. Ambrose, "could not be lost."

This third kind of merit is that of Mary in our regard. It should be noted that it is merit in the proper sense of the term since it is founded on the rights of friendship and presupposes the state of grace in the person meriting. The reason why it is truly and properly merit, and not something else or something less, is that the idea of merit is analogical, and admits therefore of differing senses which bear some proportion to one another. Thus there are, lower than the merits of Christ, and lower than the merits whereby the just man merits for himself, the merits *de congruo proprie,* founded not on the rights of strict equality of justice, nor even on the rights of distributive justice, but on the rights of friendship.[30]

There is a fourth member of the merit group which is merit in an improper sense of the term. It is that of the sinner in the state of mortal sin who prays to God under the impulse of an actual grace. His prayer has impetratory value; it addresses itself to God's mercy and not to His justice, and it is founded not on the

---

29. Ia IIae, q. 114, a. 6.
30. The term *merit de condigno* has sometimes been translated as merit properly so called. This is a mistake, since it implies that *merit de congruo proprie* is not properly merit at all.

rights of friendship but on the actual grace which moves the sinner to pray. It is merit *de congruo improprie*— merit of becomingness in the wide or improper sense.

Mary's Merit de Congruo for Us

Once the nature of merit *de congruo* has been explained, it is at once evident that Mary could merit for us *de congruo* just as any mother can merit for her children. Hence, it is in no way astonishing that from the 16th century on theologians have taught that Mary merited for us *de congruo proprie* all that Jesus merited for us *de condigno.* Suarez is very explicit. He shows, by appealing to a wide tradition, that though Mary merited nothing for us *de condigno,* since she was not constituted head of the Church, she co-operated in our salvation by her merits *de congruo.*[31] John of Cartagena,[32] Novatus,[33] Chr. de Véga,[34] Théophile Raynaud,[35] George of Rhodes,[36] all teach the same as Suarez. Later theologians follow this teaching also. Among the 19th and 20th century theologians the following may be mentioned: Ventura, Scheeben, Terrien, Billot, Lépicier, Campana, Hugon, Bittremieux, Merkelbach, Friethoff, and all those who have written in recent years on the universal mediation of the Blessed Virgin.

---

31. *In Iam P. S. Thomae,* t. II, disp. XXIII, sect. I, no. 4: "Quamvis B. Virgo nec nos redemerit, *nec aliquid de condigno nobis meruerit,* tamen, impetrando, *merendo de congruo,* et ad incarnationem Christi suo modo co-operando, ad salutem nostram aliquo modo co-operata est. . . . Et eisdem modis saepissime sancti Patres B. Virgini attribuunt, quod nostrae fuerit salutis causa." He then proceeds to quote St. Irenaeus, St. Augustine, St. Fulgentius, St. Anselm, St. Bernard, St. Germanus, St. Ephrem, St. Peter Damien, Richard of St. Victor, Innocent III, in support of his thesis.
32. *Opera,* t. II, p. 30 sqq.
33. *De eminentia Deiparae virginis Mariae,* Rome, 1629, t. I, pp. 379, sqq.
34. *Theologia Mariana,* Naples, 1866, t. II, pp. 441 sqq.
35. *Opera,* t. VI, pp. 224. sqq. Raynaud stresses the point that the redemption as accomplished by Jesus is of an infinite and superabundant value and does not need any complement from Mary's side.
36. *Disp. theol. schol.,* tr. VIII, *De Deipara virgine Maria,* t. II, p. 265, Lyon, 1661. George of Rhodes states that Mary merited for us *de congruo* all that Jesus merited for us *de condigno.*

We may conclude this list of authorities with the words of Pius X in his encyclical *Ad Diem Illum,* Feb. 2nd, 1904: "Mary . . . since she surpasses all creatures in holiness and union with Christ, and since she has been associated by Him with the work of salvation, has merited for us *de congruo,* as it is termed, all that Christ merited for us *de condigno,* and is the principal minister in the distribution of graces."[37]

As has been remarked[38] there is a double difference between Mary's merit *de congruo* for others and that of ordinary souls in the state of grace. The first difference is that Mary merited all graces, and not some only, in that way. The second is that she merited the acquisition of grace as well as its application, since, by her union with Jesus on Calvary, she had a share in the act of redemption itself even before interceding for us in Heaven.

The doctrine expressed by Pius X in the words quoted just now are merely an application to Mary of the commonly received doctrine regarding the nature and condition of merit *de congruo proprie.* Some theologians look on it as morally certain; others as a certain theological conclusion; others as a truth formally and implicitly revealed and capable of being defined as a dogma of faith. In our opinion, it is at least a certain theological conclusion. We shall return to the point later (pp. 207-214).

What is the Extension of Mary's Merit for Us?

To answer this question it is enough to recall what Jesus has merited for us, since Mary has been associated with Him in the whole work of redemption and since the theologians—and their teaching has the authority of Pius X to support it—teach in general that Mary merited *de congruo* all that Jesus merited for us

---

37. Denz. 3034. Concerning this text cf. Merkelbach, *Mariologia,* p. 328.
38. Merkelbach, *ib.,* p. 329.

de condigno.[39] But Jesus merited in justice all the graces required that all men should really be enabled to observe the commandments, even though in point of fact they do not observe them. He merited also all efficacious graces and their effects—that is to say, the effective accomplishment by men of the divine will. He merited finally for the elect all the effects of their predestination: their christian vocation, their justification, their final perseverance, and their eternal glory.[40]

It follows that Mary has merited all these same graces *de congruo* and that she asks for their application now in Heaven and distributes them.[41]

The foregoing points show in what an elevated, intimate and all-embracing manner Mary is our spiritual mother, Mother of all men. We can suspect too what her care must be for those who are not content to invoke her at distant intervals but who consecrate themselves to her that she may lead them to intimacy with Jesus, as St. Grignon de Montfort explains so admirably in the following extract from his *Treatise on True Devotion.*

Treatise, Ch. I, a. 2: "Mary is necessary for men that they may arrive at their final end. (Devotion to Mary is not therefore a work of supererogation, as is devotion to any particular saints: it is necessary, and when it is true, faithful and persevering, it is a sign of predestination.) That devotion is still more neces-

---

39. Under the Old Dispensation graces were given—as it were on credit—in view of the future merits of Jesus, with which were associated those of Mary. Thus, Mary's merits *de congruo* extended by anticipation to the just of the Old Dispensation.
40. Cf. IIIa, q. 24, a. 4, and the commentaries. Though we cannot merit our final perseverance for ourselves (it can be obtained by prayer, the value of which is distinct from merit, as we have shown). Our Blessed Lord has merited it in justice for those who will persevere and Our Lady has merited it also *de congruo.*
41. It follows from the principles enunciated in this section that Jesus has merited for Mary all the effects of her predestination, except the divine maternity. The reason for this exception is that to merit it would be equivalent to meriting the Incarnation, that is, to meriting Himself. Among the graces He merited for Mary are included: her initial fulness of grace, her preservation from original sin, all the actual graces by which the initial fulness was increased, final perseverance, and glory.

sary for those who are called to special perfection, and I do not think it possible that anyone can arrive at intimate union with Our Blessed Lord and perfect fidelity to the Holy Ghost without a great spirit of union with Our Blessed Lady and of dependence on her assistance . . . I have said that this will happen especially towards the end of the world . . . because then the Most High and His Holy Mother will need to form great saints. . . . These saints great, full of grace and zeal, will be chosen to oppose the enemies of God who will rage on every side, and they will be singularly devout to Our Lady, enlightened by her, nourished by her, led by her spirit, sustained by her and kept under her protection, in such wise that they fight with one hand and build with the other. . . . That will arouse many enemies, but it will also yield many victories and much glory to God."

This noble spiritual doctrine, the fruits of which we see daily more clearly, is the normal consequence, on the level of contemplation and intimate union with God, of the doctrine admitted by all theologians: that Mary has merited *de congruo* all that Jesus has merited for men *de condigno,* and especially has she merited for the elect the effects of their predestination.

Article 3

The Sufferings of Mary as Co-Redemptrix

How Did Mary Make Satisfaction For Us?

The purpose of satisfaction is to repair the offence offered to God and to make Him once more favourable to the sinner. The offence offered by mortal sin has about it a certain infinity, since offence is measured by the dignity of the person offended. Mortal sin, by turning the sinner away from God, his final end, denies in practice to God His infinite rights as the Supreme

Good and destroys His reign in souls.

It follows from this that only the Incarnate Word could offer to the Father perfect and adequate satisfaction for the offence of mortal sin.[42] For satisfaction to be perfect, it must proceed from a love and oblation which are as pleasing to God as, or more pleasing than, all sins united are displeasing to Him.[43] But every act of charity elicited by Jesus had these qualities for His Divine Person gave them infinite satisfactory and meritorious value. A meritorious work becomes satisfactory (or one of reparation and expiation) when there is something painful about it. Hence, in offering His life in the midst of the greatest physical and moral sufferings, Jesus offered satisfaction of an infinite and superabundant value to His Father. He alone could make satisfaction in strict justice since the value of satisfaction like that of merit comes from the person, and the Person of Jesus, being divine, was of infinite dignity.

It was, however, possible to associate a satisfaction of becomingness (*de congruo*) to Jesus' satisfaction, just as a merit of becomingness was associated to His merit. In explaining this point, we shall show all the more clearly the depth and extent of Mary's sufferings.

Mary offered for us a satisfaction of becomingness (de convenientia) which was the greatest in value after that of her Son.

When a meritorious work is in some way painful it has value as satisfaction as well. Thus theologians commonly teach, following upon what has been explained in the previous section, that Mary satisfied for all sins

---

42. It is easier to knock down than to build up. The offence of a creature's mortal sin has a certain infinity from the side of the Person offended, whereas the creature's love is limited because of the limitations of its principle. Besides, mortal sin destroys the life of grace, and once that has been lost, we cannot be restored to it by ourselves.

43. IIIa, q. I, a. 2, ad 2; q. 48, a. 2.

de congruo in everything in which Jesus satisfied *de condigno.* Mary offered God a satisfaction which it was becoming that He should accept: Jesus satisfied for us in strict justice.

As Mother of the Redeemer, Mary was closely united to Jesus by perfect conformity of will, by humility, by poverty, by suffering—and most particularly by her compassion on Calvary. That is what is meant when it is said that she offered satisfaction along with Him. Her satisfaction derives its value from her dignity as Mother of God, from her great charity, from the fact that there was no fault in herself which needed to be expiated, and from the intensity of her sufferings.

The Fathers treat of this when they speak of Mary "standing" at the foot of the Cross, as St. John says. (*John* 19:25). They recall the words of Simeon, "Thy own soul a sword shall pierce," and they show that Mary suffered in proportion to her love for her crucified Son; in proportion also to the cruelty of His executioners, and the atrocity of the torments inflicted on Him Who was Innocence itself.[44] The liturgy also has taught many generations of the faithful that Mary merited the title of Queen of Martyrs by her most painful martyrdom of heart. That is the lesson of the Feasts of the Compassion of the Blessed Virgin and of the Seven Dolours, as well as of the *Stabat Mater.*

Leo XIII summed up this doctrine in the statement that Mary was associated with Jesus in the painful work of the redemption of mankind.[45] Pius X calls her "the repairer of the fallen world"[46] and continues to show how she was united to the priesthood of her Son: "Not only because she consented to become the mother of the only Son of God so as to make sacrifice for the

---

44. Cf. St. Ephrem, *Oratio ad Virginem;* St. Ambrose, *De Instit. Virg.,* c. 7; *Epist. 25 ad Eccles. Vercell.;* St. Bernard, *Sermo de Passione, Sermo de duodecim stellis, Sermo Dom. infra Oct. Ass.;* St. Albert the Great, *Mariale,* q. 42; St. Bonaventure, *Sermo I de B. V.;* St. Laurence Justinian, *Sermo de nativ. Virginis.*
45. Encycl. *Jucunda Semper,* Sept. 8th, 1894: "Consors cum Christo existit laboriosae pro humano genere expiationis."
46. Encycl. *Ad diem illum,* Feb. 2nd, 1904: *"Reparatrix perditi orbis."*

salvation of men possible, but also in the fact that she accepted the mission of protecting and nourishing the Lamb of sacrifice, and when the time came led Him to the altar of immolation—in this also must we find Mary's glory. Mary's community of life and sufferings with her Son was never broken off. To her as to Him may be applied the words of the prophet: My life is passed in dolors and my days in groanings. To conclude this list of Papal pronouncements we may refer to the words of Benedict XV: "In uniting herself to the Passion and Death of her Son she suffered almost unto death; as far as it depended on her, she immolated her Son, so that it can be said that with Him she redeemed the human race."[47]

The Depth and Fruitfulness of Mary's Sufferings as Co-Redemptrix

Mary's sufferings have the character of satisfaction from the fact that like Jesus and in union with Him, she suffered because of sin or of the offence it offers to God. This suffering of hers was measured by her love of God Whom sin offended, by her love of Jesus crucified for our sins, and by her love of us whom sin had brought to spiritual ruin. In other words, it was measured by her fulness of grace, which had never ceased to increase from the time of the Immaculate Conception. Already Mary had merited more by the easiest acts than the martyrs in their torments because of her greater love. What must have been the value of

47. Cf. Denz. 3034, no. 4. In this same place reference is made to the words of Pius XI: "Virgo perdolens redemptionis opus Jesu Christo participavit," and to a decree of the Holy Office praising the custom of adding after the name of Jesus that of His Mother, *our Co-Redemptrix, the Blessed Virgin Mary.* The same Congregation has indulgenced (Jan. 22nd, 1914) the prayer in which Mary is addressed as Co-Redemptrix of the human race. Cf. *Dict. de Théol. Cath.,* art. *Marie,* col. 2396: "Since the word 'Co-Redemptrix' signifies of itself simple co-operation in the work of redemption, and since it has received in the theological usage of centuries the very precise meaning of secondary and dependent cooperation . . . there can be no serious objection to its use, on condition that it be accompanied by some expression indicating that Mary's role in this co-operation is secondary and dependent."

her sufferings at the foot of the Cross, granted the understanding she then had of the mystery of the Redemption!

In the spiritual light which then flooded her soul, Mary saw that all souls are called to sing the glory of God. Every soul is called to be as it were a ray of the divinity, a spiritual ray of knowledge and love, for our minds are made to know God and our wills to love Him. But though the heavens tell God's glory unfailingly, thousands of souls turn from their Creator. Instead of that divine radiation, instead of God's exterior glory and His Kingdom, there are found in countless souls the three wounds called by St. John the concupiscence of the flesh, the concupiscence of the eyes, and the pride of life: living as if there were no desirable love except carnal love, no glory except that of fame and honor, and no Lord and Master, no end, except man himself.

Mary saw all that evil, all those wounds in souls, just as we see the evils and wounds of bodies. Her fulness of grace had given her an immense capacity to suffer from the greatest of evils, sin. She suffered as much as she loved God and souls: God offended by sin and souls whom it rendered worthy of eternal damnation. Most of all did Mary see the crime of deicide prepared in hearts and brought to execution: she saw the terrible paroxysm of hatred of Him who is the Light and the Author of salvation.

To understand her sufferings, we must think too of her love, both natural and supernatural, of her only Son Whom she not only loved but, in the literal sense of the term, adored since He was her God. She had conceived Him miraculously. She loved Him with the love of a virgin—the purest, richest and most tender charity that has ever been a mother's. Nor was her grief diminished by ignorance of anything that might make it more acute. She knew the reason for the crucifixion. She knew the hatred of the Jews, His chosen people—

her people. She knew that it was all for sinners.

From the moment when Simeon foretold the Passion—already so clearly prophesied by Isaias—and her compassion, she offered and did not cease to offer Him Who would be Priest and Victim, and herself in union with Him. This painful oblation was renewed over years. Of old, an angel had descended to prevent Abraham's immolation of his son Isaac. But no angel came to prevent the immolation of Jesus.

In his sermon on the Copassion of our Lady, we read the following magnificent words of Bossuet: "It is the will of the Eternal Father that Mary should not only be immolated with the Innocent Victim and nailed to the Cross by the nails that pierce Him, but should as well be associated with the mystery which is accomplished by His death. . . . Three things occur in the sacrifice of Our Saviour and constitute its perfection. There are the sufferings by which His humanity was crushed. There is His resignation to the will of His Father by which He humbly offered Himself. There is the fruitfulness by which He brings us to the life of grace by dying Himself. He suffers as a victim who must be bruised and destroyed. He submits as a priest who sacrifices freely; *voluntarie sacrificabo tibi.* (*Ps.* 53:8). Finally He brings us to life by His sufferings as the Father of a new people. . . .

"Mary stands near the Cross. With what eyes she contemplates her Son all covered with blood, all covered with wounds, in form now hardly a man! The sight is enough to cause her death. If she draws near to that altar, it is to be immolated there: and there, in fact, does she feel Simeon's sword pierce her heart. . . .

"But did her dolors overcome her, did her grief cast her to the ground? *Stabat juxta crucem:* she stood by the Cross. The sword pierced her heart but did not take away her strength of soul: her constancy equals her affliction, and her face is the face of one no less resigned than afflicted.

"What remains then but that Jesus who sees her feel His sufferings and imitate His resignation should have given her a share in His fruitfulness. It is with that thought that He gave her John to be her son: Woman, behold thy son. Woman, who suffer with me, be fruitful with me, be the mother of my children whom I give you unreservedly in the person of this disciple; I give them life by my sufferings, and sharing in the bitterness that is mine your affliction will make you fruitful."

In the sermon, of which the paragraphs I have quoted are the opening, Bossuet develops the three main points outlined and shows that Mary's love for Jesus was enough to make her a martyr: "One Cross was enough for the well-beloved Son and the mother." She is nailed to the Cross by her love for Him. Without a special grace she would have died of her agony.

Mary gave birth to Jesus without pain: but she brings the faithful forth in the most cruel suffering. "At what price she has bought them! They have cost her her only Son. She can be mother of christians only by giving her Son to death. O agonizing fruitfulness! It was the will of the Eternal Father that the adoptive sons should be born by the death of the True Son. . . . What man would adopt at this price and give his son for the sake of strangers? But that is what the Eternal Father did. We have Jesus' word for it: God so loved the world as to give His only begotten Son. (*John* 3:16).

"(Mary) is the Eve of the New Testament and the mother of all the faithful; but that is to be at the price of her Firstborn. United to the Eternal Father she must offer His Son and hers to death. It is for that purpose that providence has brought her to the foot of the Cross. She is there to immolate her Son that men may have life. . . . She becomes mother of christians at the cost of an immeasurable grief. . . ."

We should never forget what we have cost Mary. The

thought will lead to true contrition for our sins. The regeneration of our souls has cost Jesus and Mary more than we can ever think.

We may conclude this section by noting that Mary the Co-Redemptrix has given us birth at the foot of the Cross by the greatest act of faith, hope and love that was possible to her on such an occasion. One may even say that her act of faith was the greatest ever elicited, since Jesus had not the virtue of faith but the beatific vision. In that dark hour when the faith of the Apostles themselves seemed to waver, when Jesus seemed vanquished and His work annihilated, Mary did not cease for an instant to believe that her Son was the Saviour of mankind, and that in three days He would rise again as He had foretold. When He uttered His last words "It is consummated" Mary understood in the fulness of her faith that the work of salvation had been accomplished by His most painful immolation. The evening before, Jesus has instituted the Eucharistic sacrifice and the christian priesthood; she sees now something of the influence the sacrifice of the Cross will exercise. She knows that Jesus is the true Lamb of God who takes away the sin of the world, that He is the conqueror of sin and the demon, and that in three days He will conquer death, sin's consequence. She sees the hand of God where even the most believing see only darkness and desolation. Hers was the greatest act of faith ever elicited by a creature, a faith higher than that of the angels when they were as yet in their period of trial.

Calvary saw too her supreme act of hope at a moment when everything seemed lost. She grasped the force of the words spoken to the good thief: "This day thou shalt be with me in paradise;" Heaven, she realised, was about to be open for the elect.

It was finally her supreme act of charity: so to love God as to offer His only Son in the most painful agony:

to love God above everything at the moment when He tried her in the highest and deepest of her loves, even in the object of her adoration—and that because of our sins.

It is true that the theological virtues grew in Mary up to the time of her death, for these acts of faith, hope and charity were not broken off but continued in her as a kind of state. They even expanded in the succeeding calm, like a river which becomes more powerful and majestic as it nears the ocean. The point which theology wishes to stress is not that of Mary's subsequent growth in the virtues but the equality between her sacrifice and her merits at the foot of the Cross itself: both her sacrifice and her merits were of inestimable value and their fruitfulness, while not approaching that of Christ's sacrifice and merits, surpasses anything the human tongue can utter. Theologians express this by saying that Mary made satisfaction for us *de congruo* in proportion to her immense charity, while Jesus made satisfaction *de condigno*.

Even the saints who have been most closely associated with the sufferings of the Saviour did not enter as Mary did into the most secret depths of the Passion. St. Catherine de Ricci had every Friday during twelve years an ecstasy of pain which lasted twenty-eight hours and during which she lived over again all the sufferings of the way of the Cross. But even such sufferings fell far short of those of Mary. Mary's heart suffered in sympathy with all the agony of the Sacred Heart to such a point that she would have died of the experience had she not been especially strengthened. Thereby she became the consoler of the afflicted, for she had suffered more than all, and patroness of a happy death. We have no idea how fruitful these sufferings of hers have been during twenty centuries.

Mary's Participation as Co-Redemptrix in the Priesthood of Christ

Though Mary may be termed Co-Redemptrix in the sense we have explained, there can be no question of calling her a priest in the strict sense of the word since she has not received the priestly character and cannot offer Holy Mass nor give sacramental absolution. But, as we have seen already, her divine maternity is a greater dignity than the priesthood of the ordained priest in the sense that it is more to give Our Saviour His human nature than to make His body present in the Blessed Eucharist. Mary has given us the Priest of the sacrifice of the Cross, the Principal Priest of the sacrifice of the Mass and the Victim offered on the altar.

It is more also, and more perfect, to offer her only Son and her God on the Cross as Mary did, by offering herself with Him in community of suffering, than to make the body of Our Lord present and to offer It on the altar as the priest does at Holy Mass.

We must affirm, too, as has recently a careful theologian who has devoted years to the study of these questions[48] that "it is a certain theological conclusion that Mary co-operated in some way in the principal act of Jesus' priesthood, by giving, as the divine plan required, her consent to the sacrifice of the Cross as it was accomplished by the Saviour." In another context he writes: "If we consider only certain immediate effects of the priest's action such as the eucharistic consecration or the remission of sins in the sacrament of penance, it is true that the priest can do certain things which Mary, not having the priestly power, cannot. But to look at the matter so as not to compare dignities but merely particular effects which are produced by a power which Mary lacks and which do not necessarily indicate a higher dignity."[49]

---

48. *E. Dublanchy, Dict. de Théol. Cath.,* art. *Marie,* col. 2396 sqq.
49. *Ib.,* col. 2366.

But even if Mary cannot, for the reasons given, be spoken of as priest in the strict sense of the term, it remains true, as M. Olier has said, that she has received the fulness of the *spirit* of the priesthood, which is the spirit of Christ the Redeemer. That is the reason why she is called Co-Redemptrix, a title which, like that of Mother of God, implies a higher dignity than that of the christian priesthood.[50]

Mary's participation in the immolation and oblation of Jesus, Priest and Victim, cannot be better summed up than in the words of the *Stabat Mater* of the Franciscan Jacopone de Todi (1228-1286).

The *Stabat Mater* manifests in a singularly striking manner that supernatural contemplation of the mystery of Christ crucified is part of the normal way of holiness. In precise and ardent words it speaks of the wounding of the Saviour's Heart and shows the intimate and persuasive manner in which Mary leads us to Him. Not only does Mary lead us to the divine intimacy, in a sense she produces it in us: that is what the repetition of the imperative "Fac" in the following strophes brings out:

Eia Mater, fons amoris,	O Thou Mother! Fount of love!
Me sentire vim doloris	Touch my spirit from above,
Fac, ut tecum lugeam.	Make my heart with thine accord!
Fac ut ardeat cor meum	Make me feel as thou hast felt;
In amando Christum Deum,	Make my soul to glow and melt
Ut sibi complaceam.	With the love of Christ my Lord.
Fac ut portem Christi	Let me, to my latest breath,

---

50. *Ib.,* col. 2365.

mortem	In my body bear the death
Passionis fac corsortem	Of that dying Son of thine.
Et *plagas recolere.*	

Fac me plagis vulnerari	Wounded with His every
Fac me cruce inebriari,	wound,
Et cruore Filii.	Steep my soul till it hath
	swoon'd
	In His very blood away.

—Fr. *Caswall*

This is the prayer of a soul which, under a special inspiration, wishes to know in a spiritual way the wound of love and to be associated in these painful mysteries of adoring reparation as were John and the holy women on Calvary—and Peter, too, when he shed his bitter tears. Those tears of adoration and sorrow are what the Stabat asks for in the following strophes:

Fac me tecum pie flere,	Let me mingle tears with thee,
Crucifixo condolere,	Mourning Him who mourn'd
Donec ego vixero.	for me,
	All the days that I may live.

Juxta crucem tecum	By the cross with thee to
stare,	stay.
Et me tibi sociare	There with thee to weep and
In planctu desidero.	pray,
	Is all I ask of thee to give.

—Fr. *Caswall*

Mary exercised therefore a universal mediation on earth by meriting *de congruo* all that Jesus merited *de condigno* and also by making similar satisfaction in union with Him. For both Jesus and Mary, the mediation exercised on earth is the foundation of that now exercised in Heaven of which we shall speak in the next chapter.

❧ Chapter 3 ❧

Mary's Universal Mediation in Heaven

Mary's mediation in Heaven which she has exercised since the Assumption has as purpose to obtain for us the application at the appropriate time of Jesus' merits and hers, acquired during their life on earth and especially on Calvary. We shall speak in this connection of Mary's power of intercession, of the way in which she distributes graces or the mode of her influence on us, and finally of the universality of her mediation and of its definability.

Article 1

Mary's Power of Intercession

Even during her life on earth, Mary appears in the gospels as distributing graces. Jesus sanctifies the precursor through her when she comes to visit her cousin Elisabeth. Through her He confirms the faith of His disciples at Cana by performing the miracle for which she asked. Through her He confirms John's faith on Calvary, saying: "Son, behold thy mother." Through her finally the Holy Ghost gave Himself to the Apostles, for we read in the Acts (*Acts* 1:14) that she prayed with them in the Cenacle while they prepared themselves for the apostolate and for the light and strength and graces of Pentecost.

With still greater reason is Mary powerful in her intercession now that she has entered Heaven and has been lifted up above the choirs of the angels. The Christian sense of the faithful assures us that a mother in

187

Heaven knows the spiritual needs of the children she has left behind her on earth, and that she prays for their salvation. It is a universal practice in the Church for the faithful to recommend themselves to the prayers of the saints in Heaven. As St. Thomas says,[1] when the saints were on earth, their charity led them to pray for their neighbor. With still greater reason do we say that in Heaven they pray for their neighbour since when their charity is inflamed by the beatific vision it is greater than it was on earth: their charity in Heaven is uninterrupted in its acts and proceeds from a fuller realization of human needs and the value of life eternal.

The Council of Trent defined that the saints in Heaven pray for us and that it is useful to invoke them (Denz. 984). Their merits and their expiation have ceased, but not their prayer—no longer a prayer of tearful supplication but one now of intercession.

St. Paul tells us that Our Blessed Lord does not cease to make intercession for us. (*Rom.* 8:34; *Heb.* 7:25). He is the principal and necessary intercessor. But Jesus Himself wishes that we should have recourse to Mary so that our prayers may have greater value through being presented by her.

As Mother of all men Mary knows the spiritual needs of all men, knows all that concerns their salvation. Because of her immense charity she prays for them. And since she is all-powerful with her Son because of the love by which they are united, she obtains from Him all the graces for which she asks—that is to say, all the graces we receive.

This power of Mary's intercession is proclaimed by the faithful each time they recite the *Hail Mary*.

Theology explains the belief of the faithful by pointing to three fundamental reasons for Mary's power of intercession.

The first of these is that since Mary is Mother of

---

1. IIa IIae, q. 85, a. II.

men she knows all their spiritual needs. It is a principle admitted by all theologians that the happiness of the blessed in Heaven would not be complete if they did not know what happens on earth to the extent to which it concerns them by reason of their office, their role, or their relations with men. Such knowledge is the object of a legitimate desire which must find its satisfaction in beatitude, and with all the more reason when the knowledge they desire is of men's spiritual needs and is therefore desired in charity: it is in charity that the saints desire men's salvation so that they may glorify God with them for all eternity and share thus in their happiness. Fathers and mothers, for example, know from Heaven the needs of their children, especially those which bear on their salvation. The same may be said of the founders of religious institutes. With all the more reason may the same be said of Our Lady, who has the highest degree of glory after her Son: as Mother of all men she must know everything which bears directly or indirectly on the supernatural life which she has been commissioned to give us and to nourish in us. This universal knowledge, certain and detailed, of all that concerns our destiny—our thoughts, desires, the dangers in which we are, the graces we need, temporal affairs which have some connection with our salvation—is a prerogative which belongs to Mary because of her motherhood of God and her spiritual motherhood of men.[2]

Knowing our spiritual needs and even the temporal needs which are connected with our salvation Mary is obviously impelled by her great charity to intercede

---

2. Cf. E. Dublanchy, *Dict. Théol. Cath.,* art. *Marie,* col. 2412: "Can it be said that even on earth Mary knew in detail all that concerned the salvation and sanctification of all men? It would appear that no satisfactory proof can be given to support an affirmative answer to the question, especially in regard to universal knowledge extending to all the details concerning every individual. But Mary has this perfect knowledge in Heaven where she exercises her universal intercession and mediation for all the graces which follow from the redemption."

for us. If a mother but suspects that her child needs her help she flies to its side. There is no question here of Mary's acquiring new merits in Heaven but simply of her obtaining that her merits—and her Son's—be applied to us at the appropriate moment.

Is Mary's prayer omnipotent? Tradition has honoured Mary with the title, *Omnipotentia supplex,* omnipotence in the order of supplication.[3]

In support of the title, we may refer to the principle that the intercession of the saints is proportioned to their degree of glory in heaven, or of union with God (Cf. IIa IIae, q. 83, a. II). It follows then that Mary, whose glory surpasses that of all the saints, must have all power in intercession. Even before the 8th century, this is the explicit teaching of St. Ephrem. In the 8th century, the most clear-cut statements are those of Andrew of Crete, of St. Germanus of Constantinople, and of St. John Damascene. Towards the end of the 11th century, St. Anselm and his disciple Eadmer affirm Mary's intercessory omnipotence, a doctrine explained by St. Bernard and transmitted to succeeding generations of theologians.

Bossuet brings out the underlying principles very well in his sermon on the Compassion of Our Lady, when he recalls the two texts: "God so loved the world, as to give his only begotten Son" (*John* 3:16) and "He that spared not even his own Son, but delivered him up for us all, how hath he not also, with him, given us all good things?" (*Rom.* 8:32). Mary in her turn has loved God and souls to the extent of delivering up her Son, Jesus, on Calvary. She is in consequence all-powerful with God the Father and with Jesus to obtain all that is necessary for the salvation of those who turn to her mediation.

One paragraph of the sermon deserves to be quoted:

---

3. For a list of extracts and references we refer the reader to Hugon, O.P., *Marie pleine de grâce,* 5th edit., 1926, pp. 160-166; also to Merkelbach, *Mariologia,* pp. 345-371.

"Intercede for us, O Blessed Virgin Mary: you have in your hands, if I may so speak, the key that opens the treasury of the divine blessings. That key is your Son: He closes and no one can open: He opens and no one can close: it is His innocent blood which makes us to be inundated with heavenly graces. And to whom will He give the right to that blood, if not to her from whom He drew all His blood. . . . For the rest, you live in such perfect union of love with Him that it is impossible that your prayer should not be heard." It is enough, as St. Bernard says, if Mary speaks to the Heart of Jesus.

The teaching of Tradition, thus formulated by Bossuet, has been proclaimed by Leo XIII in his first encyclical on the Rosary, September 1st, 1883, in which he calls Mary the dispenser of heavenly graces, *coelestium administra gratiarum.* In the encyclical *Jucunda Semper,* September 8th, 1894, the same Pope makes his own the two statements of St. Bernard: that God in His great mercy has made Mary our Mediatrix and that He has willed that all graces should come to us through her. The same teaching will be found in the encyclical *Ad Diem Illum,* February 2nd, 1904, where Mary is spoken of as "the dispenser of all the graces which have been acquired for us by the Blood of Jesus." Jesus is the source of these graces: Mary is, as it were, the aqueduct, or—to use another image— as it were the neck which unites the Head to the members and transmits the vital impulse to them: "Ipsa est collum capitis nostri, per quod omnia spiritualia dona corpori ejus mystico communicantur." Benedict XV has consecrated this teaching by approving the Mass and the liturgical Office of Mary, Mediatrix of all graces, for the universal Church.

As Fr. Merkelbach indicates,[4] three points are to be noted.

First of all, it is of faith that Mary prays for us, and

---

4. *Mariologia,* pp. 345-349.

even for each one of us, in her capacity as Mother of the Redeemer and of all men, and that her intercession is very useful for us. This follows from the general dogma of the intercession of the saints (Council of Trent: Session 25). In support of this assertion we may refer to the practice of the Church in praying, *Sancta Maria, ora pro nobis:* Holy Mary, pray for us. *Legem credendi lex statuat supplicandi:* dogma and prayer have one and the same law (Denz. 139).

In the second place, Tradition teaches us as certain that Mary's powerful intercession can obtain for all those who invoke her with the proper dispositions all the graces required for salvation[5] and no one is saved without her intervention. Thus the Church repeats: *Sentiant omnes tuum juvamen:* Let all be cognizant of your assistance.

In the third place, it is common and safe doctrine, taught by different Popes, by the liturgy, and by preachers throughout the world, that no grace is granted us without Mary's intervention. This is contained clearly in the Mass and Office of Mary, Mediatrix of all graces, and it would be at least rash to deny it.

Historically, this doctrine will be found implicit in the doctrine of Mary's universal mediation up to the 8th century. It becomes more explicit as we draw nearer to the 15th century, in the form of the affirmation that all God's gifts come to us through Mary as intermediary. From the 16th century onwards, the question has been examined under all its aspects. Even the graces of the sacraments are considered to fall under Mary's universal mediation in the sense that the dispositions which we must bring to the reception of the

---

5. An obstacle to grace may arise through lack of proper dispositions or, if the prayer be for another, through that other's lack of dispositions. It should be noted that for the exercise of Mary's mediation of intercession it is not necessary that one pray explicitly to her. By the fact that one prays to God or to the saints, one prays implicitly to Mary according to the present plan of our redemption. Besides, many graces are given us without our praying for them at all, for example, the actual grace required to begin to pray. However, prayer offered explicitly to Mary with the proper dispositions has a greater guarantee of calling down God's grace.

sacraments are obtained through her intercession.[6] Besides, if Mary has merited *de congruo* all that Jesus has merited for us *de condigno,* it follows that she has merited the sacramental graces themselves.

It is clear therefore that Mary's intercession is much more powerful and efficacious than that of all the other saints—even taken all together—for the other saints obtain nothing without her. Their mediation is included under her universal mediation, while hers is, in its turn, subordinated to that of Jesus. There is another point to be noted: it is that Mary has merited all the graces which she asks for us, whereas the saints often ask for graces for others which they have not merited themselves. Their prayer could not then have the same efficacy as Mary's.

Regarding the efficacy of Mary's prayer, a principle which applies to the prayer of Christ may well be recalled. The prayer of Christ is always heard when the thing prayed for is asked absolutely and in conformity with the divine intentions which He knows so well;[7] it is not so heard, however, when the thing prayed for is asked conditionally, as happened in the case of the prayer of the Garden of Olives. In the case of Mary's prayer, she obtains infallibly from her Son all that she asks absolutely and in conformity with the divine intentions: these intentions she knows, and her will is in complete accord with them.

What has been said in this section is sufficient to show that Mary's omnipotence in intercession, resting as it does on the merits of the Saviour and on His love for His Mother, is far from derogating from His own universal mediation. On the contrary it is one of its brightest manifestations, and throws into clearer relief the marvellous way in which Jesus redeemed and adorned her who was so intimately associated with Him in the redemption of men.

---

6. Cf. *Dict. Théol. Cath.,* art. *Marie,* col. 2403.
7. Cf. IIIa, q. 21, a. 4.

Article 2
Mary and the Distribution of Grace

Does Our Lady distribute grace only in the sense that she intercedes for each one of us and so obtains that the fruits of the merits of her Son be applied to each one of us at the appropriate moment, or does she transmit graces to us in the way in which the Sacred Humanity does? According to the teaching of St. Thomas and many other theologians, the Sacred Humanity is a physical instrumental cause of grace, an instrument always united to the divinity and higher than the sacraments, which are instruments separated from the divinity.

St. Thomas has treated of this question in many places in so far as it refers to Christ, the Head of the Church.[8] It is but reasonable to ask if something similar to what he says about the Head may be affirmed of her who is, according to the teaching of Tradition, as it were the neck of the Mystical Body which unites the Head to the members and transmits the vital impulse to them.

In this connection theologians commonly admit that Mary exercises moral causality by her past merits and satisfaction and by her present intercession. But very many stop there and do not admit that she exercises any physical instrumental causality.[9] Other theologians admit physical instrumental causality in subordination to the Sacred Humanity. They rely in support of their thesis on the traditional doctrine of Mary as the neck of the Mystical Body, uniting Head and members, and transmitting the vital influence to them.[10]

---

8. IIIa, q. 8, a. 2, ad 1 ; q. 13, a. 2; q. 48, a. 6; q. 49, a. 1 ; q. 50, a. 6; q. 62, a. 1, and *De Potentia,* q. 6, a. 4.

9. This negative answer is found in Suarez, III, disp. 23, sect. I, no. 2. Contemporary theologians who adopt the same position are Scheeben, Terrien, Godts, Bainvel, Campana, de la Taille, Bittremieux, Friethoff, Grabmann, Van der Meersch, Merkelbach.

10. This is the position adopted by Hugon, O.P., *La causalité physique instrumen-*

It is certain that St. Thomas taught explicitly that the Sacred Humanity and the sacraments of the New Law are physical instrumental causes of grace. God alone is its principal cause, since it is a participation in His inner life. But there is no similar statement of his about Our Lady. There are even theologians—with whom we do not agree—who hold that he explicitly denied her any such causality.[11] In his explanation of the *Ave Maria,* he attributes to Mary a fulness of grace which overflows on souls and sanctifies them, but he does not say explicitly that this overflowing is anything more than moral causality.

However, since physical instrumental causality was not an impossibility for the Sacred Humanity nor for the sacraments—for example, for the words of the priest at the consecration or when giving absolution—in the opinion of St. Thomas and his commentators, neither is it an impossibility for Mary.[12] St. Thomas even admits that a miracle-worker is sometimes instrumental cause of a miracle, for example, when it is worked through a blessing.[13] Not only can he obtain the miracle by his prayer, he may even perform it as God's instrument.

It is not possible therefore to be certain that Mary did not exercise a similar influence in regard to grace. We must also allow for the fact that God's masterpieces—among which we must include Mary—are

---

tale, 1907, pp. 194-205; de Gommer, *De munere Matris Dei in Ecclesia gerendo;* Lépicier, Girerd, Gernandex, Lavaud, Bernard.

11. In IIIa, q. 60, a. 8. All that is stated here is that one cannot baptise in the name of Mary, as we do in the name of the Father, Son, and Holy Ghost, since she is not operative in Baptism even though her intercession is of value to the baptised person to help him to preserve his baptismal grace.

12. Besides the arguments from Scripture and Tradition for the physical instrumental causality of the Sacred Humanity there is a theological argument: to act physically as well as morally is more perfect than to act only morally. But we must attribute what is more perfect to the Humanity of Christ, provided it is not incompatible with the redemptive Incarnation. Hence we must attribute to the Humanity of Christ the physical instrumental causality of grace. This same argument is valid, within all due limits, if applied to Mary, and establishes our thesis as probable.

13. Cf. IIae 178, *de gratia miraculorum,* a. 1, ad 1: Potest contingere quod mens miracula facientis moveatur ad faciendum aliquid, ad quod sequitur effectus miraculi, quod Deus sua virtute facit."

richer, more beautiful, more brimful of life than we can find words to describe.

But at the same time it must be admitted that it does not seem possible to prove with certainty that Mary did exercise physical causality. Theology will hardly advance beyond serious probability in this matter for the reason that it is very hard to see in the traditional texts quoted where precisely the literal sense ends and the metaphorical sense begins. Those who are in the habit of using metaphors whenever they can will not appreciate this difficulty. But anyone who is accustomed to using words in their exact and proper sense will be fully sensible of it. When Tradition tells us that Mary's position in the Mystical Body is comparable to that of the neck which unites the Head to the members and transmits the vital impulse to them, at the very least the metaphor it uses is an expressive one, but we cannot affirm with certainty that it is more than a metaphor.

However, as Father Hugon points out, the comparison does not seem to be given credit for all its force unless physical instrumental causality be admitted.[14] Fr. R. Bernard, O.P., is of the same opinion: "God and His Christ make use of her (Mary) in this sense, that they make all the graces which they destine for us pass through her. . . . By using her as intermediary, They temper Their action all the more with humanity, without in any way diminishing its divine efficacy. They make Mary live by the life we are to live by. She is first filled to overflowing with it. Grace is pre-formed in her and receives in her the imprint of a special beauty. All grace and all graces come to us thus canalised and distributed by her, impregnated with that special sweetness which she imparts to all she touches and all she does.

"By her action Mary enters therefore into our lives

---

14. *La causalité instrumentale en théologie,* p. 201.

as bearer of the divine. In the whole course of our lives, from the cradle and before it to the grave and beyond it, there is nothing of grace in which she had no part. She shapes us to the likeness of Jesus. . . . She leaves her mark on everything and adds to the perfection of what passes through her hands. I have said that we are sustained by her prayer: we are similarly sustained by her action and, if one may say it, have our spiritual being in her hands. Every christian is a child of Mary, but a child is not worthy of the name unless it is formed by its mother."[15]

By admitting that Mary not only obtains grace for us by her prayers but transmits it to us by her action, a fuller meaning is given to her titles of treasurer and dispensatrix of all graces. This same fuller meaning seems to be suggested by certain strong and beautiful expressions found in the Liturgy, especially in the Stabat, where the repetition of the imperative Fac implies that Mary in some way produces the grace of intimacy with Christ in us.[16]

Mary's influence on our souls remains, it is true, shrouded in mystery, but it appears probable that it is more than moral: she seems to enter into the production of grace as a free and knowing instrument, somewhat as a miracle-worker can perform a miracle by his contact and his blessing. Even in the natural order a smile, a look, the tone of the voice, communicate something of the life of the soul.

In addition to the argument drawn from the traditional formulae there are theological ones which have a certain weight.

As Fr. Hugon says:[17] "Once it is granted that the angels and the saints are frequently physical secondary causes of miracles, it seems quite natural to postulate

---

15. *Le Mystère de Marie,* 1933, p. 462.
16. Cf. the strophes quoted on pp. 197-198.
17. *La causalité instrumentale en théologie,* 1907, pp. 195 sqq.

the same power for the Mother of God and in a higher degree." And if she is the physical instrumental cause of miracles which God alone produces as Principal Cause, what reason can there be for not admitting that she causes grace in the same manner? Fr. Hugon continues: "Every prerogative which is possible in itself and which harmonises with the role and dignity of the Mother of God should be found in Mary. . . . She receives under a secondary title everything that Jesus has under a full and primary title—merits, satisfaction, intercession. Why should this relation between Mother and Son not extend to the order of physical causality? What necessitates an exception?[18] Would it not appear that the supernatural parallelism between Jesus and Mary should be continued to the very end, and that the Mother should be secondary instrument wherever the Son is first and conjoined instrument? . . . It seems but natural that Mary's acts of which God makes continual use in the order of intercession should be elevated and transformed by His infinite fecundity and commissioned to communicate the life of grace instrumentally to souls."

Another argument may be drawn from the fact that the priest who absolves is instrumental cause of grace by reason of his union with the Redeemer. But Mary is no less closely united to the Redeemer since she is Mother of God and Co-Redemptrix.

The influence which Jesus, Head of the Mystical Body, exercises is itself most mysterious since it is supernatural. No wonder then if that which Mary exercises over and above her intercession is also a mystery. We may note before concluding that Mary's influence seems to be exercised especially on our sensibility—which is sometimes so rebellious or so distracted—to calm it, to subordinate it to our higher

---

18. To justify the exception it would appear that there should be some positive reason.

faculties, and to make it easy for these latter to submit to the movement of the Head when He transmits us the divine life.[19]

Though the manner of Mary's action upon us is hidden, the fact of her influence is in no way doubtful. It is beyond question that Mary is dispensatrix of all graces, at least by her intercession. It may be added with Fr. Merkelbach[20] that Mary does not intercede in the same way as the other saints: her prayer is not such as may possibly not be heard, but rather it is like the prayer of Christ, our Mediator and Saviour, Whose intercession is effective in fact as well as in right. The intercession of Christ, says St. Thomas,[21] is the expression of His desire for our salvation which He acquired at the price of His precious blood. Since Mary was associated with the redemptive work of her Son she is associated with His intercession; she too expresses a desire which is always united to that of Jesus. In this sense she disposes of the graces which she asks for: her prayer is the efficacious cause of their being obtained, and she is united also to Christ's influence in transmitting them.

For that reason the Church sings in the hymn of Matins of the Feast of Mary Mediatrix of all graces:

Cuncta, quae nobis meruit Redemptor,
Dona partitur genitrix Maria,
Cujus ad votum sua fundit ultro
Munera Natus.[22]

She bestows on us all the graces which her Son has merited for us and which she has merited with Him.

If, as it would appear, Mary transmits to us by phys-

---

19. In this we see the application of St. Thomas's principle that the instrument disposes in preparation for the action of the principal agent.
20. *Mariologia,* p. 370.
21. *Commentarium in Ep. ad Hebr.,* vii, 25 and *ad Rom.,* viii, 34.
22. All the gifts which the Saviour merited for us are bestowed by His Mother Mary. The Son gladly loads us with benefits in answer to her prayer.

ical instrumental causality all the graces which we receive, all the actual graces which are given us to be the air which the soul breathes unceasingly, it follows that we are at all times under her influence, subordinated to the influence of Jesus the Head of the Mystical Body; she transmits to us continuously the vital influence which comes from Him.

But even if her action upon us is only the moral causality of intercession, she is present, by an affective presence, in souls in the state of grace who pray to her just as a beloved object, even if physically distant, is present to the person who loves it. Mary being physically present in body and soul in Heaven is physically distant from us on earth. But she is affectively present within the interior souls who love her.[23]

Mary's influence becomes increasingly all-embracing as souls advance in the interior life. This has been often noted by St. Grignon de Montfort. "The Holy Ghost," he says, "became fruitful on earth through Mary, His spouse. It was with her and of her that He produced His masterpiece, God-made-man, and that He produces daily till the end of the world the predestined members of the body of our adorable Head: that is why He is all the more active to produce Jesus Christ in a soul the more He finds there Mary, His dear and inseparable spouse.

"This does not mean that Mary gave the Holy Ghost His fecundity. . . . It means that the Holy Ghost manifests His fecundity by making use of Mary, even though He does not need her, to produce Jesus Christ and His members in her and through her: this is a mystery of grace unknown even to the most learned and spiritual of Christians."[24]

---

23. Cf. Ia IIae, q. 28, a. 1: "Duplex est unio amantis ad amatum. Una quidem *secundum* rem: puta cum amatum praesentialiter adest amanti. Alia vero *secundum affectum*. Secundam autem unionem facit (amor) formaliter; quia ipse amor est taus unio, vel nexus."
24. *Treatise of True Devotion*, ch. I, a. 1.

As Fr. Hugon remarks à *propos* of these words of St. Grignon de Montfort:[25] "The exterior fecundity of the Divine Paraclete is the production of grace, not in the order of moral causality—for the Holy Ghost is not a meritorious or impetratory cause—but in the order of physical causality. To reduce this fecundity to act is to produce physically grace and the other works of holiness which are appropriated to the Third Divine Person. From this it follows that the Holy Ghost produces grace physically in souls by Mary: she is the secondary physical instrument of the Holy Ghost. Such seems to us the import of these strong expressions of the saint: such the sublime doctrine which he says is a mystery of grace unknown even to the most learned and spiritual of christians." Mary's virginal motherhood reaches its completion in her transmission of the graces which she obtains by her intercession, just as the Incarnation is prolonged, in a certain sense, by the vivifying influence of Christ the Head upon His members.

St. Grignon de Montfort never expressed himself otherwise than as we have seen.[26] Reference must also be made to the work "The Mystic Union with Mary" composed by a Flemish recluse, Mary of St. Teresa (1623-1677), who had herself experience of what she taught. Such writings show that Mary exercises a very profound influence on faithful souls to lead them to ever greater intimacy with Our Blessed Lord.[27] Those who enter on this way find themselves introduced far into the mystery of the communion of saints, and come gradually to share in the sentiments Mary had at the foot of the Cross, after Jesus' death, and later on at Pentecost when she prayed for the Apostles and obtained for them the graces of light and love and strength which they needed to carry the name of Jesus

---

25. *Op. cit.*, p. 203.
26. Cf. ch. 5, a. 6; ch. 6, a. 1 ; ch. 7, a. 5, a. 6. Cf. also *L'union mystique à la Sainte Vierge*, by Father Neubert, in *La Vie Spirituelle*, Jan. 1937.
27. A French translation by L. van den Bossche of the Flemish original will be found in *Les Cahiers de la Vierge*, May, 1936.

to the limits of the earth. And now that she has entered Heaven the influence of Mary, universal Mediatrix, is still greater, more universal, and more effective.

NOTE

THE MODE OF PRESENCE OF THE BLESSED VIRGIN IN SOULS UNITED TO HER

To make clear the doctrine on this point, it is necessary to explain briefly what theologians understand by virtual contact on one hand, and by affective presence on the other.

Virtual or Dynamic Contact

With regard to the presence of God in all things or of that of the angels in the bodies on which they act, a distinction is generally made between virtual contact (*contactus virtutis*) and quantitative contact. Two bodies are present to each other by quantitative contact, i,e. by that of their own quantity or extension. A pure spirit, having no body, and consequently no quantity or extension, is present where it operates by virtual contact, by its power, the principle of its action. This is the *dynamic contact* of a spiritual force which takes possession of what it acts on.

The Power of God is not distinct from His Essence, and so God is really and substantially present, by virtual contact, in everything He Himself produces immediately, or without the intermediary of an instrument, i.e. in what He creates in the strict sense of the term *ex nihilo* and keeps immediately in existence. He is thus present in Prime Matter, in souls and in angels which can only be produced by creation *ex nihilo* and cannot be brought about by the intermediary of an instrument (cf. Ia, Q8, a. 1, 2, 3, 4; Q45, a., 5; Q104, a. 2).

For the same reason theologians admit generally that an angel, which, strictly speaking, is not in a place inasmuch as it is pure spirit, is really present where it acts, for it touches by virtual contact (*contactus virtutis*) the body which it moves locally (cf. Ia, Q52). An angel can also enlighten a human intelligence and act on it through the imagination, like a master who instructs.

The presence of the Soul of Jesus and that of the soul of the Blessed Virgin in persons united to them resembles that of the angels, but differs from it, however, under a certain respect. The difference comes from the fact that a human soul united to its body, like the Soul of Jesus and that of His Holy Mother, is really present (*definitive*) where its body is and nowhere else. Now the Body of Jesus, since the Ascension, is in Heaven alone according to its natural place, and the same must be said of Mary's body since the Assumption. And the soul, being of its nature united to its own body, acts on others only through it. In this it differs from an angel, which has no body.

But just as God can make use of angels to produce instrumentally a properly divine effect such as a miracle, He can make use also of the Soul of Jesus, of His acts, and even of His Body, or again of the soul of Mary, of her acts and of her body. When God makes use of the humanity of the Saviour as a physical instrumental cause to produce grace in us, as St. Thomas admits (IIIa, Q43, a. 2; Q48, a. 6, Q62, a. 4), *we are under the physical influence of the Humanity of Jesus.* However, It does not touch us, for It is in heaven. In the same way, if someone speaks to us from a distance by means of a megaphone, this megaphone does not touch us immediately: there is only virtual contact and not quantitative contact of the instrument and the subject on which it acts—virtual contact similar to that of the sun which gives us light and warmth from afar.

If the Blessed Virgin is a physical instrumental cause of grace, subordinate to Christ's Humanity, *we are also under her physical influence,* without her touching us, however, otherwise than by virtual contact.

It must be noted, however, that the human soul,

in so far as it is spiritual and transcends the body, is not as such in a place. From this point of view, *all souls,* in the measure in which they grow in the spiritual life and become detached from the senses, *by bringing themselves spiritually nearer to God,* bring themselves spiritually nearer to one another as well. Thus is explained the *spiritual presence* of Christ's Holy Soul and that of Mary in us, especially if we admit that they are both physical instrumental causes of the graces we receive.

Thus one can say that we are constantly under their influence in the spiritual order, as in the corporal order our body is constantly under the influence of the sun which gives us light and warmth, and under the permanent influence of the air which we breathe at all times.*

In this spiritual presence of which we have just spoken there can be united the influence of instrumental causality called physical, which is here spiritual, and the presence called affective, which we shall now explain and which for its part is not only probable but certain.

Affective Presence

Even if the Blessed Virgin were not the physical instrumental cause of the graces we receive, she would be present in us by an "affective presence" as an object known and loved is present to the lover, and

---

* The instrumental power which produces grace is of a spiritual and supernatural order. It can, however, be in a passing manner—as a vibration is—in a corporal action, for example of exterior adoration or blessing, or come through the glorious wounds of Christ's Body. It can be also in perceptible words, as in those of sacramental absolution transmitted by the sound-medium which is between the priest and the penitent. This instrumental power productive of grace can also be transmitted by the medium (air or ether) between us and the Body of Christ or that of His Holy Mother, present in Heaven.

But, as St. Thomas says (IIa IIae, q. 178, a. 1, ad 1, and *de Potentia* Q6, a. 4), God can also use as instrument a purely spiritual act, an interior prayer of the Saviour or of His Mother; in this case the instrumental power productive of grace is transmitted without a corporal medium. How God, who is present everywhere, both in spirits and in bodies, which He keeps in existence, can make present where its work is needed this instrumental power of the spiritual order, which of itself is not in any place, but which is, like the spirits, in a supra-spatial zone of reality. The Thomists say that God brings it where it has to operate. God Himself cannot play the part of medium, for a medium, like air or ether, is a material cause set in motion whereas God can be only an efficient and a final cause.

this in varying degrees of intimacy according to the depth and strength of our love.

Even a very imperfect soul is under the so-called physical influence of the Blessed Virgin if she is the physical instrumental cause of the graces received by this soul. But the deeper our love of Mary becomes, the more intimate does her affective presence in us become. It is necessary to insist on this, for the affective mode of presence is one which certainly exists, and St. Thomas has admirably explained it (Ia IIae, Q28, a. 1 and 2) where he asks whether union is the effect of love and whether a mutual inherence results from it.

He replies (a. 1): "Love, as the Areopagite has said, is a unitive force. There are two unions possible to those who love: 1—a real union, when they are really present to each other (as are two persons who are in the same place and see each other directly); 2—an affective union (as that which exists between two persons physically distant). This latter proceeds from the knowledge (derived from actual remembrance of the person loved) and the love of this person. . . . Love suffices to constitute affective union and leads to the desire for real union." There is, then, an affective union resulting from love, in spite of whatever distance may separate the persons. If St. Monica and St. Augustine, far away from each other, were nevertheless spiritually united and in that way affectively present to each other in a more or less profound manner according to the degree or intensity of their affection, how much more is a soul that grows daily closer in intimacy with our heavenly Mother affectively united to her?

St. Thomas goes further: ibid., a. 2, corp. et ad 1, he shows that a mutual spiritual inherence can be an effect of love in spite of the remoteness of the persons. And he distinguishes very well two aspects of this affective union: 1—*amatum est in amante,* the person loved is in him who loves, as being imprinted on his affection through the delight he inspires him with; 2—and on the other hand, *amans est in amato,* the lover is in the person loved, inasmuch as he rejoices greatly and intimately at what makes for his happiness.

The first mode is often the one more felt, and, with regard to God, we run the risk here of simulating such a union before the time; moreover, even when it is really the fruit of grace, it can have too strong an effect on the sensibility and thus expose one to spiritual greediness.

The more disinterested and at the same time the stronger and more intimate love is, the more does the second aspect tend to prevail. Then the soul is more in God than God in it; and there is something similar to this with regard to the Humanity of Jesus and of the Blessed Virgin.

Finally, this strong and disinterested love produces, says St. Thomas (*ibid.*, a. 3), the ecstasy of love (with or without suspension of the use of the senses), a spiritual ecstasy through which the lover goes out of himself; so to speak, because he wishes the good of his friend as his own and forgets himself.*

We see by this what can be the intimacy of this union of love and of this presence, not corporal, but affective. It is true, however, that this affective union tends to the real union which we shall enjoy in Heaven in the immediate sight of the Saviour's Humanity and of the Blessed Virgin. Even in this life there is a sort of prelude to it in the physical influence of the Humanity of Jesus and probably in that of the Blessed Virgin, when we derive a higher degree of grace and a charity which takes deeper and deeper root in our will—cf. *infra* the section dealing with Mystical Union with Mary, pp. 259-265.

---

* Ia IIae, Q28, a. 3: "Extasim secundum vim appetitivam facit amor directe, simpliciter amor amicitiae; amor autem concupiscentiae secundum quid . . . In amore amicitiae affectus alicujus *simpliciter exit extra se,* quia vult amico bonum, et operatur bonum, quasi gerens curam et providentiam ipsius propter amicum."

Article 3

The Universality of Mary's Mediation and its Definability

On this article we shall consider the universality of Mary's mediation, the degree of certainty we have concerning it, and its precise meaning.

As a matter of fact the universality of Mary's mediation follows so evidently from the principles we have established that the onus of proof lies altogether on our opponents.[28] Mary Mother of the Redeemer and Co-Redemptrix has merited *de congruo* all that Jesus has merited for us and has made satisfaction in union with and in dependence on Him. Does it not follow that she can obtain in Heaven the application of the fruits of these merits, and that she thereby obtains for us not only all graces in general but all graces in particular?

This assertion is more than pious opinion, however probable. It is theologically certain in virtue of the principles on which it rests, it has been commonly accepted by theologians, it has been part of the Church's preaching and has been confirmed by the encyclicals of different Popes. To quote but one striking papal pronouncement, we find Pope Leo XIII teaching in the encyclical *Octobri Mense* on the Rosary, September 22nd, 1891 (Denz. 3033), "Nihil nobis nisi per Mariam, Deo sic volente, impertiri:" No grace is given to us except through Mary, such being the Divine Will.

The universality of Mary's mediation is affirmed also in the prayers of the Church, which are an expression of her faith. Graces of every kind, temporal and spiritual—and among these latter all those which lead to God, from the grace of conversion to that of final perseverance—are asked through Mary. She is prayed also for the graces needed by apostolic workers, by martyrs

---

28. Among the opponents we may mention the Jansenists who wished to modify the line Bona cuncta posce of the *Ave Maris Stella,* since by it we ask Mary for all the graces which lead us to God.

in time of persecution, by confessors of the faith, by virgins that they may preserve their virginity intact, etc. The Litany of Loretto gives some idea of the many graces which the Church asks through her intercession.

Thus through her are granted all the graces all men need, in their different conditions and stages of life. It has been so for twenty centuries: it will remain so till the end of time. Mary obtains for us all we need for our journey towards eternity.

Among all the different graces that which is the most peculiar to any particular wayfarer is the grace of the moment in which he finds himself. That too comes through Mary. We pray for it daily and many times each day when we say "Pray for us sinners, now and at the hour of our death." By the word "now" we ask for the grace required to fulfil the duty of the present moment, to practise this or that virtue asked of us here and now. Even if we do not ourselves realise what grace we need, Mary in Heaven does, and it is through her intercession that we obtain it. The succession of graces of the moment, varying from one moment to the next, is like a spiritual atmosphere which we inhale and which renews our souls as air does the blood.

Mary's mediation is therefore truly universal: such is the teaching of Tradition. It extends to the whole work of our salvation, without being limited to graces of any particular kind. On this point, there is moral unanimity of the Fathers and Doctors of the Church, and of the faithful whose belief is expressed in the liturgy.

Definability of the Doctrine

It would appear that the doctrine of Mary's universal mediation is capable of being defined as a dogma of faith, for it is implicitly revealed in the different titles which Tradition gives Mary—that of Mother of God, most powerful in intercession with her Son, that of the new Eve intimately associated with the Redeemer, that of Mother of all men. Besides, it is a doctrine explicitly and formally affirmed by the morally unanimous consent of Fathers and Doctors of the Church, of preaching throughout the Church, and of the Liturgy. Leo XIII, after having stated that we receive nothing except through Mary, goes on to say that "as no one can come to the Father except by the Son, in much the same way (*ita fere*) no one can come to the Son except by Mary" (Denz. 3033). Pius X calls her "the dispensatrix of all the graces which Jesus acquired for us by His blood" (Denz. 3033). Benedict XV gave his approval to the same doctrine when he instituted the universal feast of Mary, Mediatrix of all graces (Denz. 3034).

Mary's universal mediation appears then to be capable of definition as a dogma of faith: it is at least implicitly revealed and it is already universally proposed by the ordinary magisterium of the Church.

What is the Precise Meaning of this Universality?

A number of preliminary remarks will be necessary in order to arrive at the precise meaning of Mary's universal mediation.

In the first place, all the graces received by men from the Fall up to the Incarnation were granted in view of the foreseen merits of the Saviour—with which we must associate those of His Mother—but neither Jesus nor Mary distributed or transmitted them. This limitation was removed with the coming of the Saviour on earth in human flesh. As for Mary, it is especially since her Assumption into Heaven that she knows the spiritual needs of all men and that she intercedes for them and distributes the graces they need.

Since Mary distributes all that she has merited, it follows that she distributes the graces we receive in the sacraments. She does this at least by giving us the grace of being disposed for their reception, and sometimes even by sending us a priest without whose ministry we could not have received them.[32]

Mary's universal mediation should not be understood as if it meant that no grace is given to us without our having asked it explicitly of her; that would be to confuse our prayer to her with her prayer to God. Mary does in fact ask for graces without being invoked explicitly. Many graces are given to both children and adults even before they pray for them—especially the grace of beginning to pray. The *Our Father* can be said without any explicit invocation of Mary; but she is invoked implicitly in it when it is said according to the order established by divine providence.

It should not be thought either that Mary was Mediatrix for herself. She obtained her fulness of grace through the mediation of her Son.

It would, however, be an error by defect to say that Mary merited nearly all graces, or morally all graces— say, something like eight or nine tenths of them. All graces without exception come by her mediation. Such is the general law established by divine providence, and there is no known indication of any exceptions.[33]

A point which distinguishes Mary's mediation from that of the saints is that she is mediatrix *de jure* and not simply *de facto* for all men, since she is the mother of all. This makes her intercession all-powerful. Her prayers are more efficacious than those of all the saints united. The saints can do nothing without her intercession for the reason that it is universal.[34]

Mary's universal mediation extends to the souls in Purgatory. "It is certain that the Mother of Mercy

---

32. Cf. *Dict. Théol. Cath.*, art. *Marie* (E. Dublanchy), col. 2403: The doctrine of the universal mediation of Our Lady "is true of all the supernatural graces which proceed from the Redemption. This conclusion, which is without restriction, applies to the graces of the sacraments, in this sense that the dispositions which one should bring to their reception, and on which the infusion of grace depends, are obtained through Mary's intercession."

33. Cf. Merkelbach, *Mariologia*, p. 375.

34. This is what St. Anselm taught, Or. 46:
    Te tacente, nullus (sanctus) orabit, nullus invocabit,
    Te orante, omnes orabunt, omnes invocabunt.

knows the needs of these souls. . . . She can bring her satisfaction to the support of her prayers . . . she did not need it for herself but has given it all into the hands of the Church who distributes it to souls in the form of indulgences. . . . Thus when the satisfaction of Mary is applied to the poor debtors of Purgatory, they have a kind of right to deliverance since they pay their debt with what is their own. . . . She obtains also that her children on earth pray for her clients in Purgatory, offer good works for their intention, and have the sacrifice of redemption offered for them. . . . She can obtain also that prayers destined for souls who do not need them or who are not capable of benefitting by them should be made available for the children of her special love."[35]

In the same spirit a Doctor of the Church, St. Peter Damien, assures us that on every Feast of the Assumption many thousands of the souls captive in Purgatory are delivered.[36] St. Alphonsus de Liguori adds, quoting Denis the Carthusian, that such liberations take place most particularly on the Feasts of Christmas and the Resurrection. Though these testimonies do not impose themselves on our faith for acceptance, they point to and, in their own way, explain Mary's mediation.

Some Difficulties

The objection has been raised: the mother of a king has not the right to dispose of his treasures; neither then has Mary the right to dispose of the graces which Jesus has merited.

There is no parity between the two cases.[37] The mother of a king is simply the mother of a child who subsequently became king and, more usually than not, she has not cooperated closely with him in his gov-

35. Hugon, O.P., *Marie, pleine de grâce,* edit. 5, 1926, p. 201.
36. *Ep. 52* and *Opusc.* XXIV: Disp. de variis apparit, et miraculis.
37. Cf. Merkelbach, *Mariologia,* p. 377.

ernment. But Mary is Mother of God the Redeemer, Universal King, by the simple fact of her divine maternity. She has given Him His human nature and she has been intimately associated with Him in His redemptive sufferings and in His merits. She shares therefore in His spiritual royalty and has the right, in subordination to Him, to dispose of the graces He— and she—acquired.

Another objection is that Mary's universal mediation is no more than becoming or appropriate, and therefore cannot be affirmed with certainty.

We may answer that the becomingness or appropriateness in question is more than ordinary. It is based on Mary's divine maternity, on her spiritual motherhood of men, on her union with the Redeemer, and is so connected with them that its opposite would be unbecoming. It is con-natural to the spiritual mother of all men to watch over them and to distribute to them the fruits of the Redemption. And—what is still more conclusive—Tradition shows that God has in fact disposed the scheme of our Redemption in accordance with this becomingness. This is the teaching of the Fathers of the Church, of the Doctors of the Middle ages, and of later theologians, who all in their own way have thrown the universality of Mary's mediation into clearer relief.

Conclusion

There is therefore no serious difficulty against defining Mary's universal mediation as a dogma of faith, provided it is understood as we have indicated: as a mediation subordinate to that of Jesus and depending on His merits; as a mediation which is not considered to add any necessary complement to Jesus' merits, the value of which is infinite and superabundant, but which shows forth the influence and fruitfulness of those same merits in a soul fully conformed to Him. As a matter of fact, the difficulties which are raised against Mary's universal mediation are much less serious than those raised against the Immaculate Conception in the 13th century. The Assumption is usually looked on as capable of definition; Mary's universal mediation seems to be even more certain, if we consider the principles which underlie it: the divine maternity, the motherhood of men, and the venerable tradition which contrasts Mary and Eve. Since this is so, and since the ordinary *magisterium* of the Church makes Mary's universal mediation to be theologically certain, we can only hope and pray that it be one day defined so as to increase devotion to her who is the watchful and loving Mother of all men.

Mary's mediation in no way obscures that of Jesus. Her mediation is but a share in His: her merits have been acquired under His influence, and it is He Who confers on her the dignity of being a cause in the order of salvation and sanctification. History shows, too, that devotion to Mary has been lost by those nations precisely which have lost their devotion to Jesus, whereas those which have been the first to honor Mary have also been the first in their faith in the redemptive Incarnation. When Dr. Pusey objected to Fr. Faber's statement: "Jesus is obscured because Mary is kept in the background," Newman answered that its truth "exemplified in history might be abundantly illustrated . . . from the lives and writings of holy men in modern times."[38] As examples he quoted St. Alphonsus de Liguori and St. Paul of the Cross, in whom ardent love of Jesus was inseparable from great devotion to Mary.

True cult of Mary, like her action upon us, leads surely to intimacy with Jesus. Far from diminishing our intimacy with Jesus it increases it, just as the action of the Holy Soul of Jesus increases our union

---

38. *Difficulties felt by Anglicans in Catholic Teaching,* 4th edit., p. 440.

with the Blessed Trinity.

The universality of Mary's mediation will become more evident when we consider in the next chapter that she is Mother of Mercy.

⸺ Chapter 4 ⸺

Mother of Mercy

We shall consider this title first in itself and then in its principal manifestations which are, as it were, that radiance of the revealed doctrine concerning Mary which makes it accessible to all minds.

Article 1

Greatness and Power of this Maternity

The title of Mother of Mercy is one of Mary's greatest. Mercy is not the same thing as mere emotional pity. Mercy is in the will, pity is but a good inclination of the sensibility. Pity, which does not exist in God who is a pure spirit, leads us to suffer in unison with our neighbor as if we felt his suffering in ourselves. It is a good inclination but usually a timid one, being accompanied by fear of harm to ourselves and often helpless to render effective aid.

Mercy, on the contrary, is a virtue of the will, and, as St. Thomas so well notes,[1] whereas pity is found most of all in feeble and timid beings who feel themselves threatened by the evil that has befallen their neighbor, mercy is the virtue of the powerful and the good, who are capable of giving real assistance. That is why it is found in God especially: as one of the prayers of the Missal says,[2] it is one of the greatest manifestations of His power and goodness. St. Augustine remarked that it was more glorious for God to obtain good out of evil than to create out of nothing: it is greater to convert a sinner by giving him grace than to make a whole uni-

1. Ia, q. 21, a. 3; IIa IIae, q. 30, a. 4.
2. Deus qui maxime parcendo et miserando, potentiam tuam manifestas.

215

verse, Heaven and earth, out of nothing.[3]

As Mother of Mercy, Mary reminds us that if God is Being, Truth and Wisdom, He is also Goodness and Love, and that His infinite Mercy, which is the radiation of His Goodness, flows from His love and anticipates His vindicatory Justice which proclaims the inalienable right that the Supreme Good has to be loved above every other object: "Mercy exalteth itself above justice" (*James* 2:13). She teaches us, though, that if mercy is not justice it is not opposed to it as injustice is, but unites itself to it and goes beyond it: most of all in pardoning, for to pardon is to go beyond what is demanded by justice in forgiving an offence.[4]

Every work of divine justice presupposes a work of mercy or of gratuitous goodness.[5] If God can be said to owe anything to a creature it is because of some preceding gratuitous gift: if He owes a recompense to our merits, it is because He has first of all given the grace to merit, and if He punishes, it is after having given us the assistance which made the accomplishment of His precepts really possible, for He never commands the impossible.

Mary reminds us too that God often gives us His mercy more than we need, more than He is obliged in justice to Himself to give; that He gives us more than we merit—the grace of Holy Communion, for example, which is not merited. She tells us that mercy is wedded to justice in the trials of this life. Trials are a medicine to heal us, to make us right again, to bring us to the good. She tells us finally that mercy often makes the good inequality of natural conditions among men by a correspondingly more generous distribution of graces. This is the lesson of the different beatitudes— of the poor, the meek, those that weep, those that hunger

---

3. Cf. Ia IIae, q. 113, a. 9.
4. Ia, q. 21, a. 3, ad 2.
5. *ib.* a. 4: "Opus divinae justitiae semper praesupponit opus misericordiae, et in eo fundatur."

and thirst after justice, those that are merciful, those that are pure of heart, those that are peacemakers, those that suffer persecution for justice.

Article 2

Principal Manifestations of Mercy

Mary manifests herself as Mother of Mercy by being "Health of the sick, Refuge of sinners, Comforter of the afflicted, Help of christians." The gradation of titles here is very beautiful. It shows that Mary is merciful to those who are sick of body in order to benefit their souls, and that afterwards she consoles them in their afflictions and strengthens them in the midst of all the difficulties they have to overcome. Among creatures no one is higher than Mary, and yet no one is more approachable, more helpful, and more gentle.[6]

Health of the Sick

Mary is Health of the Sick by the many providential or miraculous cures which have been obtained through her intercession in Christian sanctuaries up to our own days. So many have these cures been that it may be said that Mary is a fathomless ocean of miraculous healing. But it is to help the infirmity of the soul that she cures the body. Her most important cures are those of the four spiritual wounds which we have suffered as a result of original sin and our personal sins—the wounds of concupiscence, of weakness, of ignorance, and of malice.

She heals concupiscence—a wound of our sensibility—by diminishing the ardour of our passions and by

---

6. These points are developed by the Polish Dominican, Justin of Miéchow, in his *Collationes in Litanias B. Mariae Virginis,* translated into French by A. Ricard under the title *Conférences sur les litanies de la Très Sainte Vierge,* 3rd edit., Paris, 1870. We shall draw much of our inspiration for the following pages from this work.

breaking our sinful habits. She helps the sinner to begin to will what is right with sufficient firmness to enable him to reject evil desires as well as the appeal of honors and riches. In this way she cures the concupiscence of the flesh and that of the eyes.

She heals the wound of weakness too, our feeble pursuit of the good, our spiritual sloth. She makes the will constant and firm in its practice of virtue and helps it to despise the attractions of this world by throwing itself into the arms of God. She strengthens those who falter and lifts up those who have fallen.

She heals the wound of ignorance by lighting up the darkness of our minds and providing us with the means to escape from error. She calls to our minds the simple and profound truths of the *Our Father,* thereby lifting our minds up to God. St. Albert the Great, to whom she gave the light to persevere in his vocation and to see through the wiles of Satan, said frequently that she preserves us from losing rightness and firmness of judgement, that she helps us not to grow weary in the pursuit of truth, and that she leads us eventually to a relish of the things of God. He himself speaks of her in his *Mariale* with a spontaneity, an admiration, a freshness, and a fluency which are rarely found in the works of great students.

She heals us finally of the wounds of malice, by urging our wills Godwards, sometimes by gentle advice, sometimes by stern reproaches. Her sweetness checks anger, her humility lowers pride and restrains the temptations of the evil one. In a word, she heals us of the wounds which we bear as a result of original sin and which our personal sin has made all the more dangerous.

Sometimes this healing power of hers works in a miraculous manner by producing its effects instantaneously. An example is the conversion of the young Alphonse Ratisbonne, at the time a Jew and far removed from the faith, who visited the Church of Sant' Andrea delle Frate in Rome through curiosity. Mary appeared to him there, as she is represented on the miraculous medal, with rays of light issuing from her hands. She indicated gently to him to kneel. He obeyed, and while on his knees lost the use of his senses. When he returned to himself he expressed an intense desire for baptism. He was baptised and later, with his brother who had been converted before him, founded the congregation of the Fathers of Sion and that of the Religious of Sion, to pray, suffer, and work for the conversion of the Jews, saying daily at Holy Mass: "Father, forgive them, for they know not what they do."

Refuge of Sinners

Mary is Refuge of sinners precisely because she is so holy. Detesting sin, which does so much harm to souls, she welcomes sinners and wishes to bring them to repentance. She frees them from the bonds of sinful habits by the power of her intercession; she obtains their reconciliation with God by the merits of her Son, and reminds the sinner too of the same merits. Once converted to penance, she protects them from Satan, against everything which could lead to fresh falls. She helps them to learn of the sweetness of penance.

To her, after Jesus, all sinners now in Heaven owe their salvation. She has converted them in countless numbers, especially in places of pilgrimage—at Lourdes where she issued the invitation "Pray and do penance," and more recently at Fatima where the number of conversions since 1917 is known to God alone. There are many condemned criminals who owe to her their conversion at the last moment. She has inspired the foundation of religious orders consecrated to prayer, to penance, and to the apostolate of the conversion of sinners—those of St. Dominic and of St. Francis, the Redemptorists, the Passionists, and so many others.

What sinners are there whom she does not protect? Those only who despise God's mercy and call down His malediction on themselves. She is not the refuge of those who are obstinate in evil—in blasphemy, perjury, impurity, avarice, pride of the spirit. But even to them she sends from time to time, as Mother of Mercy, graces for the mind and the will, and if they accept them they will be led from grace to grace and finally to the grace of conversion. To such she has suggested by the lips of a dying mother that they should say at least one Hail Mary each day, and often it has happened that though they made no other effort than that to change their lives, the feeble spark of good-will it contained was enough to light them the way to a worthy and penitent reception of the Last Sacraments. They have been laborers of the last hour, called and saved by Mary.[7] For almost two thousand years Mary has been the Refuge of sinners.

Consoler of the Afflicted

Mary was Consoler of the afflicted even during her lifetime on earth: she consoled Jesus by her presence on Calvary; she consoled the Apostles in the difficulties they encountered in the conversion of the pagan world and obtained for them a spirit of strength and holy joy in their sufferings. She must have helped St. Stephen by her prayers when he was being stoned to death. She obtained for many the grace to bear persecution patiently and without giving way to cowardly fears. Though she saw the dangers which threatened the infant Church, she did not waver; her face was ever calm, for her soul was tranquil and confident. Sadness never took possession of her heart. What we know of the intensity of her love of God assures us that she remained joyous in affliction, that she did not

_____

7. This was the case in France of the immoral writer Armand Silvestre.

complain of poverty or privations, that insults had no power to alter her meekness. Her example alone was enough to hearten many a despairing soul.

She has given to many saints the grace to be themselves consolers of the afflicted. Such were St. Genevieve, St. Elizabeth, St. Catherine of Siena, St. Germaine de Pibrac.

The Holy Ghost is called the Consoler most of all because He makes us shed tears of contrition, thereby to wash away our sins and to restore to us the joy of God's friendship. For the same reason the Blessed Virgin is the Consoler of the afflicted when she prompts them to bewail their sins from a contrite heart.

Mary is particularly attentive to our inner or secret poverty: she knows how little are the resources of our hearts, and she comes to their assistance. She knows all the needs of soul and body: she has consoled christians in persecution, she has delivered the possessed, she has assisted and strengthened the dying by calling to their minds the infinite merits of her Son. She lessens the rigours of purgatory, and obtains for those who suffer there that the faithful pray and have Masses offered on their behalf.

In a sense, Mary's power as Consoler of the afflicted is felt even in the terrible regions of Hell. For St. Thomas tells us that the damned suffer less than they deserve[8] since the divine mercy is found even in the strictest exercise of divine justice. Whatever less there is of the pain of Hell than there might be is due to the merits of Jesus and Mary. St. Odilon of Cluny says in his sermon on the Assumption that the Feast of the Assumption brings some slight alleviation of pain to Hell's torments.

Mary has been Consoler of the afflicted throughout the ages in the most varied ways, because of her great knowledge of the many trials through which men pass.

---

8. Ia, q. 21, a. 4, ad I.

Help of Christians

Mary is Help of christians. Help is an effect of love, and Mary has now consummated fulness of love. She loves the souls redeemed by Jesus' blood. She helps them in their difficulties and assists them in the practice of the virtues.

The thought of Mary, Help of christians, inspired St. Bernard in the well-known passage from his second homily on the *Missus est:* "If the tempest of temptation rages, if the torrent of tribulation carries you away, look at the star, look at Mary. If the waves of pride and ambition, of slander and jealousy, buffet you and almost engulf you, look at the star, look at Mary. If anger or avarice or passion tosses the frail bark of your soul and threatens to wreck it, look once more at Mary. Let her memory be ever in your heart and her name always on your lips. . . . But remember that to obtain the benefit of her prayer you must walk in her footsteps."

She has been the refuge of whole peoples as well as of individuals. Baronius tells us that Narses, general of the armies of the Emperor Justinian, delivered Italy by her help in 553 from bondage to Totila the Goth. He tells us also that in 718 the city of Constantinople was rescued from the Saracens, who had been put to flight on many similar occasions already with Mary's aid. In the 13th century, Simon, Count of Montfort, defeated a powerful Albigensian army near Toulouse while St. Dominic invoked the Mother of God. In 1513 the city of Dijon was delivered miraculously through her. On the 7th of October, 1571, a Turkish fleet, much more numerous and powerful than that of the christians, was defeated at Lepanto, at the entrance of the Gulf of Corinth, through the help of Mary invoked in the Rosary. Finally, Mary's title of Our Lady of Victories reminds us how often her intervention on the battlefield has been decisive in favor of oppressed christian peoples.

The four invocations of the Litany of Loreto, Health

of the Sick, Refuge of Sinners, Consoler of the Afflicted, Help of Christians, recall unceasingly to the faithful how truly Mary is Mother of divine grace and Mother of mercy. The Church sings that she is our hope: Hail, Holy Queen, Mother of mercy! Hail, our life, our sweetness, and our hope! She is our hope in that she has merited, with her Son, all that we need of help from God, and in that she transmits it to us now by her intercession. She is therefore the living expression and the instrument of God's helping Mercy, which is the formal motive of our hope. Confidence, or firm hope, is certain in its tendency to salvation,[9] and its certainty increases with our growth in grace. This certainty derives from our faith in the goodness of God Omnipotent and in His fidelity to His promises. Thence comes that almost constant sense of His watchful Paternity which we find in the saints. Mary's influence leads us gradually to this perfect confidence and makes its motive ever more clear.

Mary is even called Mother of holy joy and Cause of our joy, for she obtains for generous souls the hidden treasure or spiritual joy in the midst of suffering. She obtains for them from time to time the grace to carry their cross with joy after the Lord Jesus. She initiates them into love of the cross. And even though they do not experience that joy uninterruptedly themselves, she helps them to communicate it to others.

NOTE

In *La Vie Spirituelle,* April, 1941, p. 281, Fr. M. J. Nicolas, O.P., has written of a holy religious, Fr. Vayssière, who died as Provincial of the Dominicans at Toulouse: "The grace of intimacy with Mary that he received, he owed first of all to the state of littleness to which he had been reduced and to which he

---

9. IIa IIae, q. 18, a. 4: 'Spes certitudinaliter tendit ad suam finem, quasi participans certitudinem a fide."

had consented. But he owed it as well to his Rosary. During the long days of solitude at Sainte-Baume, he had acquired the habit of saying several Rosaries in the day, sometimes as many as six. He often said the whole of it kneeling. And it was not a mechanical and superficial recitation: his whole soul went into it, he delighted in it, he devoured it, he was persuaded that he found in it all that one could seek for in prayer. 'Recite each decade', he used to say, 'less reflecting on the mystery than communicating through the heart in its grace, and in the spirit of Jesus and Mary as the mystery presents it to us. The Rosary is the evening Communion (elsewhere he calls it the Communion of the whole day) and it translates into light and fruitful resolution the morning Communion. It is not merely a series of *Ave Marias* piously recited; it is Jesus living again in the soul through Mary's maternal action.' Thus he lived in the perpetually moving cycle of his Rosary, as if 'surrounded' by Christ and by Mary, communicating, as he said, in each of their states, in each aspect of their grace, entering thus into and remaining in the depth of God's Heart: 'The Rosary is a chain of love from Mary to the Trinity.' One can understand what a contemplation it had become for him, what a way to pure union with God, what a need, like to that of Communion."

⌘ Chapter 5 ⌘

Mary's Universal Queenship

In the language of the Church, both in the Liturgy and in her universal preaching, Mary is not only Mother and Mediatrix but Queen of all men and even of the angels and the whole universe. In what sense is she a queen? In a true or in a merely metaphorical sense? It should be recalled first that God alone has universal kingship over all things through His Essence: He governs all things and leads them to their end. Jesus and Mary share in this Divine Kingship. Even as man, Jesus shares in it for three reasons: because of His Divine Personality,[1] because of His fulness of grace which overflows on men and angels, and because of His victory over sin, Satan and death.[2] He is King of all men and of all creatures including the angels, who are *"His* angels." Thus He says (*Mark* 13:26): "And then they shall see the Son of man coming in the clouds, with great power and glory. And then shall He send his angels. . . ." For Jesus is Son of God by nature, whereas the angels are but God's servants and adopted sons. Jesus has said too of Himself: "All power is given to me in Heaven and on earth" (*Matt.* 28:18), and we read in the Apocalypse that He is "King of Kings and Lord of Lords." (*Apoc.* 19:16).

---

1. Cf. Pius XI, encyc. *Quas primas,* Dec. 11th, 1925 (Denz. 2194): "Eius principatus illa nititur unione admirabili, quam hypostaticam appellant. Unde consequitur, non modo ut Christus ab angelis et hominibus Deus sit adorandus, sed etiam ut eius imperio Hominis angeli et homines pareant et subjecti sint: nempe ut vel solo hypostaticae unionis nomine Christus potestem in universas creaturas obtineat." Because of its personal union with the Word the Humanity of Christ is entitled to adoration and participation in God's universal kingship over all creatures. Christ as Man has been predestined to be Son of God by nature, not by adoption, whereas angels and men are only adoptive sons.
2. Since He accepted the humiliations of His Passion in love *"God also hath exalted Him, and given Him a name which is above all names: That in the name of Jesus every knee should bow, of those that are in Heaven, on earth, and under the earth"* (*Phil.* 2:9-10).

225

Article 1

Her Queenship in General

Can it be said of Mary, since her Assumption especially, and her crowning in Heaven, that she shares in
God's universal Kingship in the sense that she is Queen
of all creatures in subordination to Christ?[3]

She could certainly be called a queen in the wide
sense of the term by reason of her spiritual qualities
and her fulness of grace, of glory and of charity which
raise her above all other creatures. It is quite customary to use the words king and queen to designate persons of such eminence. Her motherhood of Christ the
King would also entitle her to be called a queen—still
in a wide sense of the term at least.

But would it not appear that she is a queen in the
literal sense of the term by the fact of having received
royal authority and power? Has she not, in dependence
on Jesus and through Him, not only a primacy of honor
in regard to the angels and saints, but a real power
to command both angels and men? This is, in fact,
what emerges from an examination of Tradition as
expressed in the preaching of the universal Church,
the Fathers, the statements of different Popes, the
Liturgy. There are theological arguments besides in
favor of the affirmative answer.

The Fathers of both East and West referred frequently to Mary under such titles as *Domina, Regina,
Regina nostrae salutis*. It is sufficient to mention a few
among many: in the East SS. Ephrem, Germanus of
Constantinople, Andrew of Crete, John Damascene; in
the West St. Peter Crysologus, the Venerable Bede, St.
Anselm, St. Peter Damien, St. Bernard. The same titles
occur also in the works of the theologians: in St. Albert

---

3. Cf. De Gruyter, *De B. Maria Regina*, Buscoduci, 1934: Garénaux, *La Royauté de Marie*, Paris, 1935; M. J. Nicholas, *La Vierge Reine*, in the *Revue Thomiste*, 1939; Merkelbach, *Mariologia*, 1939, p. 382.

the Great,[4] St. Bonaventure, St. Thomas,[5] Gerson, St. Bernadine of Siena, Denis the Carthusian, St. Peter Canisius, Suarez, St. Grignon de Montfort, St. Alphonsus. Different Sovereign Pontiffs have often used the same expressions.[6]

The Roman and Oriental liturgies proclaim Mary Queen of the heavens, Queen of angels, Queen of the world, Queen of all the saints. Among the mysteries of the Rosary commonly recited in the Church since the 13th century the last of all is that of the crowning of Our Lady in Heaven—a scene represented in one of Fra Angelico's most beautiful frescoes.

The arguments adduced by theologians to prove that Mary has universal Queenship in the proper, non-metaphorical sense of the term, are conclusive. They may all be reduced to the following three.

Jesus Christ is King of the universe, even as man, in virtue of His Divine Personality. But Mary as Mother of God made man belongs to the hypostatic order and shares in the dignity of her Son, for His Person is the term of her divine motherhood. Hence she shares connaturally, as Mother of God, in His universal Kingship.[7] Our Blessed Lord owes it to Himself to recognise His Mother's title in gratitude.

A second argument is that Jesus is King of the universe by His fulness of grace and by the victory which He won over Satan and sin by His humility and His

---

4. *Mariale,* q. 43, 2: "Virgo assumpta est in salutis auxilium et regni consortium . . . habet coronam regni triumphantis et militantis Ecclesiae, unde . . . est regina et domina angelorum . . . imperatrix totius mundi . . . ; in ipsa est plenitudo potestatis coelestis perpetuo ex auctoritate ordinaria . . . ; legitima dominandi potestas ad ligandum et solvendum per imperium; totam habet B. Virgo potestatem in coelo, in purgatorio et in inferno . . . *B. Virgo vere et jure et proprie est domina omnium quae sunt in misericordia Dei, ergo proprie est regina misericordiae . . . ipsa enim ejusdem regni regina est cujus ipse est rex."* Cf. *Ibid.* qq. 158, 162, 165.
5. *In expos. Salut. Angelicae.*
6. In his letter to St. Germanus of Constantinople read at the 2nd Council of Nicaea (787), Pope Gregory II terms Mary *Domina Omnium,* and the council itself approves of statues erected in Mary's honor. Leo XIII frequently spoke of Mary as *Regina* and *Domina universorum* in his encyclicals. Similarly Pius X in the encyclical *Ad diem Illum:* "Maria adstat regina a dextris ejus."
7. Cf. Merkelbach, op. cit., p. 385.

obedience unto death, "For which cause God hath exalted Him. . . ." But Mary was associated with His victory over Satan, sin, and death by her union with Him in His humiliations and sufferings. She is therefore really associated with Him in His Kingship.

The same conclusion may be arrived at by considering the close relationship in which Mary stands to God the Father, of whom she is the first adoptive daughter and the highest in grace, and God the Holy Ghost through whose operation the word took flesh in her womb.

It has been objected that the mother of a king, the queen-mother, is not by that simple fact queen in the strict sense of the term: she has nothing of royal power. Neither then has Mary. We have answered this objection already. There is no parity between the two cases. A queen-mother is simply the mother of a child who later became king. But Mary is the mother of Him who from the instant of His conception is King of the universe by His hypostatic union and His fulness of grace. Besides, Mary was associated closely with the victory by which He obtained universal kingship as a right of conquest, even though He possessed it already as Son of God. Mary is therefore associated with His Kingship in a true, even if in a subordinate, manner.

Many consequences follow from this truth. As universal King, Jesus has power to establish and promulgate the New Law, to propose revealed doctrine, to judge the living and the dead, to give souls sanctifying grace and all the virtues.[8] Mary shares in this universal kingship especially by dispensing in an interior and hidden manner the graces which she merited in dependence on Jesus. She participates in it exteriorly also by the fact that she gave on earth the example

---

8. Cf. Encyc. Quas primas (Denz. 2194) and Ia IIae, q. 106, a. 1. Jesus is all the more King of minds, hearts and wills, by the fact that the New Law is not primarily a written law, but one imprinted on the soul by grace.

of all the virtues, that she helped to enlighten the Apostles, and that she continues to enlighten us when, for example, she manifests herself exteriorly in sanctuaries such as those of Lourdes, La Salette, and Fatima. Theologians note that she does not seem to share in any special way in the royal judicial power of inflicting punishment for sin, for Tradition calls her not the Mother of justice but the Mother of mercy, a title which is hers in virtue of her mediation of all graces.[9] Jesus seems to have kept to Himself the reign of justice[10] as is becoming Him who is the "judge of the living and the dead."[11]

Mary has a radical right to universal queenship by the fact of her divine motherhood, but the divine plan was that she should merit it also by her union with her suffering Son, and that she should not exercise it fully before being crowned queen of all creation in Heaven. Her royalty is spiritual and supernatural rather than temporal and natural, though it extends in a secondary way to temporal affairs considered in their relation to salvation and sanctification.

We have seen how Mary exercises her queenship on earth. She exercises it in Heaven also. The essential glory of the blessed depends on Jesus' merits and hers. She contributes to their accidental glory—as well as to that of the angels—by the light she communicates to them, and by the joy they have in her presence and in the realization of what she does for souls. To both the angels and the saints she manifests Christ's plan for the extension of His Kingdom.

Mary's queenship extends to purgatory, for she prompts the faithful on earth to pray for the souls detained there and to have Masses offered for them. She herself offers their prayers to God, thereby increasing their value. She applies the fruits of the merits of

---

9. Cf. *Mariale,* q. 43, 2.
10. *John* 5:22-27: ". . . the Father . . . hath given all judgement to the Son."
11. *Acts* 10:42; cf. IIIa, q. 59, a. 1.

Jesus and of herself to the Holy Souls in Jesus' name.

Her queenship extends to the demons too who are obliged to recognise her power, for she can make their temptation cease, can save souls from their snares, and can repulse their attacks. "The demons suffer more," says St. Grignon de Montfort, "from being conquered by the humility of Mary than by the Omnipotence of God." Her reign of mercy extends to Hell itself, as we have seen, in the sense that the lost souls are punished less than they deserve,[12] and that on certain days—including possibly the Assumption—their sufferings become less fearful.

Thus Mary's queenship is truly universal. There is no region to which it does not extend in some way.

Article 2
Special Aspects of Mary's Queenship

Mary's universal queenship comes home to us in a more concrete form if we consider its different aspects as presented in the Litany of Loreto: Queen of angels, of patriarchs, of prophets, of martyrs, of confessors, of virgins, of all the saints, of peace.

Queen of Angels

Mary is Queen of the angels since her mission is higher than theirs. They are but servants, whereas she is the Mother of God. She is as much above them as the word "mother" surpasses the word "servant." She alone with the Father can say to Jesus: "Thou art my Son, I have begotten thee."

She is higher than the angels also by her fulness of

---

12. Ia, q. 21, a. 4, ad 1: "In damnatione reproborum apparet misericordia non quidem totaliter relaxans, sed aliqualiter allevians, dum (Deus) *punit citra condignum*" This intervention of Divine Mercy is not independent of the merits of Jesus and Mary.

grace and glory, which surpasses that of all the angels united. She is purer than they, for she has received purity for others as well as for herself. She was more perfect than they and more prompt in her obedience to God's commandments and in following His counsels. By her co-operation in the redemption she merited *de congruo* for the angels themselves the accidental graces by which they help us to save our souls and the joy which they experience in doing so.

As Justin of Miéchow well remarks,[13] if the angels have served Our Lord, how much more did not Mary serve Him, she who conceived and bore Him, who cared for Him, who carried Him into Egypt to escape Herod's anger?

She surpasses the angels in this also, that they have each care of one soul or one community, but she is the guardian of all men and of earth in particular. She is, more than they, the messenger of God who brought us not a created word but the Uncreated Word.

Archangels are appointed to protect this or that city: Mary protects all cities and all churches in them. Principalities are the custodians of provinces: Mary has the whole Church under her protection. Powers repel demons: Mary has crushed the serpent's head; she is terrible to the demons by the depth of her humility and the ardour of her charity. Virtues perform miracles as God's instruments: but the greatest miracle was to conceive the Incarnate Word for our salvation. Dominations command the lower angels: Mary commands all the heavenly choirs. The Thrones are those angels in whom God dwells in a specially intimate way: Mary, who gave birth to Jesus, is the Seat of Wisdom, and the Blessed Trinity reside in her more familiarly than in the highest angel—that is to say, in a way proportionate to her consummated grace.

She surpasses even the Cherubim and Seraphim.

13. *Collationes;* circa invocationem: Regina angelorum.

The Cherubim shine with the splendor of their knowledge: but Mary has penetrated deeper than they into the divine mysteries since she has the light of glory in a degree far above theirs. She has carried in her womb Him in whom are hidden all the treasures of wisdom and knowledge. She lived with Him for thirty years on earth, and in Heaven she is nearest of all to Him.

The Seraphim burn with the flame of love: but more ardent still is the living flame of Mary's charity. She loves God more than all creatures together, for she loves Him not only as Creator and Father but as her Infant and her treasured Son.

She is therefore the Queen of angels. They serve her faithfully, surround her with veneration, marvel at her tender solicitude for each one of us and for the whole Church. Her charity, her zeal for the glory of God and the salvation of souls are the objects of their intense admiration.

Such is the substance of Justin of Miéchow's treatise on Mary, Queen of Angels.

Queen of Patriarchs

The superiority of Mary to Adam in the state of innocence is clear from all that has been said thus far. She was higher in grace than he, and had as well the principal effects of original justice: subordination of the sensibility to the higher faculties, and subordination of these latter to God. Mary's charity was greater from the first instant of her conception than that of Adam in the state of innocence, and she had in addition the special grace of freedom from all sin however slight, even though she was conceived in passible and mortal flesh.

Her intimacy with God was much closer than that of Abel, Noah, Abraham, Isaac, Jacob, or Joseph. Abraham's most heroic act was that of preparing himself to immolate his son Isaac, the son of the promise. It was far more for Mary to offer Jesus who was dearer to her than her own life: nor did an angel come to arrest Jesus' immolation as one did in the case of Isaac. Her title of Mother of God, her charity and the heroicity of all her virtues make Mary shine as a star without compare among the patriarchs.

Queen of Prophets

Prophecy in the strict sense of the term is the gift of knowing with certainty and predicting the future under divine inspiration. It was given to many in Old Testament times. In the New Testament St. John and St. Paul were both prophets and apostles. Sacred Scripture tells us of certain holy women also who received the gift of prophecy: Mary the sister of Moses, Deborah, Anne, mother of Samuel, Elisabeth, mother of John the Baptist.

Mary is Queen of prophets. She foretold the future in the *Magnificat* when she sang: "Behold from henceforth all nations shall call me blessed." Of her the prophets spoke when they announced the mystery of the Incarnation. She bore in her womb Him of Whom the prophets spoke, and she heard from His own lips the mysteries of the kingdom of God.

She had the gift of prophecy in the highest degree after Our Blessed Lord, and at the same time she had perfect understanding of the fulness of the revelation which He communicated to the world.

Queen of Apostles

In what sense is Mary Queen of the twelve Apostles? Her dignity as Mother of God surpasses theirs. The apostolate is a form of ministry.[14] But according to

---

14. "Let a man so account of us as the ministers of Christ" (*1 Cor.* 4:1).

the phrase of St. Albert which we have quoted already, Mary is not simply God's minister since as Mother of the Saviour she is still more closely associated with Him. After the Ascension the Apostles had need of direction, of counsel, and no one was better equipped than Mary to give it to them. She consoled them in their grief at the departure of Our Lord when they felt lonely and helpless in face of the task of the evangelisation of the pagan world. Jesus had left them His mother to help them. She was for them, it has been said, a second paraclete, a visible paraclete, a mediatrix; she was their guiding star in the midst of the tempest of persecution that raged about them. She was truly a mother to them. None of them ever left her side without having been enlightened and consoled, without having been strengthened. By her example in suffering calumnies, by her experience of the things of God she sustained them in times of trial and persecution.

There was no one who could talk as she did of the virginal conception of Christ, of His birth, His infancy, His hidden life, of what took place in His soul on the cross. This is what prompted St. Ambrose to say: "It is not strange that St. John should have spoken better of the mystery of the Incarnation than the others did; he lived at the source of heavenly secrets."[15] He lived in Mary's company what he speaks of in the fourth gospel.[16]

Queen of Martyrs

The title of Queen of Martyrs has been applied to Mary by SS. Ephrem, Jerome, Ildephonsus, Anselm and Bernard. The implied allusion is to her martyrdom of heart of which Simeon spoke: "Thy own soul a sword shall pierce."

---

15. *De Institutione Virginis*, c. ix.
16. These remarks are a summary of the corresponding section of Justin de Miéchow's work.

Mary's grief was proportionate to her love for her Son. She suffered when He was called a seducer, a violator of the Law, one possessed by a devil; she suffered inexpressibly when Barabbas was preferred to Him, when He was nailed to the cross, when He was tortured by the crown of thorns, when He was parched with thirst; she shared in all the anguish of His priestly and victim soul. She felt as it were all the blows Jesus received in His scourging and crucifixion, for her love made her one with Him. As Bossuet exclaims: "One cross was enough to make martyrs of Him and her." They offered but one sacrifice, and since she, for her part, loved Jesus more than herself, she suffered more than if she herself had been the victim. All this she endured so as to confess her faith in the mystery of the redemptive Incarnation, and in her the faith of the Church was strong at that moment, stronger and more ardent than in all the other martyrs.

We should remember that Mary's sufferings had the same cause as her Son's—the accumulated sins of men and their ingratitude which made the sufferings to be partly of no avail. We must remember too that she suffered from the time of the conception of the Saviour, still more after Simeon's prophecy, still more as she saw the opposition to Jesus mounting, and most of all at the foot of the cross. But even then, even when her soul was inundated with grief, her zeal for the glory of God and for the salvation of souls caused her a holy joy at the sight of her Son consummating His redemptive work by the most perfect of holocausts.

Lastly, she has helped the martyrs in their torments. She is Our Lady of a happy death because of her care for the dying who call on her. Much more does she help those who die to profess their faith in the Redeemer.

Queen of Confessors
Mary and Priests

She is Queen of all who confess their faith in Jesus for she herself confessed the same faith more than any other creature.

But we shall speak principally in this section of what she is to the priests of Our Blessed Lord. To represent Jesus truly, the priest who brings Him down on the altar and offers Him sacramentally in Holy Mass should unite himself more and more to His sentiments, to the oblation which is always living in the Heart of Jesus "always living to make intercession for us." In addition, he should, through the different sacraments, distribute the grace which is the fruit of the merits of Jesus and Mary.

Because of the work to which they are called, Mary is specially zealous for the sanctification of priests. She sees that they share in the priesthood of her Son and she watches over their souls that the grace of their ordination may bear fruit in them, that they become living images of the Saviour. She protects them against the dangers which surround them and lifts them up if they happen to stumble. She loves them as sons of predilection, just as she loved St. John who was committed to her on Calvary. She attracts their heart to herself to raise it up and to lead them to greater intimacy with Jesus, so that one day they may be able to say in all truth: "I live, now not I, but Christ liveth in me."

Mary helps priests in a special way at the altar so that they may become more fully conscious of their union with the Principal Offerer. She is spiritually present at that sacramental oblation which perpetuates the substance of the sacrifice of the Cross, and she distributes to the priest the actual graces he needs to minister with recollection and in a spirit of self-donation. In that way she helps the priest to share in Jesus' victimhood as well as in His priesthood. All this means to form priests to the image of the Heart of Jesus.

With Jesus she arouses priestly vocations and cultivates them. She knows that where there are no priests there is no Baptism, no Confession, no Mass, no christian Marriage, no Extreme Unction, no christian life: without the priest the world returns to paganism.

Our Lord who has willed to have need of Mary in the work of salvation has willed also to have need of priests, and Mary forms them in holiness. We can see her action clearly in some of the saints who were priests—St. John the Evangelist, St. Bernard, St. Dominic, the Apostle of the Rosary, St. Bernardine of Siena, St. Grignon de Montfort, St. Alphonsus.

Queen of Virgins
Mary and Consecrated Souls

Mary is Queen of Virgins since she had the virtue of virginity in the most eminent degree and preserved it in the conception, birth, and after the birth of the Saviour. She teaches souls the value of virginity. It is a true virtue, a spiritual force, something more than a mere good inclination of the sensibility. She teaches them that virginity consecrated to God is higher than simple chastity since it promises integrity of the body and purity of the heart for the whole of life—a consideration which led St. Thomas to say that virginity stands in much the same relation to chastity as munificence does to simple liberality, since it is a perfect gift of self, and sign of a perfect generosity.

Mary safeguards virgins from danger, she supports them in their difficulties and leads them, if they are faithful, to great intimacy with her Son.

What is her role in regard to consecrated souls? The Church calls such souls "spouses of Christ." It follows that Our Lady is their perfect model. Following her example they should live a life of prayer and of reparation in union with Our Blessed Lord. They should become also consolers of the afflicted, remembering that the consolation which they afford in a supernatural spirit to the suffering members of Christ is afforded to Himself and makes amends for the ingratitude, coldness, and even hatred of so many. Thus, these souls are called to reproduce the virtues of Mary and to continue in some measure her work for Our Blessed Lord and for souls.

If consecrated souls but know and follow Mary's guidance they find through her a wonderful compensation for the privations their lives impose on them, and which, though all accepted in advance, are felt most keenly only as they come one by one, day after day. Through Mary they can aspire to a certain spiritual motherhood, which is an image of her own, in regard to all— the poor, the afflicted, sinners—who are in need of spiritual care. Our Blessed Lord alluded to that spiritual motherhood when He said: "I was hungry, and you gave me eat; I was thirsty, and you gave me to drink; I was a stranger, and you took me in: naked, and you covered me: sick, and you visited me: I was in prison and you came to me." (*Matt.* 25:35-36).

Spiritual motherhood in the life of contemplation and reparation may be practised also by the apostolate of prayer and suffering which makes fruitful the exterior apostolate for the conversion of sinners and the extension of the reign of Christ. A hidden, interior apostolate can be one of great sufferings; but Our Lady will show how to bear them and she will afford some glimpse of their effects in souls.

Another work of Mary's is to help christian mothers to bring up their children to a life of faith, confidence in God, and love. She helps them also to win back their erring children, as St. Monica did St. Augustine.

Thus, we see the universality of Mary's Queenship. She is Queen of all the saints by virtue of her unique mission in God's providential plan, and her fulness of grace and glory. She is Queen of all the saints, the unknown as well as the known, the uncanonised as well as the canonised, the Queen of all those who strive after holiness on earth, whose trials and joys are so well known to her, and the crown of whose merits she foresees even now.

∽Chapter 6∾

True Devotion to Our Lady

In this chapter we shall speak of: 1st—the cult of hyperdulia which is due to the Mother of God; 2nd— the usual forms of Marian devotion, especially the Rosary as a school of contemplation; 3rd—Consecration to Our Lady as explained by St. Grignon de Montfort; 4th—Intimate and mystical union with Mary.

Article 1

The Cult of Hyperdulia and the Benefits It Confers[1]

Cult in general means honor paid in a spirit of submission and dependence to a superior because of his excellence.[2] Whether it be merely interior, or exterior as well, cult differs according to the position or excellence of the person to whom it is paid. Since the excellence of God is infinite, He being First Principle and Supreme Master of all things, the cult to which He has a right is supreme. It is known as *latria* and to pay it is an exercise of the virtue of religion. This same cult is due to the Sacred Humanity of Our Blessed Lord considered as belonging to the uncreated Person of the Word, and in a relative manner it is due to crucifixes and to pictures and statues which represent Him.

Created persons who have a certain excellence are entitled to the cult called *dulia:* a cult of respect. Thus, in the natural order respect is due to parents, kings,

---

1. Merkelbach, *Mariologia,* pp. 392-413. E. Dublanchy, *Dict. Théol. Cath.* art. *Marie,* col. 2439-2474.
2. IIa IIae, q. 81, a. 1, ad 4 and a. 4; q. 92, a. 2. Cult is something more than honor: it is honor paid by an inferior to a superior, God honors the saints but He does not offer them cult.

teachers; in the super natural order it is due to the saints, the heroicity of whose virtues has been recognised. The latter cult paid to God's servants honors God Himself who is revealed to the world in the saints and draws us by them to Himself.[3]

It is commonly taught in the Church that the Blessed Virgin is entitled to a cult of hyperdulia, or supreme dulia, because of her eminent dignity as Mother of God.[4]

Nature and Foundation of the Cult of Mary

There have been two opposed false tendencies in regard to the cult of Mary. According to the testimony of St. Epiphanius (*Haer.*, 78-79) the Collyridians wished to pay her divine cult and to offer sacrifice to her. This error might be termed Mariolatry. It was of brief duration. Opposed to it is the Protestant contention that the cult offered to Mary by Catholics is a form of superstition.

To answer this charge, we must insist that the cult of *latria* or adoration can be and is offered to God alone. If we adore the Sacred Humanity, it is because of Its personal union with the Word; if we offer relative cult of adoration to the crucifix, it is because it represents Our Saviour,[5] for it is quite clear that the crucifix and other representations of Our Saviour have no other excellence than that of representing Him. Were relative adoration to be offered to Our Lady

---

3. IIa IIae, q. 103, a. 4.
4. According to J. B. de Rossi, *Roma sotteranea christiana*, Rome, 1911, t. III, pp. 65 sqq, and 252, and Marucchi, *Eléments d'archéologie chrétienne*, 2nd edit., 1911, p. 211 sqq. the first representations of the Blessed Virgin holding the child Jesus in her arms which are found in the Roman catacombs date back to the 2nd, 3rd, and 4th centuries. The institution of special feasts in Mary's honor appears to be traceable to the 4th century, from which time St. Epiphanius (*Haer.*, 79) speaks of her cult while condemning the error of the Collyridians who transformed it into adoration. St. Gregory of Nazianzen mentions her cult also (*Orat.* XXIV, xi) as well as St. Ambrose (*De instit. virginis*, XXX, 83). There are 11 prayers to her attributed to St. Ephrem (d. 378) in Assemani's edition of his works. The cult of Mary became general in both East and West in subsequent times.
5. IIIa, q. 25, a. 3 and a. 5.

because of her connection with the Word made flesh, it might easily be mistaken for adoration offered to her because of her own intrinsic excellence, and would therefore be an occasion of grave error and of idolatry, as St. Thomas remarks.[6]

The cult due to Our Lady is therefore one of *dulia.* This statement is of faith, because of the teaching of the universal *magisterium* of the Church; hence the condemnation of the opposed propositions of Molinos.[7] It is common and certain doctrine that Mary is entitled to a special kind of *dulia* known as *hyperdulia,* which is due to her considered as Mother of God. This doctrine is traditional. It is found quite explicitly in the works of St. Modestus in the 7th century, of St. John Damascene in the 8th, and later in the works of St. Thomas,[8] St. Bonaventure,[9] Scotus,[10] Suarez[11] and almost all Catholic theologians.[12]

The cult of *hyperdulia* is due to Mary formally because she is Mother of God since the dignity of her divine motherhood belongs by its term to the hypostatic order and is therefore very much higher than that which follows upon her degree of grace and glory. If Mary had received only the fulness of grace and glory without having been made the Mother of God, if, in other words she were higher than the other saints only through her degree of consummated glory, a special cult of *hyperdulia* would not be due to her.[13]

It is the more common and more probable opinion that *hyperdulia* differs from *dulia* not in degree only but in kind, just as the divine maternity belongs by

6. *Ib.* a. 3, ad 3.
7. Denz. 1255 sqq., 1316.
8. IIa IIae, q. 103, a. 4, ad 2; IIIa, q. 25, a. 5.
9. In *III Sent.,* d. 9, a. 1, q. 3.
10. In *III Sent.,* d. 9, q. un.
11. In IIIam, disp. XXII, sect. II, n. 4.
12. Cf. *Dict. Théol. Cath.,* art. *Marie,* cols. 2449-2453.
13. In this matter, Vasquez differs from the great majority of theologians by holding that the cult of *hyperdulia* is due to Mary principally because of her eminent holiness. This view of his is a consequence of his holding that sanctifying grace has a dignity higher than that of the divine maternity.

its term to the hypostatic order, which is specifically distinct from that of grace and glory.[14]

The cult of *hyperdulia* is offered to Mary since she is Mother of the Saviour. But we should remember that for the same reason she is Mother of men, universal Mediatrix and Co-Redemptrix.

What are the Fruits of this Cult?

By rendering Mary the cult of *hyperdulia* we move her to look down on us with still greater love, and for our part are drawn to imitate her virtues. The cult of *hyperdulia* leads effectively to salvation, for Mary can obtain the grace of final perseverance for all those who pray faithfully to her for it. For this reason true devotion to Our Lady is commonly looked on as one of the signs of predestination: though it does not give absolute and infallible certainty of salvation—a possibility ruled out by the authority of the Council of Trent (Denz. 805)—it gives rise to a firm hope. This firm hope rests on Mary's great power of intercession and her special love for those who invoke her.[15] In this sense St. Alphonsus asserts (*The Glories of Mary,* Part I, ch. viii) that it is morally impossible that they should be lost who have the desire to amend their lives and who honor the Mother of God faithfully and commit themselves to her protection. Those who have no serious desire to amend their lives cannot, of course, look on the fact that they keep up a certain appearance of devotion to Our Lady as a probable sign of predestination. But a sinner who tries to give up sin and turns to Mary for assistance will find that she will not fail him. This is the opinion of St. Alphonsus (*Ib.,* ch. I, 4) and of most modern theologians.[16]

The cult offered to Mary in the Church confirms in

---

14. This is the opinion of Fr. Merkelbach, *op. cit.,* pp. 402, 405.
15. *Dict. Théol. Cath.,* art. *Marie,* col. 2458.
16. Cf. Terrien, *op. cit.,* t. IV, pp. 291 sqq.

a general way the foundations of our faith since it derives from the Redemptive Incarnation. Thereby it destroys heresies: "Cunctas haereses interemisti in universo mundo." The same cult leads to holiness by suggesting the imitation of Mary's virtues, and it glorifies the Son by honoring the Mother.

Objections

The objection raised by some Protestants, that cult offered to Mary is derogatory to the divine cult, can be answered without much difficulty. The Catholic Church teaches that the cult of *latria* or adoration is offered to God alone and that the cult of Mary, far from taking from the cult of the Godhead, promotes it by recognising God as the Author of all the gifts with which Mary is endowed. The honor paid to the Mother redounds to the glory of the Son, and Mary the Mediatrix of all graces helps us to know better God, the Author of all graces. Experience has shown that faith in the divinity of Christ has best been preserved in those countries which are marked by devotion to Mary. All the saints were devout to both Jesus and Mary.

Since the cult of Mary is more sense-perceptible, there are some who perform its acts with more intensity than those pertaining to the cult of the Godhead. But even for such persons the cult of the Godhead is higher in kind, for they love God above all things with a love of preference (*amour d'estime*), and this love in its turn becomes more intense according as they advance in holiness and live a life more detached from the senses.

Confidence in Mary increases our confidence in God. The confidence that pilgrims had in the Cure of Ars, for example, increased their confidence that God would help them through his instrumentality.

It would be a real lack of humility, as St. Grignon de Montfort says, to pass over the mediators whom

God has given us because of our weakness. Far from lessening our intimacy with God, they prepare us for its increase. Just as Jesus does nothing in souls except in order to lead them to His Father, so also Mary works on minds and hearts solely in order to lead them nearer to her Son. God has willed to make continual use of Mary for the sanctification of souls.

Article 2

The Rosary: A School of Contemplation

From among the many customary devotions to Our Lady, such as the Angelus, the *Office of the Blessed Virgin,* the Rosary, we shall speak especially of the last in so far as it prepares us for and leads us up to contemplation of the great mysteries of salvation. After Holy Mass it is one of the most beautiful and efficacious forms of prayer, on condition of understanding it and living it.

It sometimes happens that its recitation—reduced to that of five mysteries—becomes a matter of routine. The mind, not being really gripped by the things of God, finds itself a prey to distractions. Sometimes the prayer is said hurriedly and soullessly. Sometimes it is said for the purpose of obtaining temporal favors, desired out of all relation to spiritual gain. When a person says the Rosary in such a way, he may well ask himself in what way his prayer is like that of which Pope Leo XIII spoke in his encyclicals on the Rosary, and about which Pius XI wrote one of his last apostolic letters.

It is true that to pray well it is sufficient to think in a general way of God and of the graces for which one asks. But to make the most out of our five mysteries, we should remember that they constitute but a third of the whole Rosary, and that they should be accompanied by meditation—which can be very simple—on the Joyful, Sorrowful and Glorious Mysteries, which recall the whole life of Jesus and Mary and their glory in Heaven.

The Three Great Mysteries of Salvation

The fifteen mysteries of the Rosary thus divided into three groups are but different aspects of the three great mysteries of our salvation: the Incarnation, the Redemption, Eternal Life.

The mystery of the Incarnation is recalled by the joys of the Annunciation, the Visitation, the Birth of the Saviour, His Presentation in the Temple and His finding among the doctors. The mystery of the Redemption is recalled by the different stages of the Passion: the Agony in the garden, the Scourging, the Crowning with thorns, the Carrying of the Cross, the Crucifixion. The mystery of eternal life is recalled by the Resurrection, the Ascension, Pentecost, the Assumption of Our Lady and her crowning as Queen of Heaven.

Thus, the Rosary is a *Credo:* not an abstract one, but one concretised in the life of Jesus who came down to us from the Father and who ascended to bring us back with Himself to the Father. It is the whole of christian dogma in all its splendor and elevation, brought to us that we may fill our minds with it, that we may relish it and nourish our souls with it.

This makes the Rosary a true school of contemplation. It raises us gradually above vocal prayer and even above reasoned out or discursive meditation. Early theologians have compared the movement of the soul in contemplation to the spiral in which certain birds— the swallow, for example—move when they wish to attain to a great height.[17] The joyful mysteries lead to the Passion, and the Passion to the door of Heaven.

---

17. Cf. IIa IIae, q. 180, a. 6. The spiral movement lifts itself up to God progressively by the consideration of the different mysteries of salvation, all of which lead to Him.

The Rosary well understood is, therefore, a very elevated form of prayer which makes the whole of dogma accessible to all.

The Rosary is also a very practical form of prayer for it recalls all christian morality and spirituality by presenting them from the sublime point of view of their realization in Jesus and Mary. The mysteries of the Rosary should be reproduced in our lives. Each of them is a lesson in some virtue—particularly in the virtues of humility, trust, patience and charity.

There are three stages in our progress towards God. The first is to have knowledge of the final end, whence comes the desire of salvation and the joy to which that desire gives rise. This stage is symbolised in the joyful mysteries which contain the good news of the Incarnation of the Son of God who opens to us the way of salvation. The next stage is to adopt the means—often painful to nature—to be delivered from sin and to merit Heaven. This is the stage of the sorrowful mysteries. The final stage is that of rest in the possession of eternal life. It is the stage of Heaven, of which the glorious mysteries allow us some anticipated glimpse.

The Rosary is therefore most practical. It takes us from the midst of our too human interests and joys and makes us think of those which center on the coming of the Saviour. It takes us from our meaningless fears, from the sufferings we bear so badly, and reminds us of how much Jesus has suffered for love of us and teaches us to follow Him by bearing the cross which divine providence has sent us to purify us. It takes us finally from our earthly hopes and ambitions and makes us think of the true object of christian hope—eternal life and the graces necessary to arrive there.

The Rosary is more than a prayer of petition. It is a prayer of adoration inspired by the thought of the Incarnate God, a prayer of reparation in memory of the Passion of Our Saviour, a prayer of thanksgiving that the glorious mysteries continue to reproduce themselves in the uninterrupted entry of the elect into glory.

The Rosary and Contemplative Prayer

A more simple and still more elevated way of reciting the Rosary is, while saying it, to keep the eyes of faith fixed on the living Jesus who is always making intercession for us and who is acting upon us in accordance with the mysteries of His childhood, or His Passion, or His glory. He comes to us to make us like Himself. Let us fix our gaze on Jesus who is looking at us. His look is more than kind and understanding: it is the look of God, a look which purifies, which sanctifies, which gives peace. It is the look of our Judge and still more the look of our Saviour, our Friend, the Spouse of our souls. A Rosary said in this way, in solitude and silence, is a most fruitful intercourse with Jesus. It is a conversation with Mary too which leads to intimacy with her Son.

We sometimes read in the lives of the saints that Our Blessed Lord reproduced in them first His childhood, then His hidden life, then His apostolic life, and finally His Passion, before allowing them to share in His glory. He comes to us in a similar way in the Rosary and, well said, it is a prayer which gradually takes the form of an intimate conversation with Jesus and Mary. It is easy to see how saintly souls have found in it a school of contemplation.

It has sometimes been objected that one cannot reflect on the words and the mysteries at the same time. An answer that is often given is that it is not necessary to reflect on the words if one is meditating on or looking spiritually at one of the mysteries. The words are a kind of melody which soothes the ear and isolates us from the noise of the world around us, the fingers being occupied meanwhile in allowing one bead after another to slip through. Thus, the imagination is kept tranquil and the mind and the will are set free to be united to God.

It has also been objected that the monotony of the many repetitions in the Rosary leads necessarily to routine. This objection is valid only if the Rosary is said badly. If well said, it familiarises us with the different mysteries of salvation and recalls what these mysteries should produce in our joys, our sorrows, and our hopes. Any prayer can become a matter of routine—even the Ordinary of the Mass. The reason is not that the prayers are imperfect, but that we do not say them as we should—with faith, confidence and love.

The Spirit of the Rosary as St. Dominic Conceived It

To understand the Rosary better it is well to recall how St. Dominic conceived it under the inspiration of Our Lady at a time when southern France was ravaged by the Albigensian heresy—a heresy which denied the infinite goodness and omnipotence of God by admitting a principle of evil which was often victorious. Not only did Albigensianism attack christian morality, but it was opposed to dogma as well—to the great mysteries of creation, the redemptive incarnation, the descent of the Holy Ghost, the eternal life to which we are called.

It was at that moment that Our Blessed Lady made known to St. Dominic a kind of preaching till then unknown, which she said would be one of the most powerful weapons against future errors and in future difficulties. Under her inspiration, St. Dominic went into the villages of the heretics, gathered the people, and preached to them the mysteries of salvation —the Incarnation, the Redemption, Eternal Life. As Mary had taught him to do, he distinguished the different kinds of mysteries, and after each short instruction he

had ten *Hail Marys* recited—somewhat as might happen even today at a Holy Hour. And what the word of
the preacher was unable to do, the sweet prayer of the
Hail Mary did for hearts. As Mary had promised, it
proved to be a most fruitful form of preaching.[18]

If we live by the prayer of which St. Dominic's preaching is the example our joys, our sorrows, and our hopes
will be purified, elevated and spiritualized. We shall
see that Jesus, Our Saviour and Our Model, wishes to
make us like Himself, first communicating to us something of His infant and hidden life, then something of
His sorrows, and finally making us partakers of His
glorious life for all eternity.

Article 3
Consecration to Mary

In his *Treatise of True Devotion to the Blessed Virgin,* St. Grignon de Montfort has distinguished a number of different degrees of true devotion to the Mother
of God. He speaks only briefly of the forms of false
devotion—that which is altogether exterior, or pre-
sumptuous, or inconstant, or hypocritical, or self-inter-
ested—since his main concern is true devotion.

Like the other christian virtues, true devotion grows
in us with charity, advancing from the stage of the
beginner to that of the more proficient, and continuing up to the stage of the perfect. The first degree or
stage is to pray devoutly to Mary from time to time,
for example, by saying the *Angelus* when the bell rings.
The second degree is one of more perfect sentiments
of veneration, confidence and love; it may manifest
itself by the daily recitation of the Rosary—five decades
or all fifteen. In the third degree, the soul gives itself

---

18. The first fruit of the Rosary was the victory of Simon of Montfort over the Albi-
gensians, obtained while St. Dominic implored Mary's help in prayer.

fully to Our Lady by an act of consecration so as to belong altogether to Jesus through her.[19]

What does this Consecration mean?

This act of consecration consists in promising Mary to have constant filial recourse to her and to live in habitual dependence on her, so as to attain to more intimate union with Our Blessed Lord and through Him with the Blessed Trinity present in our souls. The reason for making it lies, St. Grignon de Montfort says, in the fact that God has willed to make use of Mary for the sanctification of souls, having already made use of her to bring about the Incarnation *(Treatise of True Devotion,* ch. I, a. 1, no. 44).

The saint continues: "I do not think that anyone can attain to great union with Our Blessed Lord or perfect fidelity to the Holy Ghost without being closely united to Our Lady and depending very much on her help. . . . She was full of grace when she was saluted by the Archangel Gabriel, she was superabundantly filled with grace by the Holy Ghost when He overshadowed her, she so advanced in grace from day to day and from moment to moment as to arrive at an inconceivable summit of grace; on which account the Most High has made her His unique treasurer and the unique dispenser of His graces, so that she may ennoble, enrich and elevate whom she wills, and make whom she wills enter the narrow gate of Heaven. . . . Jesus is everywhere and always the Son and the fruit of Mary; Mary is everywhere the true tree which bears the fruit of life and the true mother who produces it."

In the same chapter, a little earlier, we read: "We may apply to Mary with even more truth than St. Paul

---

19. That is why St. Grignon de Montfort speaks in his formula of "Consecration of oneself to Jesus by the hands of Mary." In the course of his treatise he usually says more briefly, "Consecration to Mary," meaning thereby consecration to Jesus through her.

applies them to himself the words: 'My little children, of whom I am in labour again, until Christ be formed in you. I am in labour daily with God's children till Jesus be formed in them in the fulness of His age.' St. Augustine says that the predestined are in this world hidden in the womb of Mary in order to become conformed to the image of the Son of God; and there she guards, nourishes, and supports them and brings them forth to glory after death, which is the true day of their birth—the term by which the Church always speaks of the death of the just. O mystery of grace unknown to the reprobate and little understood by the predestined!" Mary is truly the mother of the just, conceiving them spiritually and bringing them forth after death by their entry into glory, which is their definitive spiritual birth. It is clear then that it would be a falling short in humility to neglect to have frequent recourse to the Universal Mediatrix whom Divine Providence has given us as our true spiritual mother to form Christ in us. It is clear also that theology cannot but recognize that it is lawful and more than lawful to consecrate oneself to Mary, Mother and Queen of all men.[20]

Consecration to Our Lady is a practical form of recognition of her universal mediation and a guarantee of her special protection. It helps us to have continual childlike recourse to her and to contemplate and imitate her virtues and her perfect union with Christ. In the practice of this complete dependence on Mary, there may be included—and St. Grignon de Montfort invites us to it—the resignation into Mary's hands of everything in our good works that is communicable to other souls, so that she may make use of it in accordance with the will of her Divine Son and for His glory. "I choose thee this day, O Mary, in the presence of the whole court of Heaven, as my Mother and Queen. I

---

20. Cf. *Dict. de Théol. Cath.*, art. *Marie,* cols. 2470 sqq. Pius X has made his own the teaching of St. Grignon de Montfort, and sometimes of his very expressions, in the Encyclical *Ad diem illum* on Mary, universal Mediatrix.

give and consecrate to you as your slave my body and my soul, my interior and exterior possessions, and even the value of my past, present and future good actions, allowing you the full right to dispose of me and of all that belongs to me, without any exception whatever, according to your good pleasure, for the greater glory of God, in time and in eternity." This offering is really the practice of the so-called heroic act, there being question here not of a vow but of a promise made to the Blessed Virgin.[21]

We are recommended to offer our exterior possessions to Mary, that she may preserve us from inordinate attachment to the things of this world and inspire us to make better use of them. It is good also to consecrate to her our bodies and our senses that she may keep them pure.

The act of consecration gives over to Mary also our soul and its faculties, our spiritual possessions, virtues and merits, all our good works past, present and future. It is necessary, however, to explain how this can be done. Theology gives us the answer by distinguishing what is communicable to others in our good works from what is incommunicable.

What in our good works is communicable to others?

To begin at the other end of the problem, our merits *de condigno* which constitute a right in justice to an increase of grace and to eternal glory are incommunicable. Our merits *de condigno* differ in that from those of Our Blessed Lord. He was Head of the human race and could in justice communicate His merits to us. If, therefore, we offer our merits *de condigno* to Mary, it is not in order that she may give them to oth-

---

21. Even religious who have taken solemn vows of poverty, chastity and obedience can make this offering which will introduce them further into the mystery of the Communion of saints.

ers but that she may keep them for us, that she may help us to make them bear fruit, and, if we have the misfortune to lose them by mortal sin, that she may obtain for us the grace of really fervent contrition.

There is, however, something in our good works which we can communicate to others whether on earth or in purgatory.[22] There is in the first place the merit *de congruo proprie,* founded on the rights of friendship with God by grace. God gives grace to some because of the good intentions and good works of others who are His friends. There are, in the second place, our prayers; we can and should pray for our neighbor, for his conversion and his spiritual progress; we should pray also for the dying, for the souls in purgatory. There are finally our acts of satisfaction. We can make satisfaction *de congruo* for others, for example, by accepting our daily crosses to help to expiate for their sins. We may even, if God moves us to do so by His grace, accept the penalty due to their sins as Mary did at the foot of the Cross, and thereby draw down the divine mercy on them.[23] This the saints did frequently. An example is found in the life of St. Catherine of Siena. To a young Sienese whose heart was full of hate of his political enemies she said: "Peter, I take on myself all your sins, I shall do penance in your place; but do me one favor; confess your sins." "I have been frequently to Confession," answered Peter. "That is not true", replied the saint. "It is seven years since you were at Confession," and she proceeded to enumerate all the sins of his life. Confounded, he repented and pardoned his enemies. Even without having all St. Catherine's generosity, we can accept our daily crosses to help other souls to pay the debt they owe to the divine justice.

We can also gain indulgences for the souls in purgatory, opening to them the treasury of the merits and

---

22. Cf. *Treatise of True Devotion,* ch. iv, a. 1.
23. Cf. IIIa, q. 14, a. 1; q. 48, a. 2; Suppl., q. 13, a. 2: "Unus pro alio satisfacere potest, in quantum duo homines sunt unum in caritate."

satisfactions of Christ and the saints and hastening the day of their liberation.

There are, therefore, three things which we can share with others: our merits *de congruo,* our prayers, our satisfaction. And if we put these in Mary's hands for others, we ought not to be surprised if she sends us crosses—proportionate, of course, to our strength—to make us really work for the salvation of souls.

Who are those who may be advised to make this act of consecration? It certainly should not be recommended to people who would make it for merely sentimental reasons or through spiritual pride, and would not understand its true meaning. But those who are truly spiritual may be recommended to make it for a few days at first and then for some longer time; when finally they are prepared they may make it for their whole lives.

Someone may say that to give everything to Our Lady is to strip oneself, to leave one's own debts unpaid, and so to add to one's term in Purgatory. This is in fact the difficulty the devil suggested to St. Brigid of Sweden when she thought of making the act of donation to Mary. Our Blessed Lord explained, however, to the saint that the objection sprang from self-love and made no allowance for Mary's goodness. Mary will not be outdone in generosity: her help to us will far exceed what we give her. The very act of love which prompts our donation will itself obtain remission of part of our Purgatory.

Others wonder if making the act of donation to Mary leaves them free to pray for relatives and friends afterwards. They forget that Mary knows the obligations of charity better than we do: she would be the first to remind us of them. There may even be some among our relatives and friends on earth and in purgatory who have urgent need of prayers and satisfactions, without our knowing who they are. Mary, however, knows who they are, and she can help them out of our good works if we have put them at her disposal.

Thus understood, consecration and donation make us enter more fully, under Mary's guidance, into the mystery of the Communion of Saints. It is a perfect renewal of the baptismal promises.[24]

Fruits of this Consecration

"This devotion," St. Grignon de Montfort tells us,[25] "gives us up altogether to the service of God, and makes us imitate the example of Our Blessed Lord, who willed to be 'subject' in regard to His Blessed Mother. (*Luke* 2:51). It obtains for us the special protection of Mary, who purifies our good works and adorns them when she offers them to her Divine Son. It leads us to union with Our Blessed Lord; it is an easy, short, perfect and safe way. It confers great interior freedom, procures great benefits for our neighbor, and is an excellent means of assuring our perseverance." The saint develops each of these points in a most practical way.

He speaks of the easiness of the way in ch. 5, a. 5: "It is an easy way, one followed and prepared for us by Our Blessed Lord in His own coming, one where there are no obstacles in reaching Him. It is true that one can arrive at union with God by following other roads; but there will be many more crosses and trials, and many more difficulties which it will not be easy to surmount—there will be combats and strange agonies, steep mountains, sharp thorns, fearful deserts. But the way of Mary is sweeter and more peaceful.

"Even along the way of Mary there are stern battles and great difficulties; but our good Mother makes herself so near and present to her faithful servants to enlighten them in their doubts, to strengthen them in their fears, and to sustain them in their battles, that in truth the Virgin's way to Jesus is a way of roses and

---

24. Cf. *Treatise of True Devotion*, ch. iv, a. 2.
25. *Ib.*, ch. v.

honey compared with all others." The saint adds that
the truth of this can be seen from the lives of the saints
who have followed this way most particularly: St.
Ephrem, St. John Damascene, St. Bernard, St. Bonaventure, St. Bernardine of Siena, St. Francis de Sales.

A little further on in the same chapter, the saint
states that Mary's servants "receive from her Heaven's
greatest graces and favors which are crosses; but it is
the servants of Mary who bear the crosses with most
ease, merit and glory; and what would hold back another
makes them advance," for they are more aided by the
Mother of God, who obtains for them the unction of
love in their trials. It is wonderful how Mary makes
the cross at the same time easier to bear and more
meritorious: easier to bear because she helps us, and
more meritorious because she obtains for us greater
charity, which is the principle of greater merit.

"It is a short way . . . one advances more in a little
while of submission to and dependence on Mary than
in many years of self-will and self-reliance. . . . We can
advance with giant strides along the path by which
Jesus came to us. . . . In a few years we shall arrive
at the fulness of the perfect age."[26]

"It is a perfect way, chosen by God Himself . . . The
Most High descended to us by way of the humble Mary
without losing anything of His divinity; it is by Mary
that little ones can rise perfectly and divinely to the
Most High without fear."

It is finally a safe way, for the Blessed Virgin preserves us from the illusions of the devil and our imagination. She preserves us from sentiment as well,
calming and ruling our sensibility, giving it a pure and
holy object, and subordinating it to the rule of the will
vivified by charity.

---

26. St. Francis of Assisi learned one day in a vision that his sons were endeavour-
ing vainly to reach Our Blessed Lord by a steep ladder which led directly to Him.
St. Francis was shown instead a ladder much less steep, at the top of which was
Mary, and he heard the words: "Tell your sons to make use of the ladder of My
Mother."

In consecration to Mary, we find great interior liberty: this is the reward of putting ourselves in such complete dependence on Mary. Scruples are banished; the heart dilates with confidence and love. The saint confirms this point by referring to what he read in the life of the Dominican, Mother Agnes de Langeac, "who, suffering great anguish of soul, heard a voice which said to her that if she wished to be delivered and to be protected from her enemies, she should make herself at once the slave of Jesus and His Holy Mother. . . . When she had done so all her anguish and scruples ceased, and she found herself in a state of great peace, as a result of which she determined to teach the devotion to others . . . among whom was M. Olier, the founder of the seminary of Saint-Sulpice, and many other priests of the same seminary." It was in the same seminary that St. Grignon de Montfort received his priestly formation.

"Finally, this devotion is one which procures the good of our neighbor and it is for those who live by it an admirable means of persevering in grace . . . for by it one gives to Mary, who is faithful, all that one has. . . . It is on her fidelity that reliance is placed . . . that she may preserve and increase our merits in spite of all that could make us lose them. . . . Do not commit the gold of your charity, the silver of your purity, the waters of heavenly graces, or the wine of your merits and virtues . . . to broken vessels such as you yourselves are; else you will be despoiled by robbers, that is by the demons, who watch day and night for a favorable opportunity. . . . Put all your treasures, all your graces and virtues, in the womb and in the heart of Mary: she is a spiritual vessel, a vessel of honor, a singular vessel of devotion.

"Souls who are not born of blood nor of the will of the flesh nor of the will of man, but of God and of Mary, understand and relish what I say; and it is for them that I write. . . . If a soul gives itself to Mary

without reserve, she gives herself to it without reserve"
and helps it to find the road which leads to the eternal goal.

Such are the fruits of this consecration: Mary loves
those who commit themselves to her fully; she guides,
directs, defends, protects, supports and intercedes for
them. It is good to offer ourselves to her so that she
may offer us to her Son according to the fulness of her
prudence and her zeal.

There are also fruits of a higher order which this
devotion produces, fruits which are strictly mystical,
as we shall explain in the next section.[27]

Article 4

Mystical Union with Mary

A soul faithful to the devotion of which we have
been speaking performs all its actions through Mary,
in Mary and for Mary, and attains thereby to great
intimacy with Our Lord.[28] To consider only humility,
the theological virtues, and the gifts of the Holy Ghost,
the following are the more precious fruits of consecration to Mary when it is lived fully: a gradually increas-

---

27. According to St. Grignon de Montfort (ch. I, a. 2, no. 3), devotion to Our Blessed
Lady will be more specially necessary in the last ages of the world, when Satan
will make an effort such "as to deceive (if possible) even the elect" (*Matt.* 24:24).
"If the predestined", he says, "enter with the grace and light of the Holy Ghost
into the interior and perfect practice of this devotion, they will see clearly as far
as faith permits this beautiful star of the sea, and they will arrive safely in harbour, in spite of pirates and tempests. They will learn the greatness of their
Queen, and they will consecrate themselves entirely to her service, as her sub-
jects and slaves of love" to combat what St. Paul calls the slavery of sin (cf. *Rom.*
6:20). They will have experience of her motherly tenderness, and they will love
her as her well-beloved children.

The expression "holy slavery" used by the saint has been sometimes criticised.
This is to forget that it is a slavery of love which accentuates rather than dimin-
ishes the filial character of our love of Mary. Besides, as Mgr Garnier, Bishop of
Luçon, remarked in a pastoral letter of March 11th, 1922, if there are in the
world slaves of human respect, of ambition, of money, and of shameful passions,
there are also, thank God, slaves of conscience and of duty. The holy slavery
belongs to this group. The expression "holy slavery" is a striking metaphor, opposed
to the slavery of sin.

28. *Treatise of True Devotion,* ch. viii, a. 2.

ing participation in Mary's humility and faith, great confidence in God through her, the grace of pure love, and the transformation of the soul to the image of Jesus.[29]

Participation in Mary's Humility and Faith

By the light of the Holy Ghost the soul consecrated to Mary will come to learn of all the evil that is in itself; it will see by experience that it is naturally incapable of every salutary and supernatural good and that through self-love it opposes many obstacles to the work of grace within it. Thus, it will attain to that contempt of self of which St. Augustine speaks in the *City of God* (Bk. XIV, ch. 28): "Two loves have built two cities. The love of self even to the degree of despising God has built the city of Babylon, and the love of God even to the degree of despising self has built the city of God." "The humble Mary", says St. Grignon de Montfort,[30] "will make you a sharer in her deep humility, so that you will despise yourself and no one else, and you will love to be despised.

"She will give you a share in her faith also, which was greater than the faith of the patriarchs, the prophets, the apostles, and all the saints. She herself has that faith no longer, for she sees all things clearly in God in the light of glory; but she keeps it . . . in the Church militant for her most faithful servants.

"The more you win her love . . . the more you will have a pure faith, which will make you set little store by the sense-perceptible and the extraordinary; a faith living and animated by charity which will make you act from a motive of pure love; a faith firm and immovable as a rock which will make you constant in the midst of storms and afflictions; a faith active and pierc-

---

29. *Ib.,* ch. vii.
30. *Ib.,* ch. vii, a. 1.

ing which, like a mysterious master-key, will give you entry to all the mysteries of Jesus, the final destiny of man, and the heart of God Himself; a courageous faith which will make you undertake and bring to achievement great things for God and the salvation of souls; a faith that will be your flaming torch, your divine life, your hidden treasure of divine wisdom, your all-powerful weapon, yours to use for the enlightenment of those who are in darkness and the shadow of death, for the inflaming of those who are lukewarm and who need the purified gold of charity, for the restoration to life of those who are dead by sin, for touching and uprooting by your sweet and powerful words the hearts of marble and the cedars of Lebanon, and finally for resisting the devil and all the enemies of salvation."[31] These wonderful pages are the fruit of the full development of the virtue of faith, lit up by the gifts of understanding and wisdom—*fides donis illustrata,* as theologians say.

Great Confidence in God through Mary

By confidence we mean that firm hope which tends towards eternal glory with sureness of direction. According to St. Grignon de Montfort,[32] the Blessed Virgin inspires great confidence in God and in herself: 1st— since through consecration we approach Jesus no longer alone but in the company of His Mother; 2nd—having given Mary all our merits, graces and satisfactions to dispose of as she wills, she in return will communicate to us her virtues and clothe us with her merits; 3rd—since we have given ourselves to Mary she will give herself to us. We can say to Mary: "I belong to you, O Holy Virgin. Save me." And to God we can say with the psalmist (*Ps.* 130:1): "Lord, my heart is not

31. *Ib.,* ch. vii, a. 2.
32. *Ib.,* a. 4.

exalted: nor are my eyes lofty. Neither have I walked in great matters, nor in wonderful things above me. No, but I keep my soul in calm and silence; as a child that is weaned (from the pleasures of the world, and resting) on its mother's breast (and trusting in her)." Through Mary we receive more and more the inspirations of the gift of knowledge which shows us the emptiness of the things of this world and our frailty, and contrasts them with the reward of eternal life and the divine assistance.

The Grace of Pure Love and of Transformation of Soul

Those who walk by the way of Mary grow in charity under the influence of her who is called the "Mother of fair love." (*Ecclus.* 24:24). "She will take out of your heart every scruple and servile fear; she will expand it so that you will run in the commandments of her Son (*Ps.* 118:32) with the holy freedom of the children of God. She will introduce into your heart that pure love of which she has all the treasures so that you will no longer serve the God of love in fear as you have done, but in pure love. You will look on Him as your good Father whom you will try to please at all times, with whom you will converse in all confidence. If you have the misfortune to offend Him . . . you will at once ask forgiveness humbly, you will stretch out your hands to Him . . . and you will continue your journey towards Him with unshaken confidence."[33]

Mary's soul will be communicated to yours to glorify the Lord and to rejoice in Him, to live the *Magnificat*. The faithful christian "inhales Mary in a spiritual manner just as his body inhales the air".[34] So well is her spirit of wisdom communicated that her

---

33. *Ib.,* ch. vii, a. 3.
34. *Ib.,* a. 5.

fully faithful servant and child becomes a living image of her mother.

Through this communication the soul is transformed to the image of Jesus Christ. "St Augustine calls the Blessed Virgin the mould of God, *forma Dei* . . .[35] Whoever is cast in this mold is soon formed in Christ . . . Some directors are like sculptors who, placing their trust in their art, deal blow after blow with hammer and chisel to a hard stone or a piece of wood in order to shape it into a representation of Jesus, and sometimes do not succeed . . . one badly-aimed blow can botch the whole work. But those who accept the secret of grace of which I write are like the artists who work from a mould. Having found the beautiful mould of Mary, where Jesus was formed naturally and divinely, they do not trust their own industry but only the fidelity of the mould, and cast and lose themselves in Mary, becoming thus images of Christ . . . But remember that you can cast in a mould only what has been melted to a liquid: that is to say, you must destroy and melt down the old Adam, to become the new Adam in Mary." [36]

The way of Mary increases purity of intention. By it a person renounces his own peculiar intentions, even if good, to be lost in those of the Blessed Virgin. "One enters thus into the sublimity of her intentions which were so pure that she gave more glory to God by the least of her actions—for example, by winding her distaff, or by some needlework—than St. Laurence did on the gridiron by his martyrdom, or even all the saints by their most heroic acts . . . or all the angels. . . . By deigning to receive into her virginal hands the gift of our actions she gives them a beauty and splendor which glorify Our Blessed Lord much more than if we offered them to Him ourselves. . . . Finally, you never think of Mary but she thinks of God for you. . . . She is all

---

35. Sermon 208, which has been attributed to St. Augustine. "Si formam Dei te appellem, digna existis."
36. *Treatise of True Devotion,* ch. vii, a. 6.

she is relative to God . . . she is the echo of God, who says and repeats but 'God'. . . .When she is praised God is loved and praised. We give to God through and in Mary."[37]

Grace of Intimacy with Mary

Some souls are favored with a special grace of union with Mary. Fr. E. Neubert, the Marianist, has gathered a number of significant testimonies in this connection.[38] Reference must also be made to the work "Mystic Union with Mary", written by a Flemish recluse, Marie de Sainte-Thérèse (1623-1677), who had personal experience of the subject on which she wrote.

Fr. Chaminade, who exercised the priestly ministry at Bordeaux with great zeal during the French Revolution and who founded the Marianists, had the same experience. He wrote: "There is a gift of the habitual presence of the Blessed Virgin even as there is a gift of the habitual presence of God—very rare, it is true, but obtainable through great fidelity." As Fr. Neubert explains, this text refers to normal and habitual mystical union with Mary. The Ven. L. Ed. Cestac had the same gift. "I do not see her", he said, "but I feel her presence as the horse feels the hand on the rein." Thus these souls are conscious of the influence which Mary exercises on us continually by transmitting actual graces to our souls.

Marie de Sainte-Thérèse has words to the same effect: "That sweet mother has taken me under her maternal direction just as a teacher takes in her own the hand of the child she is teaching to write. . . . She remains almost uninterruptedly before my soul, drawing me to herself in so loving and motherly a manner, stimulating me, guiding me, instructing me in the way

---

37. *Ib.,* ch. vii, a. 7.
38. *La Vie Spirituelle,* January 1937: "L'Union mystique à la Sainte Vierge," pp. 15-29.

of the spirit and in the perfect practice of the virtues. And I do not lose for a single instant the charm of her presence along with that of the God head. . . . She produces the divine life in me by an imperceptible inflow of different graces. . . . It is of the nature of love to unite itself to the object loved. . . . Thus tender, burning and unifying love draws the soul which loves Mary to live in her, to be united to her, and to other effects and transformations. . . . Then God shows Himself in Mary and by her as in a mirror." Such was a great part of the life of this servant of God.

Some souls who have had great intimacy with Mary say that they never experienced her presence in them, but rather her presence very near them—as near as possible, in fact—and that they felt a great joy at knowing of her happiness. We have known a saintly Carthusian who said: "I suffer, but she is happy."

Finally, many holy souls have had, in the midst of their sufferings, a gift of deep intimacy with Mary which was the source of their strength even though they have left no account of it. Many of them have experienced, were it only for an instant, her presence like that of a mother who peeps into the room where her children are. In such experiences she communicates an indescribable holiness, and prompts to more generous sacrifices, such as lead the soul into the depths contained in the *Magnificat and the Stabat Mater.*

Article 5

The Consecration of the Human Race to Mary for the Peace of the World

The gravity of the events of these latter years, since the Russian Revolution, the Spanish Civil War and the World War, shows that the faithful should have recourse to God more and more through the great mediators He has given us on account of our weakness. The horror of these events shows in a singularly striking manner to what men can come if they wish to do absolutely without God, and organise their life without Him, far from Him and against Him. When, instead of believing in God, hoping in Him and loving Him above all and our neighbor in Him, we wish to believe in humanity, hope in it, and love it in a purely earthly manner, it does not take long to show itself to us with all its blemishes and gaping wounds: the pride of life, the concupiscence of the flesh, the concupiscence of the eyes, and all the brutality that ensues from them. When, instead of making our last end God, who can be simultaneously possessed by all, we seek our final end in earthly goods, we are not long in finding out that they divide us profoundly; for the same house, the same field, the same territory, cannot belong simultaneously and integrally to several owners. The more life is materialized, the more the lower appetites are excited, without any subordination to a superior love, the more the conflicts between individuals, classes and peoples become acute, till finally earth becomes a veritable Hell.

The Lord shows thus to men what they can be without Him. It is a striking commentary on these words of the Saviour: "Without me you can do nothing" (*John* 15:5); "He that is not with me is against me: and he that gathereth not with me, scattereth" (*Matt.* 12:30); "seek ye first the kingdom of God and his justice, and all these things shall be added unto you." (*Matt.* 6:33). The psalmist in the same way says: "Unless the Lord build the house, they labor in vain that build it. Unless the Lord keep the city, he watcheth in vain that keepeth it." (*Ps.* 126:1).

The two great evils of the age, as Pope Pius XI said, are on the one hand materialistic and atheistic communism according to the programme of the "God-less," and on the other hand, an unbounded nationalism which aims at establishing the supremacy of the stronger nations over the weaker, without respect for divine and natural law. Hence the bitter conflict in which the entire world is plunged.

As a remedy for these evils, the best and most zealous among catholics in nations actually on opposite sides feel the need for common prayer which will re-unite before God the souls of true christians in all countries, to obtain that the reign of God and of His Christ be established more and more in the place of the reign of pride and covetousness. To this end, masses are daily offered along with adoration of the Blessed Sacrament; which latter has been established in different countries in so speedy and widespread a manner that one must consider it the fruit of a great grace from God.

Exterior peace will not be obtained for the world except by the interior peace of souls, bringing them back to God and working to establish the reign of Christ in the depths of their intellects, of their hearts and of their wills. For this return of straying souls to Him who alone can save them, it is necessary to have recourse to the intercession of Mary, Universal Mediatrix and Mother of all men. It is said of sinners who seem for ever lost that they must be confided to Mary: it is the same for christian peoples who stray. All the influence of the Blessed Virgin has as its end to lead souls to her Son, just as that of Christ, the Universal Mediator, has as its end to lead them to His Father.

Mary's prayer, especially since she was assumed into Heaven, is universal in the widest sense of the term. She prays not only for individual souls on earth and in Purgatory, but also for families and for all nations, which ought to live beneath the rays of the Gospel's light and the influence of the Church. Moreover, her prayer is all the more powerful in that it is more enlightened and proceeds from a love of God and of souls which nothing can weaken or interrupt. The merciful love of Mary for men surpasses that of all the angels and saints united, and so does the power of her intercession with the Heart of her Son.

That is why on all sides many interior souls, before the unprecedented disorders and tragic sufferings of the hour, feel the need for recourse to the redeeming Love of Christ through the intercession of Mary Mediatrix.

In many countries, especially in convents of fervent contemplative life, it is remembered that many French bishops united at Lourdes, at the second national Marial Congress, on the 27th of July, 1929, expressed to the Sovereign Pontiff their desire for a consecration of the human race to the Immaculate Heart of Mary. It is remembered also that Father Deschamps, SJ., in 1900, Cardinal Richard, Archbishop of Paris, in 1906, Fr. Le Doré, Superior General of the Eudists, in 1908 and 1912, and Fr. Lintelo, S.J., in 1914, took the initiative in the matter of petitions to the Sovereign Pontiff to obtain the consecration of the human race to the Immaculate Heart of Mary.

By a collective act, the bishops of France, at the beginning of the war of 1914, in December of the same year, consecrated France to Mary. Cardinal Mercier in 1915, in his Pastoral Letter on Mary Mediatrix, saluted the Blessed Virgin, Mother of the human race, as Queen of the World. Fr. Lucas, new Superior General of the Eudists, obtained finally in a few months more than three hundred thousand signatures to hasten by this consecration the peace of Christ in the reign of Christ.

The strength that we need in the present upheaval is the prayer of Mary, Mother of all men, who will obtain it for us from the Saviour. Her intercession is very powerful against the spirit of evil which ranges individuals, classes and peoples one against the other. If a formal pact, fully consented to, with the demon, can have dire consequences in the life of a soul and send it to eternal damnation, what spiritual effect will a consecration to Mary not have, made in a deep spirit of faith and often renewed with still greater fidelity?

One may remember how in December, 1836, the venerable curé of Our Lady of Victories in Paris, while celebrating Mass at the altar of the Blessed Virgin, heartbroken at the thought of the apparent failure of his ministry, heard these words: "Consecrate your parish to the Holy and Immaculate Heart of Mary," and how once the consecration was made the parish was transformed.

Mary's prayer for us is that of a Mother very enlightened, very loving and very strong, who watches ceaselessly over her children, over all men, called to receive the fruits of the Redemption. This is the experience of anyone who daily consecrates to Mary all his works, material and spiritual, and all his undertakings. He recovers faith and confidence when all seems lost.

Now, if the individual consecration of a soul to Mary obtains for it daily great graces of light, love and strength, what will not be the fruits of a consecration of the human race made to the Saviour by Mary herself, at the request of the common Father of the faithful, the supreme Pastor? What will not be the effect of a consecration thus made, especially if the faithful among the different peoples unite, so as to conform their lives to it, in fervent prayer often renewed at Holy Mass?

To obtain that the Sovereign Pontiff perform this act, it is necessary that a sufficient number of the faithful understand the recent lessons given us by Divine Providence. In other words, a sufficient number must have seized the meaning and the import of the consecration asked for. Otherwise it will not be able to produce the required effects. In the divine plan, trials end when they have produced the effect they were intended to produce, when souls have profited by them—just as Purgatory ends when the soul is purified.

As a saintly religious used to say:[39] "We do not live
for ourselves; we must see everything as it is in God's
plan; our present sufferings—even were they to rise
to their peak and were we ourselves to be sacrificed
in the disaster—gain and prepare the future assured
triumphs of the Church. . . . The Church goes thus
from struggle to struggle and from victory to victory,
each succeeding the other until Eternity, which will be
the final victory." "Ought not Christ to have suffered
these things and so to enter into His glory?" (*Luke*
24:26). The Church and souls must go along the same
road. The Church does not live only for a day; when
the martyrs fell like snowflakes in winter, might one
not have believed that all was lost? No, their blood
was preparing the triumphs of the future.

In the difficult period we are going through the
Church has need of very generous souls, of real saints.
It is Mary, Mother of Divine Grace, Mother most pure,
Virgin most prudent and strong, who must shape them.

From various sides the Lord suggests to interior
souls a prayer of which the form may differ but of
which the substance is always the same: "In this time
when a spirit of pride pushed to the point of atheism
seeks to spread itself among the peoples, O Lord, be
Thou as the soul of my soul, the life of my life; grant
me a deeper understanding of the mystery of the
Redemption and of Thy holy self-abasement, the remedy of all pride. Grant me a sincere desire to participate, in the measure intended for me by Providence,
in these salutary humiliations and make me find in
this desire the strength, peace and—when Thou desirest
it—the joy, to stir up my courage and the confidence
of those around me."

To enter thus practically into the depths of the mystery of the Redemption, it is necessary that Mary, who

---

39. Mère Marie de Jésus, foundress of the Society of the Daughters of the Heart of
Jesus: "Pensées de la Servante de Dieu, Mère Marie de Jésus" (1841-1884), Rome,
1918, pp. 43 sqq., 50.

at the foot of the Cross entered into them deeper than did any other creature, should teach us interiorly and reveal to us in the words of the Gospel the spirit in which she herself lived so fully.

May the Mother of the Saviour deign by her prayer to place all the faithful of the different nations beneath the rays of these words of Christ: "The glory which thou hast given me I have given to them; that they may be one, as we also are one." (*John* 17:22).

It is to be hoped that one day, when the hour appointed by Divine Providence will have come, and when souls are prepared, the Supreme Pastor, in answer to the prayers of the bishops and the faithful, will consecrate the human race to the merciful and Immaculate Heart of Mary,* that she may offer us all the more appealingly to her Son and so obtain peace for the world. This would be a new affirmation of the universal mediation of the Blessed Virgin.

Let us go to her with the greatest confidence: she has been called "the hope of the hopeless," and by going to her as to the best and the most enlightened of mothers we shall go to Jesus as to our sole and merciful Saviour.

---

* This has been done since the publication of this book.

∽Chapter 7∽

The Predestination of St. Joseph and His Eminent Sanctity

"He that is lesser among you all, he is the greater."
—*Luke* 9:48

One cannot write a book on Our Lady without referring to the predestination of St. Joseph, his eminent perfection, the character of his special mission, his virtues, and his role in the sanctification of souls.

His Pre-eminence over the other Saints

The opinion that St. Joseph is the greatest of the saints after Our Lady is one which is becoming daily more commonly held in the Church. We do not hesitate to look on the humble carpenter as higher in grace and eternal glory than the patriarchs and the greatest of the prophets—than St. John the Baptist, the apostles, the martyrs and the great doctors of the Church. He who is least in the depth of his humility is, because of the interconnection of the virtues, the greatest in the height of his charity: "He that is the lesser among you all, he is the greater."

St. Joseph's pre-eminence was taught by Gerson[1] and St. Bernardine of Siena.[2] It became more and more common in the course of the 16th century. It was admitted by St. Teresa, by the Dominican Isidore de Isolanis, who appears to have written the first treatise on St. Joseph,[3] by St. Francis de Sales, by Suarez,[4] and

---

1. *Sermo in Nativitatem Virginis Mariae,* IVa consideratio.
2. *Sermo I de S. Joseph,* c. iii, Opera, Lyon, 1650, t. IV, p. 254.
3. *Summa de donis S. Joseph,* ann. 1522. There is a new edition by Fr. Berthier, Rome, 1897.
4. *In Summam S. Thomae,* IIIa, q. 29, disp. 8, sect. I.

later by St. Alphonsus Liguori,[5] Ch. Sauve,[6] Cardinal Lépicier[7] and Mgr Sinibaldi;[8] it is very ably treated of in the article "Joseph" in the *Dict. de Théol. Cath.* by M. A. Michel.

The doctrine of St. Joseph's pre-eminence received the approval of Leo XIII in his encyclical *Quamquam pluries,* August 15th, 1899, written to proclaim St. Joseph patron of the universal Church. "The dignity of the Mother of God is so elevated that there can be no higher created one. But since St. Joseph was united to the Blessed Virgin by the conjugal bond, there is no doubt that he approached nearer than any other to that super-eminent dignity of hers by which the Mother of God surpasses all created natures. Conjugal union is the greatest of all; by its very nature it is accompanied by a reciprocal communication of the goods of the spouses. If then God gave St. Joseph to Mary to be her spouse He certainly did not give him merely as a companion in life, a witness of her virginity, a guardian of her honor, but He made him also participate by the conjugal bond in the eminent dignity which was hers."

When Leo XIII said that Joseph came nearest of all to the super-eminent dignity of Mary, did his words imply that Joseph is higher in glory than all the angels? We cannot give any certain answer to the question. We must be content to restate the doctrine which is becoming more and more commonly taught: of all the saints Joseph is the highest after Jesus and Mary; he is among the angels and the archangels. The Church mentions him immediately after Mary and before the Apostles in the prayer *A cunctis.* Though he is not mentioned in the Canon of the Mass,* he has a proper preface, and the month of March is consecrated to him as protector and defender of the universal Church.

---

5. *Sermone di S. Giuseppe,* Discorsi Morali, Naples, 1841.
6. *Saint Joseph Intime,* Paris, 1920.
7. *Tractatus de Sancto Joseph,* Paris, 1908.
8. *La Grandezza di San Giuseppe,* Rome, 1927, pp. 36 sqq.
* St. Joseph's name was added to the Canon in 1962.—*Publisher,* 2007.

The multitude of Christians in all succeeding generations are committed to him in a real though hidden manner. This idea is expressed in the litanies approved by the Church: 'St. Joseph, illustrious descendant of David, light of the Patriarchs, Spouse of the Mother of God, guardian of her virginity, foster-father of the Son of God, vigilant defender of Christ, head of the Holy Family; Joseph most just, most chaste, most prudent, most strong, most obedient, most faithful, mirror of patience, lover of poverty, model of workers, glory of domestic life, guardian of virgins, support of families, consolation of the afflicted, hope of the sick, patron of the dying, terror of demons, protector of the Holy Church." He is the greatest after Mary.

The Reason for St. Joseph's Pre-eminence

What is the justification of this doctrine which has been more and more accepted in the course of five centuries? The principle invoked more or less explicitly by St. Bernard, St. Bernardine of Siena, Isidore de Isolanis, Suarez, and more recent authors is the one, simple and sublime, formulated by St. Thomas when treating of the fulness of grace in Jesus and of holiness in Mary: "An exceptional divine mission calls for a corresponding degree of grace." This principle explains why the holy soul of Jesus, being united personally to the Word, the Source of all grace, received the absolute fulness of grace. It explains also why Mary, called to be Mother of God, received from the instant of her conception an initial fulness of grace which was greater than the initial fulness of all the saints together: since she was nearer than any other to the Source of grace she drew grace more abundantly. It explains also why the Apostles who were nearer to Our Blessed Lord than the saints who followed them had more perfect knowledge of the mysteries of faith. To preach the gospel infallibly to the world they received at Pentecost the gift of a most eminent, most enlightened, and most firm faith as the principle of their apostolate.

The same truth explains St. Joseph's pre-eminence. To understand it we must add one remark: all works which are to be referred immediately to God Himself are perfect. The work of creation, for example, which proceeded entirely and directly from the hand of God was perfect. The same must be said of His great servants, whom He has chosen exceptionally and immediately—not through a human instrument—to restore the order disturbed by sin. God does not choose as men do. Men often choose incompetent officials for the highest posts. But those whom God Himself chooses directly and immediately to be His exceptional ministers in the work of redemption receive from Him grace proportionate to their vocation. This was the case with St. Joseph. He must have received a relative fulness of grace proportionate to his mission since he was chosen not by men nor by any creature but by God Himself and by God alone to fulfil a mission unique in the world. We cannot say at what precise moment St. Joseph's sanctification took place. But we can say that, from the time of his marriage to Our Lady, he was confirmed in grace, because of his special mission.[9]

To What Order Does St. Joseph's Exceptional Mission Belong?

St. Joseph's mission is evidently higher than the order of nature—even by angelic nature. But is it simply of the order of grace, as were that of St. John the Baptist who prepared the way of salvation, and that the Apostles had in the Church for the sanctification of souls, and that more particular mission of the founders of religious orders? If we examine the ques-

---

9. *Cf. Dict. Théol. Cath.*, art. *Joseph*, col. 1518.

tion carefully we shall see that St. Joseph's mission surpassed the order of grace. It borders, by its term, on the hypostatic order, which is constituted by the mystery of the Incarnation. But it is necessary to avoid both exaggeration and understatement in this matter.

Mary's unique mission, her divine motherhood, has its term in the hypostatic order. So also, in a sense, St. Joseph's hidden mission. This is the teaching of many saints and other writers. St. Bernard says of St. Joseph: "He is the faithful and prudent servant whom the Lord made the support of His Mother, the foster-father of His flesh, and the sole most faithful co-operator on earth in His great design."[10]

St. Bernardine of Siena writes: "When God chooses a person by grace for a very elevated mission, He gives all the graces required for it. This is verified in a specially outstanding manner in the case of St. Joseph, Foster-father of Our Lord Jesus Christ and Spouse of Mary. . . ."[11] Isidore de Isolanis places St. Joseph's vocation above that of the Apostles. He remarks that the vocation of the apostles is to preach the gospel, to enlighten souls, to reconcile them with God, but that the vocation of St. Joseph is more immediately in relation with Christ Himself since he is the Spouse of the Mother of God, the Foster-father and Protector of the Saviour.[12] Suarez teaches to the same effect: "Certain offices pertain to the order of sanctifying grace, and among them that of the apostles holds the highest place; thus they have need of more gratuitous gifts than other souls, especially gratuitous gifts of wisdom. But there are other offices which touch upon or border on the order of the Hypostatic Union . . . as can be seen clearly in the case of the divine maternity of the Blessed Virgin, and it is to that order that the

---

10. *Homil. II super Missus est.*
11. *Sermo I de S. Joseph.*
12. *Summa de donis sancti Joseph,* Pars IIIa, c. xviii. This work was very highly praised by Benedict XIV.

ministry of St. Joseph pertains."[13]

Some years ago Mgr Sinibaldi, titular Bishop of Tiberias and secretary of the Sacred Congregation of Studies, treated the question very ably. He pointed out that the ministry of St. Joseph belonged, in a sense, because of its term, to the hypostatic order: not that St. Joseph co-operated intrinsically as physical instrument of the Holy Ghost in the realization of the mystery of the Incarnation—for under that respect his role is very much inferior to that of Mary—but that he was predestined to be, in the order of moral causes, the protector of the virginity and the honor of Mary at the same time as foster-father and protector of the Word made flesh. "His mission pertains by its term to the hypostatic order, not through intrinsic physical and immediate cooperation, but through extrinsic moral and mediate (through Mary) co-operation, which is, however, really and truly co-operation."[14]

St. Joseph's Predestination is One with the Decree of the Incarnation

St. Joseph's pre-eminence becomes all the clearer if we consider that the eternal decree of the Incarnation covered not merely the Incarnation in abstraction from circumstances of time and place but the Incarnation here and now—that is to say, the Incarnation of the Son of God who by the operation of the Holy Ghost was to be conceived at a certain moment of time by the Virgin Mary, espoused to a man of the family of David whose name was Joseph: "The angel Gabriel was sent from God into a city of Galilee, called Nazareth, to a virgin espoused to a man whose name was Joseph, of the house of David." (*Luke* 1:26-27).

All the indications are therefore that St. Joseph

---

13. *In Summam S. Thomae*, q. 29, disp. 8, sect. I.
14. *La Grandezza di San Giuseppe*, Rome, 1927, pp. 36 sqq.

was predestined to be foster-father of the Incarnate Word before being predestined to glory; the ultimate reason being that Christ's predestination as man to the natural divine sonship precedes the predestination of all the elect, since Christ is the first of the predestined.[15] The predestination of Christ to the natural divine sonship is simply the decree of the Incarnation, which, as we have seen, includes Mary's predestination to the divine motherhood and Joseph's to be foster-father and protector of the Incarnate Son of God.

As the predestination of Christ to the natural divine sonship is superior to His predestination to glory and precedes it, and as the predestination of Mary to the divine motherhood precedes (*in signo priori*) her predestination to glory, so also the predestination of St. Joseph to be foster-father of the Incarnate Word precedes his predestination to glory and to grace. In other words, the reason why he was predestined to the highest degree of glory after Mary, and in consequence to the highest degree of grace and of charity, is that he was called to be the worthy foster-father and protector of the Man-God.

The fact that St. Joseph's first predestination was one with the decree of the Incarnation shows how elevated his unique mission was. This is what people mean when they say that St. Joseph was made and put into the world to be the foster-father of the Incarnate Word and that God willed for him a high degree of glory and grace to fit him for his task.

The Special Character of St. Joseph's Mission

This point is explained admirably by Bossuet in his first panegyric of the saint: "Among the different vocations, I notice two in the Scriptures which seem directly

---

15. Cf. IIIa, q. 24, a. 1, 2, 3, 4.

opposed to each other: the first is that of the Apostles, the second that of St. Joseph. Jesus was revealed to the Apostles that they might announce Him throughout the world; He was revealed to St. Joseph who was to remain silent and keep Him hidden. The Apostles are lights to make the world see Jesus. Joseph is a veil to cover Him; and under that mysterious veil are hidden from us the virginity of Mary and the greatness of the Saviour of souls . . . He who makes the Apostles glorious with the glory of preaching, glorifies Joseph by the humility of silence." The hour for the manifestation of the mystery of the Incarnation had not yet struck: it was to be preceded by the thirty years of the hidden life.

Perfection consists in doing God's will, each one according to his vocation; St. Joseph's vocation of silence and obscurity surpassed that of the Apostles because it bordered more nearly on the redemptive Incarnation. After Mary, Joseph was nearest to the Author of grace, and in the silence of Bethlehem, during the exile in Egypt, and in the little home of Nazareth he received more graces than any other saint.

His mission was a dual one.

As regards Mary, he preserved her virginity by contracting with her a true but altogether holy marriage. The angel of the Lord said to him: "Joseph, son of David, fear not to take unto thee Mary thy wife, for that which is conceived of her is of the Holy Ghost." (*Matt.* 1:20; *Luke* 2:5). Mary is truly his wife. The marriage was a true one, as St. Thomas explains (IIIa, q. 29, a. 2) when showing its appropriateness. There should be no room for doubt, however light, regarding the honor of the Son and the Mother: if ever doubt did arise Joseph, the most informed and the least suspect witness, would be there to defend it. Besides, Mary would find help and protection in St. Joseph. He loved her with a pure and devoted love, in God and for God. Their union was stainless, and most respectful on the side of St. Joseph. Thus he was nearer than any other saint to the Mother of God and the spiritual Mother of men—and he too was a man. The beauty of the whole universe was nothing compared with that of the union of Mary and Joseph, a union created by the Most High, which ravished the angels and gave joy to the Lord.

As regards the Incarnate Word, Joseph watched over Him, protected Him, and contributed to His human education. He is called His foster-father, but the term does not express fully the mysterious supernatural relation between the two. A man becomes foster-father of a child normally as a result of an accident. But it was no accident in the case of St. Joseph: he had been created and put into the world for that purpose: it was the primary reason of his predestination and the reason for all the graces he received. Bossuet expressed this well:[16] "If nature does not give a father's heart, where will it be found? In other words, since Joseph was not Jesus' father, how could he have a father's heart in His regard?

"Here we must recognise the action of God. It is by the power of God that Joseph has a father's heart, and if nature fails God gives one with His own hand; for it is of God that it is written that He directs our inclinations where he wills. . . . He gives some a heart of flesh when He softens their nature by charity. . . . Does He not give all the faithful the hearts of children when He sends to them the Spirit of His Son? The Apostles feared the least danger, but God gave them a new heart and their courage became undaunted. . . . The same hand gave Joseph the heart of a father and Jesus the heart of a son. That is why Jesus obeys and Joseph does not fear to command. How has he the courage to command his Creator? Because the true Father of Jesus Christ, the God who gives Him birth from all eternity,

---

16. *First Panegyric of St. Joseph,* edit. Lebarcq, t. II, pp. 135 sqq.

having chosen Joseph to be the father of His only Son in time, sent down into his bosom some ray or some spark of His own infinite love for His Son; that is what changed his heart, that is what gave him a father's love, and Joseph the just man who feels that father's heart within him feels also that God wishes him to use his paternal authority, so that he dares to command Him who he knows is his Master." That is equivalent to saying that Joseph was predestined first to take the place of a father in regard to the Saviour who could have no earthly father,[17] and in consequence to have all the gifts which were given him that he might be a worthy Protector of the Incarnate Word.

Is it necessary to say with what fidelity St. Joseph guarded the triple deposit confided to him: the virginity of Mary, the Person of Jesus Christ, and the secret of the Eternal Father, that of the Incarnation of His Son, a secret to be guarded faithfully till the hour appointed for its revelation?

In a discourse delivered in the Consistorial Hall on the 19th of March, 1928, Pope Pius XI said, after having spoken on the missions of St. John the Baptist and St. Peter: "Between these two missions there appears that of St. Joseph, one of recollection and silence, one almost unnoticed and destined to be lit up only many centuries afterwards, a silence which would become a resounding hymn of glory, but only after many years. But where the mystery is deepest it is there precisely that the mission is highest and that a more brilliant cortège of virtues is required with their corresponding echo of merits. It was a unique and sublime mission, that of guarding the Son of God, the King of the world, that of protecting the virginity of Mary, that of entering into participation in the mystery hidden from the eyes of ages and so to co-operate in the Incarnation

---

17. We read that Jesus was subject to Mary and Joseph. Joseph in his humility must have been confounded that he, the least of the three, should be the head of the Holy Family.

and the Redemption." That is equivalently to state that
Divine Providence conferred on St. Joseph all the graces
he received in view of his special mission: in other
words, St. Joseph was predestined first of all to be as
a father to the Saviour, and was then predestined to
the glory and the grace which were becoming in one
favored with so exceptional a vocation.

The Virtues and Gifts of St. Joseph

St. Joseph's virtues are those especially of the hidden life, in a degree proportioned to that of his sanctifying grace: virginity, humility, poverty, patience,
prudence, fidelity, simplicity, faith enlightened by the
gifts of the Holy Ghost, confidence in God and perfect
charity. He preserved what had been confided to him
with a fidelity proportioned to its inestimable value.

Bossuet makes this general observation about the
virtues of the hidden life:[18] "It is a common failing of
men to give themselves entirely to what is outside and
to neglect what is within; to work for mere appearances and to neglect what is solid and lasting; to think
often of the impression they make and little of what
they ought to be. That is why the most highly esteemed
virtues are those which concern the conduct and direction of affairs. The hidden virtues, on the contrary, which
are practised away from the public view and under the
eye of God alone, are not only neglected but hardly
even heard of. And yet this is the secret of true virtue
. . . a man must be built up interiorly in himself before
he deserves to be given rank among others; and if this
foundation is lacking, all the other virtues, however
brilliant, will be mere display . . . they will not make
the man according to God's heart. Joseph sought God
in simplicity; Joseph found God in detachment; Joseph
enjoyed God's company in obscurity."

---

18. *Second Panegyric on St. Joseph.*

St. Joseph's humility must have been increased by the thought of the gratuity of his exceptional vocation. He must have said to himself: why has the Most High given me, rather than any other man, His Son to watch over? Only because that was His good pleasure. Joseph was freely preferred from all eternity to all other men to whom the Lord could have given the same gifts and the same fidelity to prepare them for so exceptional a vocation. We see in St. Joseph's predestination a reflection of the gratuitous predestination of Jesus and Mary. The knowledge of the value of the grace he received and of its absolute gratuitousness, far from injuring his humility, would strengthen it. He would think in his heart: "What have you that you have not received?"

Joseph appears the most humble of the saints after Mary —more humble than any of the angels. If he is the most humble he is by that fact the greatest, for the virtues are all connected and a person's charity is as elevated as his humility is profound. "He that is lesser among you all, he is the greater." (*Luke* 9:48).

Bossuet says well: "Though by an extraordinary grace of the Eternal Father he possessed the greatest treasure, it was far from Joseph's thought to pride himself on his gifts or to make them known, but he hid himself as far as possible from mortal eyes, enjoying with God alone the mystery revealed to him and the infinite riches of which he was the custodian.[19] Joseph has in his house what could attract the eyes of the whole world, and the world does not know him; he guards a God-Man, and breathes not a word of it; he is the witness of so great a mystery, and he tastes it in secret without divulging it abroad."[20]

His faith cannot be shaken in spite of the darkness of the unexpected mystery. The word of God communicated to him by the angel throws light on the

---

19. *First Panegyric on St. Joseph.*
20. *Second Panegyric on St. Joseph.*

virginal conception of the Saviour: Joseph might have hesitated to believe a thing so wonderful, but he believes it firmly in the simplicity of his heart. By his simplicity and his humility, he reaches up to divine heights.

Obscurity follows once more. Joseph was poor before receiving the secret of the Most High. He becomes still poorer when Jesus is born, for Jesus comes to separate men from everything so as to unite them to God. There is no room for the Saviour in the last of the inns of Bethlehem. Joseph must have suffered from having nothing to offer to Mary and her Son.

His confidence in God was made manifest in trials. Persecution came soon after Jesus' birth. Herod tried to put Him to death, and the head of the Holy Family was forced to conceal the child, to take refuge in a distant country where he was unknown and where he did not know how he could earn a living. But he set out on the journey relying on Divine Providence.

His love of God and of souls did not cease to increase during the hidden life of Nazareth; the Incarnate Word is an unfailing source of graces, ever newer and more choice, for docile souls who oppose no obstacle to His action. We have said already, when speaking of Mary, that the progress of such docile souls is one of uniform acceleration, that is to say, they are carried all the more powerfully to God the nearer they approach Him. This law of spiritual gravitation was realized in Joseph; his charity grew up to the time of his death, and the progress of his latter years was more rapid than that of his earlier years, for finding himself nearer to God he was more powerfully drawn by Him.

Along with the theological virtues the gifts of the Holy Ghost, which are connected with charity, grew continuously. Those of understanding and of wisdom made his living faith more penetrating and more attuned to the divine. In a simple but most elevated way his contemplation rose to the infinite goodness of God. In its simplicity his contemplation was the most perfect after Mary's.

His loving contemplation was sweet, but it demanded of him the most perfect spirit of abnegation and sacrifice when he recalled the words of Simeon: "This child will be . . . a sign that will be contradicted" and "Thy own soul a sword shall pierce." He needed all his generosity to offer to God the Infant Jesus and His Mother Mary whom he loved incomparably more than himself. St. Joseph's death was a privileged one; St. Francis de Sales writes that it was a death of love.[21] The same holy doctor teaches with Suarez that St. Joseph was one of the saints who rose after the Resurrection of the Lord (*Matt.* 27:52 sqq.) and appeared in the city of Jerusalem; he holds also that these resurrections were definitive and that Joseph entered Heaven then, body and soul. St. Thomas is much more reserved regarding this point. Though his first opinion was that the resurrections were definitive[22] he taught later, after an examination of St. Augustine's arguments in the opposed sense, that this was not the case.[23]

St. Joseph's Role in the Sanctification of Souls

The humble carpenter is glorified in Heaven to the extent to which he was hidden on earth. He to whom the Incarnate Word was subject has now an incomparable power of intercession. Leo XIII, in his encyclical *Quamquam pluries* finds in St. Joseph's mission in regard to the Holy Family "the reasons why he is Patron and Protector of the universal Church. . . . Just as Mary, Mother of the Saviour, is spiritual mother of all christians . . . Joseph looks on all christians as having been confided to himself. . . . He is the defender of the Holy Church which is truly the house of God

---

21. *Treatise of the Love of God,* Bk. VII, ch. xiii.
22. Cf. in *Matt.* 27 and *IV Sent.,* dist. 42, q. 1, a. 3.
23. Cf. IIIa, q. 53, a. 3, ad 2.

and the kingdom of God on earth."

What strikes us most in St. Joseph's role till the end of time is that there are united in it in an admirable way apparently opposed prerogatives. His influence is universal over the whole Church, and yet, like Divine Providence, it descends to the least details; "model of workmen," he takes an interest in everyone who turns to him. He is the most universal of the saints, and yet he helps a poor man in his ordinary daily needs. His action is primarily of the spiritual order, and yet it extends to temporal affairs; he is the support of families and of communities, the hope of the sick. He watches over christians of all conditions, of all countries, over fathers of families, husbands and wives, consecrated virgins; over the rich to inspire them to distribute their possessions charitably, and over the poor so as to help them. He is attentive to the needs of great sinners and of souls advanced in virtue. He is the patron of a happy death, of lost causes; he is terrible to the demon, and St. Teresa tells us that he is the guide of interior souls in the ways of prayer. His influence is a wonderful reflection of that of Divine Wisdom which "reacheth from end to end mightily, and ordereth all things sweetly." (*Wis.* 8:1).

He has been clothed and will remain clothed in Divine splendor. Grace has become fruitful in him and he will share its fruit with all who strive to attain to the life which is "hid with Christ in God." (*Col.* 3:3).

FR. REGINALD GARRIGOU-LAGRANGE, O.P.

Fr. Garrigou-Lagrange, O.P.
1877-1964

Fr. Reginald Marie Garrigou-Lagrange, O.P. (1877-1964) was probably the greatest Catholic theologian of the 20th century. (He is not to be confused with his uncle, Père Lagrange, the biblical scholar.) Fr. Garrigou-Lagrange initially attracted attention in the early 20th century, when he wrote against Modernism. Recognizing that Modernism—which denied the objective truth of divine revelation and affirmed an heretical conception of the evolution of dogma—struck at the very root of Catholic faith, Fr. Garrigou-Lagrange wrote classic works on apologetics, defending the Catholic Faith by way of both philosophy and theology. Fr. Garrigou-Lagrange taught at the Angelicum in Rome from 1909 to 1960, and he served for many years as a consultor to the Holy Office and other Roman Congregations. He is most famous, however, for his writings, producing over 500 books and articles. In these he showed himself to be a thoroughgoing Thomist in the classic Dominican tradition.

Fr. Garrigou-Lagrange was best known for his spiritual theology, particularly for insisting that all are called to holiness and for zealously propounding the thesis that infused contemplation and the resulting mystical life are in the normal way of holiness or Christian perfection. His classic work in this field—and his overall masterpiece—is *The Three Ages of the Interior Life,* in which the Catholic Faith stands out in all its splendor as a divine work of incomparable integrity, structure and beauty, ordered to raise man to the divine life of grace and bring to flower in him the "supernatural organism" of Sanctifying Grace and the Seven Gifts of the Holy Ghost—the wellsprings of all true mysticism. Among his other famous theological works are *The Three Ways of the Spiritual Life, Christian Perfection and Contemplation* (a forerunner of *The Three Ages of the Interior Life), The Love of God and the Cross of Jesus, The Mother of the Saviour and our Interior Life,* and *Christ the Saviour.* His most important philosophical work was *God, His eminence and Nature: A Thomistic Solution of Certain Agnostic Antinomies.*

The works of Fr. Garrigou-Lagrange are unlikely to be equalled for many decades to come.

Books by the Author
Translated into English

God, His Existence and His Nature: A Thomistic Solution of Certain Agnostic Antinomies (1914)

Christian Perfection and Contemplation, according to St. Thomas Aquinas and St. John of the Cross (1923)

The Love of God and the Cross of Jesus (1929)

Providence (1932)

Our Saviour and His Love for Us (1933)

Predestination (1936)

*The One God (1938)

The Three Ages of the Interior Life: Prelude of Eternal Life (1938)

The Three Ways of the Spiritual Life (1938)

*The Trinity and God the Creator (1943)

*Christ the Savior (1945)

The Priesthood and Perfection (1946)

Reality: A Synthesis of Thomistic Thought (1946)

Life Everlasting (1947)

*Grace (1947)

The Priest in Union with Christ (1948)

The Mother of the Saviour and Our Interior Life (1948)

*The Theological Virtues—Vol. 1: Faith (1948)

*Beatitude (moral theology, 1951)

Last Writings (spiritual retreats, 1969)

Books by the Author
Not Translated into English

Le sens commun: la philosophie de l'être et les formules dogmatiques (1909)

Saint Thomas et le neomolinisme (booklet, 1917)

De Revelatione per ecclesiam catholicam proposita (1918)

De methodo sancti Thomae speciatim de structura articulorum summae theologicae (booklet, 1928)

Le réalisme du principe de finalité (1932)

Le sens du mystère et le clair-obscur intellectuel: nature et surnaturel (1934)

Essenza e attualità del Tomismo

Die accessible à tous (booklet, 1941)

*De Eucharistia: Accedunt de Paenitentia quaestiones dogmaticae (1942)

Les XXIV Theses Thomistes pour le 30e Anniversaire de leur Approbation (booklet, 1944)

Verite et immutabilite du dogme (booklet, 1947)

*De virtutibus theologicis (1948)

---

*Commentaries on St. Thomas Aquinas' Summa Theologia

✠ SAINT BENEDICT✝PRESS

Saint Benedict Press, founded in 2006, is the parent company for a variety of imprints including TAN Books, Catholic Courses, Benedict Bibles, Benedict Books, and Labora Books. The company's name pays homage to the guiding influence of the Rule of Saint Benedict and the Benedictine monks of Belmont Abbey, North Carolina, just a short distance from the company's headquarters in Charlotte, NC.

Saint Benedict Press is now a multi-media company. Its mission is to publish and distribute products reflective of the Catholic intellectual tradition and to present these products in an attractive and accessible manner.

 TAN·BOOKS

TAN Books was founded in 1967, in response to the rapid decline of faith and morals in society and the Church. Since its founding, TAN Books has been committed to the preservation and promotion of the spiritual, theological and liturgical traditions of the Catholic Church. In 2008, TAN Books was acquired by Saint Benedict Press. Since then, TAN has experienced positive growth and diversification while fulfilling its mission to a new generation of readers.

TAN Books publishes over 500 titles on Thomistic theology, traditional devotions, Church doctrine, history, lives of the saints, educational resources, and booklets.